5
FOCUS
ON
GRAMMAR
AN INTEGRATED SKILLS APPROACH

THIRD EDITION

SUSAN LANZANO

PEARSON
Longman

FOCUS ON GRAMMAR 5: An Integrated Skills Approach, Teacher's Manual

Pearson Education, 10 Bank Street, White Plains, NY 10606

Staff credits: The people who made up the *Focus on Grammar 5 Teacher's Manual*
    team, representing editorial, production, design, and manufacturing, are: Rhea Banker,
    John Barnes, Christine Edmonds, Nancy Flaggman, Ann France, Diana George, and
    Laura Le Dréan.
Cover images: Large shell, background, Nick Koudis, RF; large shell, center image, Kaz
    Chiba; background, Comstock Images, RF
Text design: Quorum Creative Services, Rhea Banker
Text composition: ElectraGraphics, Inc.
Text font: 10/12 New Aster, 10/13 Myriad Roman

ISBN: 0-13-191276-3

LONGMAN ON THE **WEB**

Longman.com offers online resources for
teachers and students. Access our Companion
Websites, our online catalog, and our local
offices around the world.

Visit us at **longman.com**.

Printed in the United States of America
5 6 7 8 9 10 V001 12 11

Contents

Introduction

The *Focus on Grammar* series

Written by ESL/EFL professionals, *Focus on Grammar: An Integrated Skills Approach* helps students to understand and practice English grammar. The primary aim of the course is for students to gain confidence in their ability to speak and write English accurately and fluently.

The **third edition** retains this popular series' focus on English grammar through lively listening, speaking, reading, and writing activities. The new *Focus on Grammar* also maintains the same five-level progression as the second edition:

- Level 1 (Beginning, formerly Introductory)
- Level 2 (High-Beginning, formerly Basic)
- Level 3 (Intermediate)
- Level 4 (High-Intermediate)
- Level 5 (Advanced)

What is the *Focus on Grammar* methodology?

Both controlled and communicative practice

While students expect and need to learn the formal rules of a language, it is crucial that they also practice new structures in a variety of contexts in order to internalize and master them. To this end, *Focus on Grammar* provides an abundance of both controlled and communicative exercises so that students can bridge the gap between knowing grammatical structures and using them. The many communicative activities in each Student Book unit provide opportunities for critical thinking while enabling students to personalize what they have learned.

A unique four-step approach

The series follows a four-step approach:

Step 1: Grammar in Context shows the new structures in natural contexts, such as articles and conversations.

Step 2: Grammar Presentation presents the structures in clear and accessible grammar charts, notes, and examples.

Step 3: Focused Practice of both form and meaning of the new structures is provided in numerous and varied controlled exercises.

Step 4: Communication Practice allows students to use the new structures freely and creatively in motivating, open-ended activities.

Thorough recycling

Underpinning the scope and sequence of the *Focus on Grammar* series is the belief that students need to use target structures many times, in different contexts, and at increasing levels of difficulty. For this reason, new grammar is constantly recycled throughout the book so that students have maximum exposure to the target forms and become comfortable using them in speech and in writing.

A complete classroom text and reference guide

A major goal in the development of *Focus on Grammar* has been to provide students with books that serve not only as vehicles for classroom instruction but also as resources for reference and self-study. In each Student Book, the combination of grammar charts, grammar notes, a glossary of grammar terms, and extensive appendices provides a complete and invaluable reference guide for students.

Ongoing assessment

Review Tests at the end of each part of the Student Book allow for self-assessment. In addition, the tests in the new *Focus on Grammar* Assessment Package provide teachers with a valid, reliable, and practical means of determining students' appropriate levels of placement in the course and of assessing students' achievement throughout the course. At Levels 4 (High-Intermediate) and 5 (Advanced), Proficiency Tests give teachers an overview of their students' general grammar knowledge.

What are the components of each level of *Focus on Grammar*?

Student Book

The Student Book is divided into eight or more parts, depending on the level. Each part contains grammatically related units, with each unit focusing on specific grammatical structures; where appropriate, units present contrasting forms. The exercises in each unit are thematically related to one another, and all units have the same clear, easy-to-follow format.

Teacher's Manual

The Teacher's Manual contains a variety of suggestions and information to enrich the material in the Student Book. It includes general teaching suggestions for each section of a typical unit, answers to frequently asked questions, unit-by-unit teaching tips with ideas for further communicative practice, and a supplementary activity section. Answers to the Student Book exercises and audioscripts of the listening activities are found at the back of the Teacher's Manual. Also included in the Teacher's Manual is a CD-ROM that includes PowerPoint® presentations that offer alternative ways of presenting selected grammar structures.

Workbook

The Workbook accompanying each level of *Focus on Grammar* provides additional exercises for self-study of the target grammar for each unit. Tests included in each Workbook provide students with additional opportunities for self-assessment.

Audio Programs

The Student Book Class Audio Program includes the listening activities, the Grammar in Context passages, and various other exercises. The symbol ⌒ identifies audio for the listening exercises. The symbol ⌒ next to the Grammar in Context passages and other exercises indicates that the listening is optional. Audioscripts for the listening exercises are located in the back of the Teacher's Manual.

Some Student Books are packaged with a Student Audio CD. This CD includes the listening exercise from each unit.

CD-ROM

The *Focus on Grammar* CD-ROM provides students with individualized practice and immediate feedback. Fully contextualized and interactive, the activities extend practice of the grammatical structures in the reading, writing, speaking, and listening skills areas. The CD-ROM includes grammar review, review tests, score-based remedial practice, games, and all relevant reference material from the Student Book. It can also be used in conjunction with the *Longman Interactive American Dictionary* CD-ROM.

Assessment Package (NEW)

A comprehensive Assessment Package has been developed for each level of the third edition of *Focus on Grammar*. The components of the Assessment Package are:

1. Placement, Diagnostic, and Achievement Tests

- a Placement Test to screen students and place them into the correct level
- Diagnostic Tests for each part of the Student Book
- Unit Achievement Tests for each unit of the Student Book
- Part Achievement Tests for each part of the Student Book

2. General Proficiency Tests

- two Proficiency Tests at Level 4 (High-Intermediate)
- two Proficiency Tests at Level 5 (Advanced)

These tests can be administered at any point in the course.

3. Audio CD

- Audio CDs include the listening portions of the Placement, Diagnostic, and Achievement Tests.
- The audioscripts for the tests are located in the Assessment Package.

4. Test-Generating Software

The test-bank software provides thousands of questions from which teachers can create class-appropriate tests. All items are labeled according to the grammar structure they are testing, so teachers can easily select relevant items; they can also design their own items to add to their tests.

Transparencies (NEW)

Transparencies of all the grammar charts in the Student Book are also available. These transparencies are classroom visual aids that help instructors point out and explain important patterns and structures of grammar.

Companion Website

The ***Focus on Grammar*** companion website (www. longman.com/focusongrammar) contains a wealth of information and activities for both teachers and students. In addition to general information about the course pedagogy, the website provides extensive practice exercises for the classroom, a language lab, or at home.

What's new in the third edition of the Student Book?

In response to users' requests, this edition has:

- a new four-color design
- easy-to-read color coding for the four steps
- new and updated reading texts for Grammar in Context
- post-reading activities (in addition to the pre-reading questions)
- more exercise items
- an editing (error analysis) exercise in each unit
- an Internet activity in each unit
- a Glossary of Grammar Terms
- expanded Appendices

References

Alexander, L. G. (1988). *Longman English Grammar*. White Plains: Longman.

Biber, D., S. Conrad, E. Finegan, S. Johansson, and G. Leech (1999). *Longman Grammar of Spoken and Written English*. White Plains: Longman.

Celce-Murcia, M., and D. Freeman (1999). *The Grammar Book*. Boston: Heinle and Heinle.

Celce-Murcia, M., and S. Hilles (1988). *Techniques and Resources in Teaching Grammar*. New York: Oxford University Press.

Firsten, R. (2002). *The ELT Grammar Book*. Burlingame, CA: Alta Book Center Publishers.

Garner, B. (2003). *Garner's Modern American Usage*. New York: Oxford University Press.

Greenbaum, S. (1996). *The Oxford English Grammar*. New York: Oxford University Press.

Leech, G. (2004). *Meaning and the English Verb*. Harlow, UK: Pearson.

Lewis, M. (1997). *Implementing the Lexical Approach*. Hove, East Sussex, UK: Language Teaching Publications.

Longman (2002). *Longman Dictionary of English Language and Culture*. Harlow, UK: Longman.

Willis, D. (2003). *Rules, Patterns and Words*. New York: Cambridge University Press.

About the *Focus on Grammar* Teacher's Manual

This Teacher's Manual offers a multitude of ideas for working with the material in *Focus on Grammar 5: An Integrated Skills Approach,* third edition. In this manual, you will find the following information:

- **General Teaching Tips** (pages 1–14) describe the principles underlying the course and give suggestions for teaching the activities in the Student Book. A Strategies for Teaching Grammar page offers a quick reference for some of the most common and useful grammar teaching techniques. A Frequently Asked Questions section answers some of the most common issues encountered by teachers.
- **Unit-by-Unit Teaching Tips** (pages 15–96) give you additional ideas for completing the activities unique to each unit.
- **Supplementary Activities** (pages 97–108) provide extra practice exercises for use during your presentation of a grammar point.
- **Scoring Rubrics for Speaking and Writing** are provided on pages 109 and 110 of the Teacher's Manual. You can use the rubrics to assess various speaking and writing tasks throughout the Student Book.
- **Audioscripts** and the **Student Book Answer Key** are included at the back of the Teacher's Manual for easy reference.

The **PowerPoint® presentations CD-ROM** bound into this Teacher's Manual includes additional teaching tools and resources:

- **PowerPoint® presentations** for selected units in the Student Book offer an innovative method for the contextualized instruction of grammar. These theme-based, user-friendly presentations contain a variety of colorful graphics and animations to engage a wide range of learning styles. In addition to providing a stimulating visual reinforcement of the Grammar Notes, these presentations also include interactive practice activities.
- A **PowerPoint® presentation guide,** included on the CD-ROM in PDF format, offers guidelines for using the **PowerPoint® presentations.** It contains a variety of suggestions for getting the most out of the presentations in terms of both instructional benefit and learner participation.
- **Transparencies** of all Grammar Charts in the Student Book offer an additional teaching tool for presenting the target grammar points in the classroom.
- **Graphic Organizers** can be printed out and used in the classroom or assigned as homework. The graphic organizers provide support through the steps of pre-writing and writing a first draft.
- **Rubrics for assessing speaking and writing tasks** help teachers provide helpful feedback to students. Teachers are encouraged to use the scoring system provided, as well as write specific notes based on each student's performance.

General Teaching Tips

These tips are designed to guide you in teaching the recurring sections of the Teacher's Manual and Student Book. Experimenting with the various options will enliven your classroom and appeal to students' different learning styles.

In the following section and in the Unit-by-Unit Teaching Tips, the icon ⏱ indicates an optional step you may wish to include if time permits.

Unit Overview

The Unit Overview (offered in the Teacher's Manual) highlights the most important grammar points of each unit. It also points out common grammar trouble spots for students. You may also find it helpful to review the Grammar Charts and Grammar Notes in the Student Book before teaching each unit.

Grammar in Context

Each unit of the Student Book begins with a reading selection designed to raise students' interest and expose them to the target grammar in a realistic, natural context. The selections include newspaper and magazine excerpts, websites, newsletters, advertisements, conversations, and other formats that students may encounter in their day-to-day lives. All of the texts are also available on the Audio Program.

Background Notes

Where appropriate, background notes are provided in the Teacher's Manual to explain cultural and historical terms or concepts that appear in a reading selection. You can introduce these terms and concepts to students during a warm-up discussion, or you can use the notes as a reference if questions come up as students are reading.

Following the Background Notes is a list of vocabulary words and expressions that may be unfamiliar to students. Rather than pre-teaching these terms, you may wish to wait until students have finished reading. This allows students to focus on reading for general comprehension, building their reading fluency. See the section on vocabulary below for some ideas on how to respond to students' vocabulary questions.

Before You Read (5 minutes)

This pre-reading activity creates interest, elicits students' knowledge about the topic, and encourages students to make predictions about the reading.

Suggested Procedure for Before You Read
1. Have the class cover up the text and look at the illustrations.
2. Ask students to respond to the questions. Ask these questions in a conversational way, instead of reading them from the book.

Option A
- Have students work in pairs to read the questions and discuss their answers.
- Call on pairs to share their ideas with the class.

Option B
- Ask pairs of students to think about what they want to know about the topic and/or to prepare some questions they have about the topic.
- Call on pairs to share some of their questions and write them on the board.
- Have students try to find the information as they read.

Option C
- Have students work in groups of three.
- Each student chooses a question to memorize and, with books closed, ask their partners.
- Call on various groups to share their answers with the class.

Reading (15–25 minutes)

Depending on the needs of your class, have students complete the reading in class or at home (procedures for both options are given below). Whichever option you choose, encourage students (1) to read with a purpose; (2) to read the passage through once or twice without stopping for unknown words; and (3) to identify and deal with new vocabulary.

Comprehension questions and discussion topics are offered in the Unit-by-Unit Teaching Tips to supplement the grammar-focused activities of the Student Book.

Suggested Procedure for Reading

1. Play the audio and have students follow along in their books.
2. Write the comprehension questions from the Unit-by-Unit Teaching Tips on the board.
3. Have students read the passage again silently, looking for answers to the questions.
4. ⏱ Have students discuss their answers with a partner or in small groups.
5. Call on individuals to share their answers with the class.
6. Spend a few minutes going over any unfamiliar vocabulary terms. (See suggested procedures for Vocabulary.)
7. ⏱ Put students in pairs or small groups to discuss the reading. Invite them to respond to the reading in a way that is meaningful to them: What was most interesting? What did they learn? Refer to the Discussion Topics in the Unit-by-Unit Teaching Tips to help generate ideas for discussion.

Option A (At Home/In Class)

- Write the comprehension questions on the board for students to copy, or prepare them as a handout for students to take home.
- Have students read the passage and answer the questions at home.
- ⏱ Have students write a few additional questions about the reading.
- In class, have students work in pairs or small groups to discuss their answers.
- ⏱ Have students take turns asking and answering questions they prepared at home.
- Follow steps 5–7 in the Suggested Procedure for Reading above.

Option B (In Class)

- Have students work in pairs. Divide the reading in half, and have each student in the pair read one half.
- Have students summarize the information in their half of the reading for their partner.
- Follow steps 5–6 in the previous notes for Suggested Procedure for Reading.

Vocabulary

After students have read the passage and answered the comprehension questions, spend a few minutes going over any unfamiliar vocabulary terms. In addition to using the definitions provided in the Unit-by-Unit Teaching Tips, you may wish to use illustrations in the Student Book or pictures that you supply to illustrate the meaning of new words.

Suggested Procedure for Vocabulary

1. Have students make lists of the words in the reading they need help with.
2. Allow them to use their dictionaries or to work with other students to discuss, search for and find the meanings, or ask you for assistance.
3. ⏱ Write the new vocabulary items on the board, or have students write them, and provide definitions.
4. Encourage students to keep a record of vocabulary items by using a notebook or by making vocabulary cards. The entries should include a definition and an example sentence. Suggest that they be on the lookout for other examples of these items and add any new examples they find to their notebooks or cards.

Where appropriate, encourage students to draw pictures on the card or to record any information that helps them remember the vocabulary item. It may be helpful for students to include a translation of the new term in their own language.

Here's one way to do a vocabulary card:

```
                                              [front]
_____
_____
_____
                 thrill (n., v., adj.)
_____
_____
_____
_____
_____
_____
```

```
                                               [back]
(n) + (adj) a strong feeling of excitement
and pleasure; (v) to feel or make someone
feel strong excitement or pleasure
(n) My grandmother always gets a thrill
when I call her.
(v) The skaters thrilled their fans with their
high jumps.
(adj) I was thrilled to hear the good news.
```

Option A
- Write new vocabulary and definitions on the board, but do not write the definitions next to the corresponding words.
- Ask students to find the appropriate match.

Option B
- If classroom time is limited, allow students to consult their dictionaries as they are reading.
- Remind them that they will not necessarily need to know the meaning of every word in order to understand the meaning of the passage.

After You Read (5 minutes)

These post-reading questions help students focus on the meaning of the target grammar without explicitly presenting the grammar point.

Suggested Procedure for After You Read
1. Have students work individually to answer the questions.
2. Tell students to compare answers with a partner.
3. Call on volunteers to read their answers aloud.

Grammar Presentation

There are many ways to teach the material in the Grammar Presentation. As a general rule, the more varied and lively the classroom activities, the more engaged students will be—and the more learning will occur! Approaching grammar from different angles and trying out different classroom management options can help increase student motivation.

The Strategies for Teaching Grammar on page 11 provides some guidelines to keep in mind when presenting a new grammar point. In addition to these strategies and the procedures outlined below, you can find specific suggestions for presenting the unit's grammar in the Unit-by-Unit Teaching Tips.

Identify the Grammar (5–10 minutes)

This section in the Teacher's Manual provides support for you to help students identify the target grammatical structures embedded in the reading. This helps students learn the usage of the target grammar point and helps you make a smooth transition from Grammar in Context to the Grammar Presentation.

Suggested Procedure for Identify the Grammar
1. Choose an example of the target grammar from the reading and write it on the board. The Unit-by-Unit Teaching Tips provide examples that focus on specific features of that grammar point.
2. Point out that the target grammar is presented in boldfaced type in the reading for easy identification. Elicit more examples from students and write them on the board.
3. Find out what your students may already know about that grammar point. List the information you have elicited on the board. As students continue with the Grammar Presentation, encourage them to compare these notes with the information presented in the Grammar Charts and Grammar Notes.

After studying the target grammar in context, students should be ready to study the isolated forms, meanings, and usage. You can use the charts, notes, and examples to present and review the grammatical structures in a straightforward and comprehensive way.

Note that common grammatical terms are used throughout the Grammar Presentations because they help make the explanations clearer and because students often have learned them in their own language. If students are having trouble understanding the grammatical terms, encourage them to use the Glossary provided in the back of the Student Book.

Grammar Charts (5–10 minutes)

The Grammar Charts provide a clear reference of all the forms of the target grammar. Students also become familiar with grammatical terminology. The charts also enable you to pre-teach some of the Grammar Notes that follow. In addition to the charts in the Student Book, you may want to use the Focus on Grammar Transparencies (on the CD-ROM in the back of this Teacher's Manual) to help direct all of your students' attention to the same focus point.

Suggested Procedure for Grammar Charts

1. Using the examples you wrote on the board (see Identify the Grammar above) and/or Focus on Grammar Transparencies, draw students' attention to important features in the models by asking them questions or by pointing out the key features.
2. Confirm students' understanding by engaging them in some recognition activities. Try one or two activities from Strategies 3, 4, 5, or 6 (page 11).
3. Get students to manipulate the new structures through substitution or transformation drills. See Strategy 7 (page 11) for an example of a transformation drill.
4. Encourage students to make sentences that are personally meaningful using the new grammar.

Option A
- Have students study the Grammar Charts at home.
- In class, follow step 1 in the suggested procedure above.
- Move directly to the Grammar Notes section. Carry out steps 2, 3, and 4 in the suggested procedure above using the notes together with the charts.

Option B
- Assign individual students responsibility for presenting a topic to the class by combining the information in the charts and the relevant notes. Give them newsprint and a marker to prepare a display in class or at home.
- ⏱ Meet with students individually. Allow them to rehearse their presentations and provide any coaching needed.
- Call on students to present their topics to the class. Encourage class questions.
- Choose appropriate practice activities from Strategies 4–8 (page 11) OR move directly to the Grammar Notes section.

Grammar Notes (10–30 minutes)

These notes provide helpful information about meaning, use, and form of the grammatical structures that students have encountered in the introductory reading selection and Grammar Charts. They include the following features to help students understand and use the forms.
- Where appropriate, time lines illustrate the meaning of verb forms and their relationship to one another.
- *Be careful!* notes alert students to common errors among English language learners.
- *Usage Notes* provide guidelines for using and understanding different levels of formality and correctness.
- *Pronunciation Notes* are provided when appropriate.
- Below the notes and examples, references to related structures are provided.

The Grammar Notes section includes cross-references to the Focused Practice exercises in the Student Book and to the Supplementary Activities in this Teacher's Manual. Have students complete the appropriate exercises after you present each note. This breaks up the grammar presentation into manageable chunks and allows students to check their understanding of the note.

Suggested Procedure for Grammar Notes
1. Have students read each note at home and/or in class.
2. For each note, write examples on the board and elicit from students the important features of the form (see Strategy 1, page 11, for suggestions) or point out the key features yourself.
3. If possible, demonstrate the meaning of the grammatical form(s) by performing actions (see Strategy 6, page 11).

4. Model the examples and have students repeat after you so that they become comfortable with the appropriate stress, intonation, and rhythm.

5. Engage students with the grammar point by choosing appropriate activities, for example:
  • Elicit examples of the target structure.
  • Confirm students' understanding by having them categorize examples or perform actions that illustrate structure. See Strategies 5 and 6 (page 11) for examples.
  • Provide controlled practice with quick substitution or transformation drills.
  • Encourage students to make personally meaningful sentences using the new grammatical forms.
  • Use the Focused Practice exercises in the Student Book and/or the Supplementary Activities starting on page 97 of this Teacher's Manual.

6. You may want to repeat steps 2–5 for each Grammar Note. Where appropriate, the Unit-by-Unit Teaching Tips give suggestions for presenting two or more notes simultaneously.

Option
• Photocopy one set of Grammar Notes for each group of three or four students in your class. Cut them up so that the notes and their corresponding examples are not attached.
• Divide the class into groups of three or four students and give a set of cut-up notes to each group.
• Give students their task:
  1. Match the examples with the correct notes.
  2. Attach the notes and corresponding examples to a sheet of newsprint (a large piece of paper).
  3. Have students create more examples for each note.
• Circulate to ensure that students are on the right track, and provide help as needed.
• Have students post their results around the room, and invite groups to look at each other's work.
• Regroup as a whole class to answer questions.

Focused Practice

The exercises in this section provide practice for the structures in the Grammar Presentation. You may wish to have students complete the corresponding exercise immediately after you have presented the relevant Grammar Note. Another option is for students to complete one

or more of the exercises at home, using the cross-references to the Grammar Note(s) for support.

If you decide to have students complete the exercises in class, you can keep them motivated by varying the order of the exercises and/or the way you conduct them. Following are various ways of conducting the exercises. In the Unit-by-Unit Teaching Tips, you will find definitions for potentially unfamiliar words and phrases that appear in the Focused Practice exercises.

Discover the Grammar (5–10 minutes)

This opening activity gets students to identify the target grammar structures in a realistic context. This recognition-only activity raises awareness of the structures as it builds confidence.

Suggested Procedure for Discover the Grammar
1. Go over the example with the class.
2. Have students complete the exercise individually or in pairs.
3. Elicit the correct answers from students.

Controlled Practice Exercises (5–10 minutes each)

Following the Discover the Grammar activity are exercises that provide practice in a controlled, but still contextualized, environment. The exercises proceed from simpler to more complex and include a variety of exercise types such as fill-in-the-blanks, matching, and multiple-choice. Exercises are cross-referenced to the appropriate Grammar Notes so that students can review as necessary. Students are exposed to many different written formats, including letters, electronic bulletin boards, résumés, charts, and graphs. Many exercises are art-based, providing a rich context for meaningful practice.

Options
• Have students work in pairs to complete the exercises.
• If the exercise is in the form of a conversation, have students complete the exercise and then work in pairs to practice and perform the conversation for the class.
• When going over answers with students, have them explain why each answer is correct.
• Whenever possible, relate exercises to students' own lives. For example, if an exercise includes a time line, elicit from

students some important events that have happened in their own lives.

Editing (10 minutes)

All units include an editing exercise to build students' awareness of incorrect usage of the target grammar structures. Students identify and correct errors in a contextualized passage such as a student's composition, a journal entry, or an online message-board posting. The direction line indicates the number of errors in the passage.

Suggested Procedure for Editing

1. Have students read through the passage quickly to understand its context and meaning.
2. Tell students to read the passage line by line, circling incorrect structures and writing in the corrections.
3. Have students take turns reading the passage line by line, saying the structures correctly. Alternatively, read the passage aloud to the class and have students interrupt you with their corrections.
4. There are also usually examples of the correct usage of the structures in each editing exercise. After students have identified the errors, point out the correct usages and ask why they are not errors.

Communication Practice

These in-class exercises give students the opportunity to use the target structure in communicative activities. These activities help develop listening and speaking fluency and critical thinking skills, as well as provide opportunities for students to "own" the structures. As with the Focused Practice exercises, you may wish to vary the order of these activities to keep student motivation high.

Since there are many different exercise types in the Communication Practice section, specific ideas and guidelines are provided in the Unit-by-Unit Teaching Tips. Following are general suggestions for the three main types of exercises. (Note: See the FAQ on pages 12–14 for more information about setting up pair work and group work.)

Listening (10 minutes)

Each Communication Practice section begins with a listening and a comprehension exercise. Students hear a variety of listening formats, including conversations, television scripts,

weather forecasts, and interviews. After listening, students complete a task that focuses on the form or meaning of the target grammar structure. The listening exercises are included on the Student CD so that students may also complete these exercises outside of class.

Suggested Procedure for Listening

Before students listen
1. Explain the situation or context of the listening passage. Provide any necessary cultural information, and pre-teach any vocabulary students may need to know. Definitions are provided in the Unit-by-Unit Teaching Tips for words and phrases that may be unfamiliar to students. (Note that some of these words and phrases may appear in the listening, not in the exercise itself.)
2. Ask students to read the exercise questions first so that they know what to listen for.

Listening
1. Play the audio or read the audioscript aloud. If you choose to read:
   • Speak with a lot of expression and at a natural pace.
   • Change positions and tone of voice to indicate who the speaker is. Another method is to draw stick figures on the board and label them with the characters' names so that you can point to the appropriate character as you change roles.
2. Have students listen the first time with their pencils down.
3. Have students listen again and complete the task.
4. You may want to let students listen as many times as necessary to complete the task.

After students listen
1. Elicit answers for the exercise items and write them on the board. Answer any questions the students may have.
2. ⏱ Students listen a final time and review the passage.

Option A
• Make photocopies of the audioscript and hand it out to students.
• Play the audio recording and have students read along with it in chorus. Explain that this exercise will help them to hear and practice the rhythms, stresses, and clusters of English sounds.

Option B
Have students listen and complete the exercise at home or in a language lab.

Role Plays (10–20 minutes)

In these classroom speaking activities, students role-play a real-life encounter, such as a business meeting or an interview.

Advantages of Role Plays

- They are fun and motivating for most students.
- Role-playing characters often allows the more hesitant students to be more outgoing than if they are speaking as themselves.
- By broadening the world of the classroom to the world outside, role playing allows students to use a wider range of language than less open-ended activities.

Suggested Procedure for Role Plays

1. When possible, bring in props or costumes to add drama and fun.
2. Review the task so students understand what is required.
3. Perform a sample role play with a volunteer in front of the class.
4. Divide the class into the suggested groupings and give them a fixed time limit for completing the task.
5. Have students write a script for the role play. Then have them write key words on cards and perform the role play using the cards as prompts. OR Have students plan the action without a script and present it extemporaneously.
6. While students are working, circulate among the pairs or groups to answer students' questions and help them with the activity.
7. Have various pairs or groups perform their role plays in front of the class. If possible, tape-record or videotape the role plays for students' own listening or viewing. You may want to use the Speaking Rubric on page 109.

Information Gaps (10–20 minutes)

These games are designed to encourage communication between students. In these activities, each student has a different set of information. Students have to talk to their partners to solve a puzzle, draw a picture (describe and draw), put things in the right order (describe and arrange), or find similarities and differences between pictures.

Advantages of Information Gaps

- Like role plays, information gaps are motivating and fun.
- Information gaps are additionally motivating because there is a real need for

communication in order to combine the information to solve a problem and complete the task.
- Information sharing allows students to extend and personalize what they have learned in the unit.

Suggested Procedure for Information Gaps

1. Explain how the Student A and Student B pages relate to each other (how they are different or similar).
2. Refer students to the examples and to any language provided.
3. Divide the class into pairs (Student A and Student B) and have them position themselves so that they cannot see the contents of each other's books.
4. Tell the Student Bs what page to turn to, and circulate to check that they are looking at the correct page.
5. Have students read their separate instructions. Check comprehension of the task by asking each group, "What are you going to do?"
6. Remind students not to show each other the contents of their pages.
7. As students are working, circulate to answer individual questions and to help students with the activity.

Writing (15–25 minutes in-class time)

These activities give students the opportunity to develop their writing skills and provide additional practice using the target grammatical structures. There is a variety of realistic formats, including paragraphs, essays, letters, and journal entries. The themes are related to material covered in the unit so that students already have some preparation for the writing task.

A Scoring Rubric for Writing is included on page 110 so that you can assess students' general writing skills as well as their ability to apply the target grammar point within a written context. This rubric allows you to give students a holistic score from 1 to 5 that reflects how well students have responded to the topic, organized their ideas, and incorporated the new grammar points from the unit. It is best to hand out copies to students before they begin working on the assignment, so that they understand what competencies are required.

The rubric provided in this book is for classroom use. To see an example of a rubric used to evaluate writing in a formal assessment situation, you can look at the one used by raters of the writing section on the TOEFL® iBT. This is available to download at http://ftp.ets.org/pub/toefl/Writing_Rubrics.pdf.

Suggested Procedure for Writing
Pre-writing
1. Go over the requirements of the assignment to make sure students understand what they are expected to do.
2. Write some questions on the board, and have students work in pairs or small groups to brainstorm ideas for the writing assignment. The Unit-by-Unit Teaching Tips provide suggestions for questions you might write on the board.
3. Call on volunteers to answer the questions as you write key words and phrases on the board.
4. Remind students to include the grammar studied in the unit as they complete the assignment.

Composing and correcting
1. Have students compose a draft of the writing assignment at home and then submit it to you or share it with a partner in class.
2. Give students feedback on the following features:
   • Content: Has the student responded appropriately to the task? Are the main points well supported?
   • Organization: Is the flow of ideas logical and effective?
   • Accuracy: Are there any major errors in the grammar points taught in the unit? (At this stage, you may want to focus your comments on errors related to the target grammar point. Circle the errors, but let students make the corrections. If students are providing feedback to each other, encourage them to focus on content and organization.)
3. ⏱ For longer assignments, have students complete a second draft. When you check these drafts, point out any further areas needing correction, concentrating especially on errors in the target grammar point or grammar points from a previous unit.
4. Have students prepare their final draft at home.

Presentation
1. In class, have students share their final drafts. There are a variety of ways to do this:
   • Post students' work on the class bulletin board.
   • Publish it in a website or a magazine that the class creates.
   • Exchange papers with others in the class.
   • Read papers aloud.
2. ⏱ Have your students put all their corrected written work into a folder, or portfolio, which you can review at the end of the course. This will allow your students and you to see the progress they have made.

Internet Activity (20 minutes in-class time)
This activity gives students an opportunity to do research related to the content of the unit and to discuss or present their findings in class. The activity varies from unit to unit. In some cases students are given very specific questions to research, and the reporting task is brief. In other cases, the investigation is more open-ended, and there is potential for a more extensive presentation.

Suggested Procedure for Internet Activity
Before class
Try the activity yourself, and prepare a list of appropriate key words or specific websites. Note: some suggested website addresses are listed on the **Focus on Grammar** Companion Website (www.longman.com/focusongrammar).

In class: preparation
1. Go over the directions to be sure students understand them. Have students work in small groups to brainstorm ideas for their research.
2. For some projects, you may want to have students work in small groups to divide up the research tasks.
3. Ask students to think about how they would search for their topics. Discuss useful key words and/or write some suggested websites on the board. Remind students that they can find websites on the **Focus on Grammar** Companion Website (www.longman.com/focusongrammar).
4. Elicit language that students are likely to use when discussing their research results. Remind them to review language they have studied in the unit.

At home / language lab
1. Students research their topics and take notes.
2. Ask students to review the notes they made on each website and summarize the most important information.

In class: wrap-up

1. During the next class session, put students into small groups to discuss their research findings.
2. Call upon a spokesperson for each group to report what the group discussed and, if appropriate, what conclusions they came to.

Option (40–60 minutes in-class time)

- Follow the above procedure, but instead of having small group discussions, have students deliver more formal spoken presentations. You may wish to use the Speaking Rubric on page 109.
- When going over the directions to the activity, tell students that they should take notes as they do their research and prepare a short (5-minute) presentation.
- Talk with students about elements of successful spoken presentations, including the importance of making eye contact and using body language. Encourage them to practice at home and to bring in visuals if possible.
- Coach students as they present and provide feedback on their presentations. You may wish to have students complete feedback forms for other students' presentations.

Further Practice

One or more Further Practice activities (in the Teacher's Manual only) can be found at the end of every unit in the Unit-by-Unit Teaching Tips. These exercises offer additional communicative practice with the target structure of the unit. Most can be done in class with no before-class preparation.

This activity (in the Teacher's Manual only) offers ideas for how to bring "real life" into your grammar classroom. Using video, pictures, news articles, or other realia, these activities help students make the connection between the structures they learn in the classroom and their application in the real world.

From Grammar to Writing

The From Grammar to Writing section at the end of each Part of the Student Book includes a grammar point and relates this grammar point to the writing focus. Students first practice the teaching point in a controlled exercise such as fill in the blanks, identification, or editing. Following these exercises, students practice pre-writing strategies such as making charts, time lines, schedules, story maps, Venn diagrams, notes, and outlines. Finally, students apply the teaching point in a writing task. Text types include both formal and informal writing, such as personal letters, business letters, essays, summaries, and reports. The section concludes with peer review and editing.

Suggested Procedure for From Grammar to Writing
Pre-writing

1. Have students work individually to complete the controlled practice exercises. Then have them exchange books and compare answers.
2. Go over the answers as a class and answer any questions that students have at this point.
3. Explain the pre-writing task. Where appropriate, provide a model for students on the board or on an overhead.
4. Have students work in pairs or small groups to complete the pre-writing task. Circulate while they are working to answer any questions and to help them with the activity.

Composing and correcting

1. Go over the requirements of the assignment to make sure students understand what they are expected to do.
2. Have students complete the writing assignment at home.
3. In class, complete the peer review portion of the task. Circulate while students are working together to make sure they are on task and to provide appropriate feedback. (See Suggested Procedure for Writing on page 8 for examples of what kind of feedback to provide.)
4. ⏱ Have students revise their writing and turn in the second draft to you. You may wish to use the Scoring Rubric for Writing on page 110 to correct these drafts and to include the drafts as part of the students' writing portfolios.

Option

- Have students complete the controlled practice exercise(s) at home.
- In class, have students work in pairs to compare answers.
- Follow the suggested procedure, starting from step 4 in the pre-writing phase.

Review Test

The last section of each Part of the Student Book is a review feature that can be used as a self-test. These exercises test the form and use of the grammar content presented and practiced in that Part. They give students a chance to check their knowledge and to review any problematic areas before moving on to the next part. An Answer Key is provided at the back of the Student Book, with cross-references to units for easy review.

Suggested Procedure for Review Test

1. Have students complete the exercises at home and check their answers in the Answer Key.
2. During the next class, go over any remaining questions students may have.

Option

- Have students complete the exercises in class. Give them a time limit of 20–30 minutes and circulate as they work.
- Have students use the Answer Key to check and correct their answers in pairs. Or you can go over the answers as a class.

Strategies for Teaching Grammar

1. Develop awareness

- Ask questions that help students become aware of the form of the structure. For example, for the contrast between the simple past and past progressive (FOG 5, page 19, Grammar Notes 1–2), ask, "What was she studying?" *(She was studying pharmacy.)* Ask what verb form is used in that question and answer *(past progressive).* Then ask, "What happened to her when she was studying?" *(She decided to get married.)* Ask what verb form is used in this question and answer. *(past)* Ask for the difference between the verb forms used for *study* and *decide.* *(One happened over a period of time; the second took only an instant.)* The deciding interrupted the studying; so the simple past is used with *decide.* How do we decide which verb should be in the past progressive? *(We determine which action is interrupted by the other.)*
- Compare information in the Grammar Charts. For example, the comparison of the past with the present perfect (FOG 5, page 18) shows a difference between the definite and indefinite past. Ask, "What forms do we use for the definite past?" *(simple past / past progressive)* "What form do we use for the indefinite past?" *(present perfect)*

2. Present meaning

Show the meaning of a grammatical form through a classroom demonstration. For example, to illustrate the use of present perfect progressive, you could show a picture of a person carrying grocery bags full of food *(He / She has been shopping.)*.

3. Identify examples

Ask students to go back to the Grammar in Context section and label examples in the reading passage with the grammatical terms in the Grammar Charts.

4. Generate examples

Find examples from the reading or elsewhere that could fit into the Grammar Charts. An interesting way to do this is to photocopy and enlarge the Grammar Chart. White out the targeted structures and replace them with blank lines for each missing word. Make copies and distribute them to students in pairs or small groups. Have students fill in the blanks, using examples from the reading. Then generate more examples. Books can be open or closed, depending on the level of challenge desired.

5. Show understanding by categorizing

Check comprehension of a grammatical principle by asking students to label multiple examples appropriately. For example, students can label verbs "present" or "future" or they can label examples "correct" or "incorrect."

6. Show understanding by performing actions

Check comprehension of the meaning of a grammatical form by having students follow instructions. Ask students, for example, to think of and perform a set of actions that they could describe using the past progressive and the simple past. (Note that some grammatical forms lend themselves better than others to this strategy.)

7. Manipulate forms

Have students manipulate the examples in the Grammar Charts to practice the form. Drills such as substitution or transformation help students to build fluency. For example, in Unit 1 (FOG 5, pages 4–5), you might have students transform simple future statements into future progressive:

A: *I'll be traveling in Thailand.*

B: *A week from now you'll be traveling in Thailand.*

Similar drills can be done with the future perfect and the future perfect progressive on page 69.

8. Personalize

Ask students to provide personal examples. For example, on page 12 in Exercise 6, students are asked to write about their future plans. Have two or three students, in turn, share a personal plan with the rest of the class using *when* or *after*:

A: When I **get** my visa, **I'll go** to Brazil.

B: After I **finish** calculus, **I'll study** physics.

Have other students talk about plans using the future perfect.

C: By this time next year, **I'll have graduated**.

D: By this time next year, **I'll have gotten** a job.

9. Repeat, reinforce

Students need to be exposed to new grammar many times in order to internalize it completely. You can first present a new structure on the board, then point it out in the book, then have students use it in an informal oral exercise, then do a written exercise in pairs, and finally review the same structure in homework. Varying the content and focus of these activities will keep students interested, and the grammar will be reinforced almost automatically.

Frequently Asked Questions (FAQ)

1. When should I have students work in pairs or groups rather than individually or as a whole class?

Varying your classroom organization to suit particular activity types will result in more effective and more interesting classes. Many students are not accustomed to working in pairs or groups, so it is important to use these groupings only when they are most beneficial.

- **Whole-class teaching** maximizes teacher control and is especially good for:
  —presenting information, giving explanations and instructions
  —showing material in texts and pictures or on audio or videotape
  —teacher-led drills (such as substitution or transformation) or dictations
  —reviewing answers or sharing ideas after students have completed an activity
  —enabling the whole class to benefit from teacher feedback to individuals
- **Students working individually** allows quiet, concentrated attention and is most effective for:
  —processing information or completing a task at students' own pace
  —performing writing tasks

For objective exercises such as fill-in-the-blank, matching, multiple choice, and editing, vary your class organization to keep student motivation high. Students can sometimes complete these exercises individually, and sometimes they can work with a partner.

- **Students working in pairs** maximizes student speaking time, breaks up the routine and "teacher talk," and is ideal for:
  —information-gap activities
  —role plays
  —writing and/or reading dialogues
  —predicting the content of reading and listening texts
  —comparing notes on what students listen to or see
  —checking answers
  —peer assessment

Pair work can also be very effective for completing objective exercises such as fill-in-the-blank, matching, multiple-choice, and editing.

- **Students working in groups** creates ideal conditions for students to learn from each other and works well for:
  —generating ideas
  —pooling knowledge
  —writing group stories
  —preparing presentations
  —discussing an issue and reaching a group decision

2. How should I set up pair work and group work?

- **Streaming:** Grouping students according to ability or participation has certain advantages.
  —**ability:** Grouping weaker and stronger students together allows more able students to help their less fluent classmates.
  —**participation:** If you see that some students participate less than others, you could make a pair or group of weak participators. By the same token, you can also put especially talkative students together.
- **Chance:** Grouping students by chance has many benefits, especially if it results in students working with varied partners. You can group students by chance according to:
  —**where they sit:** Students sitting next to or near one another work in pairs or groups. This is the easiest option, but if students always sit in the same place, you will want to find other ways of grouping them.
  —**the "wheels" system:** Half the class stands in a circle facing outwards, and the other half stands in an outer circle facing inwards. The outer circle revolves in a clockwise direction, and the inner circle revolves in a counterclockwise direction. When you tell them to stop, students work with the person facing them. This is a very effective way to have students engage in meaningful repetition, such as asking the same question of many different partners.
  —**assigned letters:** Assign each student a letter from *A* to *E*. Then ask all the As to form a group, all the Bs to form a group, and so on.
  —**birthdays:** Students stand in a line in the order of their birthdays (with January at one end and December at the other). The first five students form one group; the second five students another group, and so on.

—**native language:** If possible, put students in groups or pairs with others who don't share a native language. This helps create an "English-only" classroom.

3. How can I make activities more successful?

Before the activity:
- **Motivate students and explain the purpose.** Make it clear that something enjoyable or interesting is going to happen. Explain the rationale for the activity. Making sure students understand the purpose of the activity is to practice what they learned and encourage them to participate.
- **Provide clear directions.** Explain what students should do in every step of the activity. Have students paraphrase or demonstrate the task to be sure they understand it.
- **Demonstrate.** Show the class what is supposed to happen in an activity. This might involve asking a student to demonstrate the activity with you or having two students role-play in the front of the room.
- **Provide a time frame.** It is helpful for students to know how much time they have and exactly when they should stop. Approximate times are given for all the activities in this Teacher's Manual.

For open-ended activities, such as the Internet Activity or writing exercises, you will also want to:
- **Stimulate thinking.** When there are choices for students to make, it is often helpful to set up small-group and/or whole-class brainstorming sessions to define the focus and/or content of their task.
- **Prepare language.** Review grammar and vocabulary that students may need to complete the task. This can be done as a follow-up to a brainstorming activity where you elicit ideas and write key language on the board.

During the activity:
- **Observe students.** Walk around the room watching and listening to pairs or groups.
- **Provide assistance as needed.** (See FAQ #5 for suggestions on giving feedback and correcting errors.)

After the activity:
- **Elicit student responses.** For some activities, you may ask for volunteers or call on students to share some of their ideas with the class. For other types of activities, a few pairs or groups can be asked to role-play

their discussions to demonstrate the language they have been using.
- **Provide feedback.** In many cases, this is most conveniently done in a whole-class setting. It may be preferable, however, for you to meet with individuals, pairs, or groups. While the principal focus in a grammar class is language use, it is also important to acknowledge the value of students' ideas. See FAQ #5 below for suggestions on feedback and error correction.

4. What can I do to encourage students to use more English in the classroom?

It is perfectly natural for students to feel the need to use their first language in an English class. There are a number of actions that teachers can take to promote the use of English.
- **Set clear guidelines:** Some teachers in monolingual classes find that activities such as providing vocabulary definitions, presenting a grammar point, checking comprehension, giving instructions, and discussing classroom methodology are best done in the students' native language.
- **Use persuasion:** Walking among the students during speaking activities and saying things like "Please speak English!" or "Try to use English as much as possible." helps to ensure that students will speak English most of the time.

5. What's the best approach to giving feedback and correcting errors?

Be selective in offering correction. Students can't focus on everything at once, so concentrate first on errors relating to the target grammar point and grammar points from units previously studied, as well as any errors that interfere with communication. Whether you respond to other errors depends on your judgment of students' readiness to take in the information. If you see a teachable moment, seize it! Rather than correct every error individual students make in the course of activities, it is generally preferable to note commonly occurring mistakes and give a short presentation for the whole class at the end of the activity.
- **Recasting.** If a student makes an error—for example, "I *didn't came* to class yesterday because I was sick."—you can recast it as, "You *didn't come* to class yesterday because you were sick?" The student ideally notices the difference and restates the original

sentence: "Right. I didn't come to class yesterday because I was sick." This process can be effective because the student has the opportunity to self-correct an error that is still in short-term memory. As a variation, you can restate but stop, with rising intonation, right before the potential error: "You didn't . . . ?"

6. What can I do to accommodate different learning styles?

Focus on Grammar recognizes different styles of learning and provides a variety of activities to accommodate these different styles. Some learners prefer an analytical, or rule-learning (deductive) approach. Others, especially younger learners, respond best to an inductive approach, or exposure to the language in meaningful contexts. Indeed, the same students may adopt different styles as they learn, or they may use different styles at different times.

As teachers, we want to help the students in our classes who prefer to follow rules become more able to take risks and to plunge into communicative activities. We also want to encourage the risk-takers to focus on accuracy. *Focus on Grammar* provides the variety to ensure that students achieve their goal: to learn to use the language confidently and appropriately.

Unit-by-Unit Teaching Tips

UNIT 1 Present and Future Time

Unit Overview

Unit 1 teaches present and future time using the simple present, present progressive, present perfect, present perfect progressive, *will / be going to,* future progressive, future perfect, and future perfect progressive. Some of this will be review for your students.

- The simple present for habitual actions (or states) contrasts with the present progressive, which describes actions in progress. The simple present is also used to narrate past events.
- The present perfect and present perfect progressive show actions and states that began in the past and continue to the present.
- The future can be expressed by *be going to, will,* the present progressive, or the simple present (for schedules). Note the contrast between *be going to* (or the present progressive), for a future action that has already been planned, and *will,* which expresses an unplanned future action.
- The future progressive is used to talk informally about a future intention, and the future perfect is used to show an action or state that will happen before a certain time in the future.

Given the amount of material covered in this unit, depending on how much of it is already familiar to your students, you will probably want to divide the grammar presentations into two or three class meetings.

Grammar in Context (pages 2–4)

Background Notes

Some Americans are quite willing to bargain, but others are nervous about it. Bargaining is probably less common in North America than in many other places in the world. However, bargaining is usually acceptable and even expected when buying expensive items like houses and cars. It is also common when buying used items from people at yard sales or garage sales.

Vocabulary

counter: to react to a statement by saying something that shows disagreement

mock: not real, but intended to be very similar to a real situation

landmarks: things that are easy to recognize, such as a tall tree or building, and that help you know where you are

souvenirs: objects that you keep to remind yourself of a special occasion or a place you have visited

not too big a deal: not very important or common

yard or garage sale: a sale of used furniture, clothes, etc., from people's houses, usually done in someone's yard or garage

intimidated: feeling worried and less confident, for example, because you are in a difficult situation or other people seem better than you

Comprehension Questions

- Why does the author give tips on bargaining? *(He wants you to learn to enjoy it.)*
- Why do some people dislike bargaining? *(They are used to paying fixed prices. They don't want to hurt the vendor's feelings by offering too low a price. They are afraid of being assertive.)*
- The author suggests that some people might want to wear sunglasses when they bargain. Why? *(to conceal their anxiety)*
- Why does the author feel the need to say, "Treat the vendor with respect"? *(People not used to bargaining may feel that vendors are trying to take advantage of them.)*
- Is bargaining common in North America? *(No, but it occurs in some places, such as yard sales and garage sales.)*

Discussion Topics

- Discuss a time you were successful or had fun bargaining for something you wanted. What did you buy? How did you bargain?

What price did the seller want? And what amount did you offer? How did you reach an agreement? Did you enjoy the process?

- Think back to a time you bought or sold something (for example, a car, chair, or television). How did you decide what the item was worth? Did you buy from or sell to a friend or a stranger? Were you comfortable in this transaction?

Grammar Presentation (pages 4–7)

Identify the Grammar

SIMPLE PRESENT
She finds one she likes and asks the price.
Souvenirs cost money.
I take a trip every year.
Do you feel more confident?

PRESENT PROGRESSIVE
A tourist is admiring the . . . rugs.
So you're visiting another country this year?

Grammar Charts

- Ask students how many time periods they see represented in the charts: by the simple present *(present and future)* and by the present progressive *(present and future)*
- How many ways do they see in the charts to express future time? *(six: will, be going to, future progressive, simple present, present progressive, future perfect, future perfect progressive)*

Grammar Notes

Notes 1 and 2   *(Exercises 2–3)*

- Write the six sentences above from the reading. Then write: *past, present, future,* and ask students to think about the time that each example expresses. Elicit their comments and help them to develop the awareness that each of these forms has multiple meanings.
- Starting with the present progressive, label the examples (1—*present* and 2—*future*).
- Moving to the simple present, label the last three examples (2—*present* [general truth], 3—*present* [habitual action], 4—*present* [state]), reviewing what students already know. Then point out how the first example shows the narration of actions in a sequence, which may be new to them.
- Have students find more examples of the narrative use of the simple present in the

reading. Have them practice this use by writing a paragraph of about five sentences that narrates a series of events, using the simple past. Then have them rewrite these sentences, putting the verbs in the simple present to show the sequence of actions.

- Following up on the Be Careful! note in Note 2, you may want to refer students to Appendices 2 and 3. (Note: Non-action verbs will be covered more fully in Unit 3.)

Notes 3–5   *(Exercises 2–4)*

- Write *present perfect* on the board. Ask students to find the first example of that form in the reading and write it below: *They've just participated in a ritual that has existed worldwide for centuries.* Again, ask students to think about the time that is expressed here *(past + present)*.
- Direct students' attention to the examples of the present perfect and present perfect progressive in the charts.
- Point out that they both show action beginning in the past and coming up to the present.
- Then help them to see the differences: The progressive emphasizes the ongoing nature of the activity, and, as is the case with other progressive forms, the present perfect progressive is not used with stative verbs.

    Could the first example ("We have visited 11 countries so far.") be expressed in the progressive? No, because while they are still visiting countries, the visiting of those 11 countries is not continuing. Could the second example be expressed without the progressive? Yes, but the ongoing quality *(We've been traveling . . .)* is better expressed with the progressive.
- Have students read the examples in Notes 3, 4, and 5, drawing attention to the way the past and present are connected in each example.

Notes 6–9   *(Exercises 2–6)*

- Have students look at the examples of *will, be going to,* and the future progressive in the charts. Point out that here *will* and *be going to* are interchangeable. In fact, *be going to* could also be used in place of *will* in the future progressive example.
- Now have them look at Note 6, where an important contrast in usage between *will* (for unplanned action) and *be going to* (for a planned or already developing situation) is explained and exemplified.

- Point out the example of *will* in the progressive in Note 7, and get students to practice forming the tense: *Marta will be cooking all night before the party*, etc.
- Go over the simple present for future as described in Note 9. Be sure students understand that the simple present can be used for future meaning only when a timetable or schedule is involved.

→ For additional practice, see the Supplementary Activities on page 97.

Note 10 *(Exercises 4–6)*
- On the board illustrate that when two future actions are described in two clauses, one independent and one dependent, the one in the dependent clause shows the earlier of the two actions and is expressed in the simple present.

        1   *2*
  We will get to Italy. Then we will rent a car.
  → *When we get to Italy, we will rent a car.*
- Write these sentences on the board:
  As soon as <u>class is over</u>, I'm going to <u>go shopping</u>.
  When I <u>get home</u>, I'll <u>make a list</u>.
  I'm going to <u>watch a movie</u> after I <u>finish dinner</u>.
- First have students identify the sequence of actions by writing *1* over the first and *2* over the second one.
- Then have them generate more examples, replacing the underlined words with their own ideas.
- You may want to refer students to Appendix 20 for a list of words that begin dependent clauses.

Note 11 *(Exercises 5–6)*
- Have students write some true sentences about themselves using the structure *When / After I . . . , I'll . . . .*
- Then have some fun with this activity by encouraging playful statements using the future perfect:
  By this time next year, I will have

graduated	*and*	*moved to Paris*
moved to ___	*and*	*become a ___*
gotten married	*and*	*bought a ___*
become a ___	*and*	*traveled to the moon*

- An alternate activity for the future perfect is to have students make predictions about the future of the Earth, for example, "By 2020 colonies will have been established on Mars."

Focused Practice (pages 7–13)

Exercise 3
dog-eared: dog-eared books have been used so much that the corners are turned down or torn

roaming: walking or traveling, usually for a long time, with no clear purpose or direction

remote: far away in space or time

mental baggage: the beliefs or opinions that someone has which make the person think in a particular way, especially a negative way

preconceived: preconceived ideas, opinions, etc., are formed before you really have enough knowledge or experience

go with the flow: to do what is easiest in your situation, and not try to do something difficult or different

Exercise 5
flea market: a market, usually in the street, where old or used goods are sold

splitting headache: a very bad headache

excuse me for living: said when someone has offended you or told you that you have done something wrong

Exercise 7
mugged: to be attacked and robbed in a public place

Communication Practice (pages 14–15)

Exercise 8
- To set the scene, ask students if they like going to museums and what they think about guided tours.
- Check students' comprehension by asking the following questions: "What time of day is it?" *(morning)* "Where are they going?" *(to a historical museum and then skating at a mall)*

Exercise 9
- To generate ideas for this discussion, begin with a brainstorming session where you ask students to propose names of the most evil people or empires they can think of and the reasons why they regard them as evil. Write these on the board.
- Discussion: After all the groups have reported their viewpoints, lead a brief class discussion about what actions or institutions they consider to be evil.

Exercise 10
- Students who would like to respond to the first question will be well prepared from the ideas generated from the preceding small group discussion.

- For those writing about their "dream vacation" here are some questions to generate ideas and elicit vocabulary:
  —What are some places you have always wanted to go?
  —What would you like to do while you are there?
  —What time of year would you go? For how long?
  —Would you go alone or with someone? Who?

Further Practice

Although bargaining is not common in the United States, a related practice, bidding at auctions, is quite widespread. Ask students what they know about auctions and bidding, and whether any of them have ever taken part in an auction. A new form of auction that is spreading rapidly in the United States and abroad is the online variety found on eBay. Founded in 1995 in Pierre Omidyar's living room in San Jose, California, by Omidyar and Jeff Skoll, eBay is now one of the biggest and richest online enterprises. It brings together potential sellers, who list an enormous array of items, and buyers, who bid on them. Ask students what they know about eBay and whether any have participated in an online auction. Have students get more information from the Internet about eBay and things offered for sale there. In class, they can share information in small groups and say what items, if any, they'd be interested in bidding on.

 **OUT OF THE BOX** . . . . . .

Travel tips galore! Bring in columns from magazines, newspapers, or websites written by travel editors. Make sure the columns include an anecdote and some travel tips. Have students work in *small groups* and hand out a different column to each group. Have students read the column, and find and underline verb forms expressing present and future time. Ask students to take some notes about the anecdote and the tips. Follow up by having students share the anecdote and some tips with the class. Have students retell the anecdote using the simple present, and encourage the use of verb forms practiced in this unit for reporting the tips.

UNIT 2 Past Time

Unit Overview

This unit shows how the following forms can work alone and together to convey a range of meanings regarding past time: the simple past, the past progressive, the present perfect, *used to / would* + base form, past progressive, past perfect progressive, and the "future in the past."
- The simple past describes completed activities; the past progressive describes action in progress in the past.
- The present perfect describes an action that began in the past and continues to the present.
- *Used to* and *would* + base form are employed to describe habitual or repeated actions.
- The past perfect and the past perfect progressive are used to talk about a past action that preceded a more recent past action.
- The "future in the past" describes plans or expectations that existed in the past. (*He knew it would rain.*)

Grammar in Context (pages 16–17)

Background Notes

The sort of arranged marriage described in the reading is extremely unusual in the United States and would be considered strange or even bizarre by other Americans.

Vocabulary

tie the knot: to get married

out of the blue: suddenly and without warning

come up with: to think of an idea or plan

look on: to watch something happening without being involved in it

Comprehension Questions

- How many Americans have arranged marriages? *(not very many)*
- Why did Weinlick choose the date of his wedding before he found a bride? *(He got tired of being asked when he was going to tie the knot.)*
- Whose idea was the selection process for a bride? *(It was the idea of his friend Steve Fletcher.)*
- Where did Runze and Weinlick get married? *(at the Mall of America in Minneapolis)*

- What qualities did Weinlick consider important to a successful marriage? *(commitment and willingness to work at the relationship)*
- What quality did Weinlick's sister consider important in a potential bride for her brother? *(being able to fit into family celebrations like Christmas)*

Discussion Topics

- Even though the idea of an arranged marriage seems "medieval" to most Americans, this marriage could not have taken place without some very modern ideas and inventions. What are they? *(the computer, the Internet, huge shopping malls, sophisticated surveys and advertising techniques, and a democratic selection process)*
- In most countries where arranged marriage is practiced, it is symbolic of individuals conforming to social expectations; however, in the case of "A Marriage Made on the Internet," individuals go <u>against</u> the norms of the larger culture.
  —What do you think of arranged marriages?
  —Do you know examples of people who have had arranged marriages?
  —Do you think individuals should have complete freedom to choose their marriage partners?

Grammar Presentation (pages 18–20)

Identify the Grammar

simple past   *simple past*
He <u>created</u> an application form and <u>asked</u> friends . . . to interview the candidates.

    past progressive
She <u>was looking for</u> someone special.

        present perfect
How many Americans <u>have</u> ever <u>considered</u> asking friends or relatives to select their spouse for them?

      past perfect progressive
Weinlick <u>had</u> apparently . . . <u>been considering</u>

    past perfect
marriage and <u>had known</u> for quite some time

     future in the past
that he <u>was going to get married</u> in June.

Grammar Charts

- Referring to the above examples, ask students which verbs in the target points refer to:
  —a specific time in the past *(created, asked)*
  —an extended time in the past *(was looking for, had been considering)*
  —something that began in the past and continues into the present *(have considered)*
  —a time before something else happened *(had been considering, had known)*
  —the future in the past *(he was going to get married)*
- Have students look at the charts and find examples of the habitual past *(She used to be a pharmacist. Some days she would work twelve hours.)*
- So that students can gain familiarity with the forms, ask them to work in pairs and generate questions for each of the examples given in the charts. (e.g., "Did she use to be a pharmacist?" "Had he met her before the wedding?")

Grammar Notes

Note 1   *(Exercises 2, 4, 6)*
- Point out the examples of general and specific time and elicit more examples of each.
- Refer students to Appendix 1 for a list of irregular verbs.

Note 2   *(Exercises 2, 6)*
- Write the example on the board: *Runze <u>was studying</u> . . . when she <u>decided to get married</u>.* Ask students to label the verb forms.
- Ask them to share stories about what they or someone they know was doing when they decided to get married.
- Then erase the verbs and elicit other examples.
- Remind students that the restrictions regarding non-action verbs in the progressive discussed in Unit 1 apply to the past progressive as well as the present progressive. Refer them to Appendices 2 and 3.

Note 3   *(Exercises 2, 6)*
- To clarify the contrast in meaning between the simple present and the present perfect, have students ask *Have you ever . . . ?* questions. When the answer is *yes,* the question *When?* can then be asked, prompting a response in the simple past with a specific time stated or implied.
- Another key point about the present perfect is that it shows the relevance of the action to the present moment.

- At 7 P.M., the question *Have you had breakfast yet?* will not be asked. However, *Have you eaten dinner yet?* would be.
- Have students work in pairs asking each other *Have you _____ yet?* questions. (Note that *Did you eat dinner yet?*, while not considered as "correct," is actually more commonly heard these days. In combination with the words *yet, already,* and *just,* the simple past is becoming increasingly more common as a substitute for the present perfect in informal speech.)

→ For additional practice, see the Supplementary Activities on pages 97–98.

Note 4   *(Exercises 3, 6)*
- To clarify the difference in usage between *would* and *used to:*
  —Write on the board:
    I used to _____. I would _____.
  —Ask students to read out loud the sentence that can be used with these cues: *have a guitar, be a good student, live in the city, have dinner with my parents.*
  —Ask students why these phrases all required *used to.* *(The verbs are stative.)*
  —Ask students, "Can *used to* be used with active verbs as well?" *(Yes.)*
- Write: *Luis used to play the guitar.* Ask, "Does he still play the guitar?" *(No.)*
  Now write: *Tania would practice the piano for hours when she was young.* Ask, "Does she still practice the piano?" *(Maybe, we don't know.)*
- Point out that in order to use *would,* we generally include a time reference such as *when she was young* above, whereas *used to* can stand alone.

Notes 5–6   *(Exercises 2, 4–6)*
- Illustrate the contrast between the simple past and the past perfect. Ask students to describe their actions on a particular day in chronological order: *At 6:30, I got up. I took a shower. Then I had breakfast.* Then show them how the usage changes when you use *by* or *by the time.* This is a point in the past, so all actions before it will use the past perfect: *By 8:30 A.M., I had gotten up, taken a shower, eaten breakfast, walked the dog, read the newspaper, and left for work.*
- Another good way to practice the past perfect is to ask students historical questions like these:
  —Had television been invented by 1900?
  —Had Columbus traveled to the New World by 1500?

- In everyday speech Americans tend to avoid both the past perfect and the past perfect progressive. *(She worked before she got married.* OR *She was working before she got married.)* But mentioning a specific time forces the use of these forms. *(She had worked / been working for five years before she got married.)*
- Here is a game you can play with your students to give them some practice using both forms: Have students tell amazing things about their childhood. (Truth is not important.) Be sure they include a specific time reference. For example:
    By the time I was four I had made my debut at Carnegie Hall and had received three marriage proposals.
    By the time I was twelve I had been making movies for six years.
- For additional practice of past perfect progressive: Draw attention to the example given in Note 6, pointing out the sequence of events. Write several similar examples on the board and have students "translate" the information into two sequential actions. Then elicit some sequential actions from students and have them combine them using the past perfect progressive.

Note 7   *(Exercise 6)*
- The term "future in the past" may be a bit difficult to understand; it simply refers to states and actions planned or expected in the past.
- Remind students that *be going to* is used to show future intention.
- Have students construct affirmative sentences about things they intended to do but didn't, along with things that they didn't intend to do.

Focused Practice (pages 21–27)

Exercise 2
blind date: an arranged date between two people who have not met each other before

opinionated: expressing very strong opinions and being sure that your opinions are always right

Exercise 3
That's a trip: used to describe an experience that is amusing and very different from normal

been there, done that: used to say that you are not interested in doing something, because you already have a lot of experience doing it

Communication Practice (pages 28–32)

Exercise 8
- Before playing the tape, have students look at the pictures and guess what the news is.
- Discussion: Ask students to tell the class about other unusual wedding ceremonies they know of.

Do you take this woman to be your lawfully wedded wife: Do you agree to marry this woman?

I now pronounce you man and wife: You are now married.

This is one for the scrapbook: This experience was memorable, but I don't have to repeat it.

Exercise 9
Discussion: Ask students what they think of the underlying idea here: "Do marriages suffer when partners are away from each other a lot?"

Exercise10
- Ask students if they think the artist intended to make a statement. If so, what was it?
- Does this picture show a negative view of marital relationships, or is this portrayal typical in situations where the people know each other well?

Further Practice
Bring in pictures of married people in your family and describe their courtship and/or marriage to the class.
- Have students think of couples they know well (e.g., their parents, their grandparents, themselves) and prepare some notes describing their courtship and marriage.
- Have students then share their stories in small groups or with the whole class. (Encourage them to use a variety of past time forms. Tell them that *would* + base form should be especially useful here!)
- Have each group select one story to tell the whole class.
  OR
  The last sentence in the reading is, "Maybe they (arranged marriages) are not such a bad idea." Is that true?
- Have students working in pairs imagine themselves to be bride and groom and write five sentences each describing what they are thinking to themselves when they see each other for the first time. Emphasize that they should strive for humor. For example:
  Bride: *I knew you were going to be strange, but I didn't know you would be totally weird!*
  Groom: *I figured you weren't going to be too attractive, but I didn't know you would be . . . .*

- Have students role-play their "private thoughts" for the class. Have the class vote on the funniest ones.

GRAMMAR OUT OF THE BOX . . . . . .

Marriage stories. Choose a movie that deals with the topic of marriage—for example, *My Best Friend's Wedding* or *Green Card.* Have students watch the movie—or parts of it—and then write a summary of what they've seen. The summary should be based on questions that use the verb forms covered in this unit. Below are some suggested questions you can write on the board. You should adapt the questions to the movie you select.
- What were the bride and the groom doing when they met each other?
- Had they ever considered marriage before meeting each other? What did they use to think about marriage before then?
- How long had the bride and the groom known each other when they decided to tie the knot?
- How long had they been seeing each other when they picked a date for the wedding?
- What expectations did they have about the wedding?
- What did they think their life would be like after the wedding?
- Did they ever get to marry?
- What happened the day of the wedding?

 Instead of a movie, you can bring in photocopies of a magazine or newspaper article about a famous couple whose marriage is in trouble. This kind of article often looks back on the couple's story, which can also be exploited with questions such as the ones above. If the article lends itself well, add some questions about the couple's future.

| UNIT 3 | **Simple and Progressive: Action and Non-Action Verbs** |

Unit Overview

The contrasts between action and non-action verbs and the dynamic and stative uses of certain verbs are the focus of this unit.

- Action verbs can be used both in simple and progressive forms and can be modified by adverbs.
- Non-action verbs are generally not used in the progressive form, and one group, verbs of bodily sensation, are normally followed by adjectives. *You look sad.*
- Some verbs, such as *have* and *be,* can be used in both stative and dynamic ways, usually with different meanings: *I have a new car.* (possess) *I'm having trouble with my car.* (experiencing)
- The construction *there + be* to show the existence of something is used only in simple, not progressive, verb forms.

Grammar in Context (pages 33–35)

Background Notes

- To report an emergency to the police or fire department, or to call an ambulance, people dial 911 on the telephone.
- The Information Age, the age in which we live, is so named because of the rapid exchange of information we enjoy today, which is made possible by modern computer technology. The Information Age is often seen in contrast with the Industrial Age that preceded it, when the new technology of that day enabled the mass production of many products, such as clothing and the automobile.

Vocabulary

downside: disadvantage of something

at the mercy of: unable to do anything to protect yourself from something

pros and cons: advantages and disadvantages

with each passing year: continuously as time passes

sold out: a concert, performance, etc. that is sold out, has no tickets left

stay in touch: to speak or write to someone when you cannot see them as often as you used to

prohibit: to officially stop an activity by making it illegal or against the rules

reluctant: slow and unwilling

device: a machine or other small object that does a special job

few and far between: rare, or not happening or available often

kidney: one of two organs in your lower back that separate waste liquid from blood and make urine

over-dependence: too much dependence

Elicit examples of new technologies. Then have students look at the photo and read the questions. Discuss the ideas as a class.

Comprehension Questions

- Does the author think technology is bad for us? *(No, but he points out the disadvantages as well as the advantages.)*
- When do people call 911? *(in emergencies)*
- Why do some students want to keep their cell phones on in class? *(They feel they have the right.)*
- According to the author, what are the benefits of cars? *(freedom, mobility, fast transportation, jobs)*
- What are some negative effects of automobiles? *(air pollution, automobile accidents, heavy traffic)*
- How does the author recommend we live with technology? *(We need to be less dependent on technology, and to learn to use it moderately.)*

Discussion Topics

- The author seems to believe that technology always has a downside. Do you think that is true? Why or why not? Give examples to support your position.
- The author says, "We need to learn how to use technology moderately. . . ." What does this really mean? Is it realistic? Can you think of technological "advances" that people or nations have refused to use? What were the circumstances? When these circumstances did not exist, have people ever used technology moderately? Why should they?

Grammar Presentation (pages 35–37)

Identify the Grammar

ACTION VERBS
  simple form
You <u>read</u> news articles.

  progressive form
You're <u>driving</u> it for the first time.

NON-ACTION VERBS

It <u>looks</u> good.
We <u>need</u> to learn how to use technology.

SOME NON-ACTION VERBS
  simple form
you <u>have</u> a new computer
if someone <u>is</u> sick

  + adj.
You <u>feel bad</u> about this.

(continued)

Grammar Charts

- Write a contrasting example next to the first sentence on the board: *You are reading news articles.* Ask students what the difference in meaning is. *(In the progressive, the action is in progress; in the simple present, it is a general practice.)*
- Ask students for a contrasting example for the second sentence that expresses the time frame. *(You drive to work every day.)*
- Point out the non-action verbs in the next two sentences on the board and the second Grammar Chart. Ask students what form this is. *(simple present)* Ask students what they know about non-action verbs. *(They are generally not used in the progressive form.)*
- Ask students to look at the sentences on the board and in the third Grammar Chart where simple and progressive forms of some non-action verbs are contrasted. After looking at the contrastive pairs in the chart, ask if they think the time period is the same or different. *(same)* Continue, asking if they can think of a reason why the progressive form is used. *(The progressive is used with a different meaning here.)*
- This provides a nice transition to the next two charts which focus on the use of adverbs with action verbs and non-action verbs with stative and active uses. Ask students to look at the last chart and tell you if the meanings of the verbs in the two columns are the same or different. *(different)*

Grammar Notes

Note 1
To review action verbs in the simple and progressive present:
- Have students work in pairs to write five contrastive pairs of sentences.
- Write some of these on the board, using the examples to assess students' grasp of the forms and correct any misunderstandings.

Note 2   *(Exercises 2, 5)*
- Refer students to the list of Non-Action Verbs in Appendix 2. Have them work in pairs to

write two sentences from each of the seven categories. Call on pairs to read a few of their favorite sentences aloud.
- Now have them turn to Appendix 3, Non-Action Verbs Sometimes Used in the Progressive. Have students work in small groups to chose ten verbs and write two contrastive sentences for each, one in the simple present, one in the present progressive. Have each group present five of these pairs to the class.

→ For additional practice, see the Supplementary Activities on page 98.

Notes 3–4   *(Exercises 2–5)*
- Have students work in small groups to come up with a list of ten adverbs and ten adjectives. Encourage them to use their imagination and be playful.
- Have each group exchange their lists with another group. Groups are now responsible for writing fifteen sentences using the adverbs and adjectives they have received.
  —five with action verbs in the simple present
  —five with non-action verbs (stative use) in the simple present
  —five with non-action verbs (active use) in the present progressive
  They will hopefully have understood the point of Note 4 and will make the right choices. You will know as soon as you see their work!

Note 5
- Have students quickly scan the reading passage to find examples of *there is / are*. Ask them to write them on the board and underline the subject and verb.
  > *There's no <u>doubt</u> that technology serves us.*
  > *There <u>are</u> countless <u>benefits</u> of cars.*
  > *There <u>are</u> other <u>negatives</u>.*
- Now ask the class to transform singular subjects into plurals and vice versa, adjusting the verbs to agree:
  > *There <u>are</u> no <u>doubts</u>.*
  > *There <u>is</u> a <u>benefit</u>.*
  > *There <u>is</u> a(nother) <u>negative</u>.*
- Practice using *there* with different tenses and different subjects, in affirmative and negative sentences with a simple transformation drill. Start with a sentence and provide cues such as these on the board:
  > *There <u>have been</u> questions.*
  > *next year: There <u>will be</u> questions <u>next year</u>.*
  > *in the last century: There <u>were</u> questions <u>in the last century</u>.*
  > *no: There <u>were</u> <u>no</u> questions. . . .*
  > *doubt: There <u>was</u> no <u>doubt</u>. . . .*

Focused Practice (pages 38–43)

Exercise 1
hearing aid: a small piece of equipment that you put in or behind your ear to make sounds louder if you cannot hear well

Communication Practice (pages 43–45)

Exercise 7
Discussion: Ask students if they have ever been victims of credit card or identity theft. What did they do? What can be done to prevent it?

Exercise 8
- Have students look over the chart. Ask them to think about some inventions that are important to them. Write these on the board. Remind them to add two inventions to their own charts.
- Have two students read the examples out loud. Afterwards, ask them if what they said is true for them. If not, have them change the information so that it is and perform the dialogue again. *I have a bicycle, and I use it all the time.* OR *I don't have a bicycle, and I don't want one.* Some students may need help with the language, so you may want to elicit benefits and disadvantages of some of the inventions and write these on the board.
- Invite a few pairs to share their favorite dialogues with the class.

Exercise 9
Questions to generate ideas and elicit vocabulary:
- What makes an invention important to people?
- Are there other inventions besides the ones listed that you think are important?
- What about the cotton gin, the sewing machine, the machine gun, antibiotics, the radio, plastic?

Further Practice
When automobiles were new, there were no laws, licenses, or regulations governing their use. Today, there must be thousands of laws governing automobile use. The cell phone is relatively new, and regulations regarding cell phone use have not yet been standardized. Should people talk on their cell phones in a restaurant, in class, while they are driving, while on a bus, an airplane, etc.?

Turn the class into a "commission of experts" whose job it is to prepare recommendations for the legislature on cell phone regulation. Divide the class into small groups, each of which considers one of the following areas: public areas such as parks, sidewalks, transportation terminals, public buildings; private areas such as hospitals, restaurants, movies, theatres; means of transportation, including automobiles, airplanes, trains, buses; schools, from public schools to universities. Each committee reports to the class on these questions: What laws have already been passed? What regulations do you recommend? How could these rules be enforced?

GRAMMAR OUT OF THE BOX ......

Get it now! Bring in catalogs of modern appliances and technological products. (You can print out online catalogs.) Have students form small groups and give each group a catalog. Have students look through the catalog and choose a product that they would like to order. Then have students use the questions below as a guide to tell their group about the product they are interested in:
- Why do you like the product you chose? Does it look fashionable? Does it sound good? Do you think it's cheap?
- Do you have one of the same kind? Is there one in your family? If so, who does it belong to?
- If you have one already, why do you want a new one? Does the old one work well, or are you having problems with it?
- Were you thinking about buying a new one before now?
- Do you really need the product you chose? Do you feel strongly about buying it? Why / Why not?

As students talk about the products they would like to buy, encourage their partners to make relevant comments, for example: *Why don't you buy this one? It looks similar, and it's cheaper. I guess this one is better.*

UNIT 4 — *Be* and Auxiliaries in Additions, Tags, and Short Answers

Unit Overview

Be and the auxiliaries are employed in forming:
• additions referring to previous information
• additions of similarity, contrast, and emphasis
• tag questions
• short answers

The function of much of the language taught in this unit is to take "shortcuts" correctly. When we make statements adding to, agreeing or disagreeing with, or confirming a previous statement, or providing a short answer, we can use the appropriate auxiliary or *be* to avoid lengthy repetition of the original statement. The little grammatical words which are the subject of this unit carry a lot of meaning, and mastery of them will greatly enhance students' communicative abilities.

Grammar in Context (pages 56–58)

Background Notes

The theme of the unit is families and family dynamics, especially those related to birth order. Although many traditional cultures around the world give special attention to firstborn children, this isn't done much in mainstream American culture. Still, there are widespread beliefs about differences between firstborns and their later-born siblings. The reading deals with the most important American book on how birth order affects people and shapes their personalities and their lives. Examples of the effects of birth order are drawn from history and contemporary culture and range from Churchill and Stalin to John Wayne, a famous film star, and Oprah Winfrey, a popular TV figure.

Vocabulary

perfectionist: someone who is not satisfied with anything unless it is perfect

enterprises: companies, organizations, or businesses, especially new ones

rule-oriented: living according to rules, rigid

assertive: behaving in a confident way so that people notice you

conscientious: showing a lot of care and attention

moralistic: having strong beliefs about what is right and wrong and how people should behave

configuration: the shape or arrangement of the parts of something

acknowledge: admit or accept that something is true or that a situation exists

Comprehension Questions

• Are Sam and Jerry birth-order researchers? *(no)*
• Why are firstborn children usually conservative? *(because they want to keep the special relationship with their parents that they enjoyed before the arrival of other children)*
• What do Winston Churchill, John Wayne, Oprah Winfrey, and Joseph Stalin have in common? *(They were firstborn children.)*
• According to Sulloway, what are the characteristics of middle children? *(They are usually more flexible and have a talent for compromise.)*
• How are firstborn children different from "only" children? *(Only children are more flexible than firstborns.)*

Discussion Topic

The reading deals with the much-discussed theory of birth order. It has not been proved that the effects of birth order actually exist, but the theory does seem to have some validity. How important is birth order in determining our personalities and political preferences? Ask students if they had heard of this theory before reading the article in this unit. Then ask what they think of the theory.

Grammar Presentation (pages 58–62)

Identify the Grammar

• *Write these sentences on the board:*
  1. *Sam is a perfectionist; so is Jerry.*
  2. *Jerry has been a leader. . . . So has Sam.*
  3. *Sam . . . tries to obey rules. Jerry does, too.*
  4. *Jerry has never liked liberal ideas. Neither has Sam.*
  5. *They're not twins or even related to each other. But they are both firstborns.*
  6. *This is all just too much of a generalization, isn't it? Yes, maybe it is.*
  7. *Shy children . . . may not become leaders even if they are firstborns.*
• Ask students to identify the grammar in these sentences according to the charts— chart 1: additions that refer back to preceding information *(1, 2, 6)*; chart 2:

(continued)

additions of similarity *(1, 2, 3, 4, 6)*; chart 3: additions of contrast and emphasis *(5, 7)*; and chart 4: tag questions *(6)*.
- Have students underline the auxiliaries and forms of *be.*
- Read the examples at normal speed, producing the spoken contractions that would normally occur in questions 1 *(Sam is → Sam's)*, 2, and 4 *(Jerry has → Jerry's).*
- Point out to students that knowing when to use spoken contractions and when not to is a key to handling additions, tags, and short answers—the subject matter of this unit.
- Ask if they noticed which words you pronounced in a contracted form and which you didn't. *(Contractions are the norm in English except in short answers, contrast and emphasis sentences, and tag questions.)*

Grammar Charts

Chart 1
- Ask students to notice where contractions are used and where they are not used. They will probably see that there are no contractions in the Addition column, and that's because the auxiliaries of *be* are always stressed in short answers. Looking at the Statement column, they will have noticed only one written contraction *(it's).*
- Ask if there are any other statements where they could make another written contraction *(He is working on this problem* becomes *He's working . . .)*
- Explain that in speech we often contract or reduce words even if they are not written that way and that auxiliaries and forms of *be* would normally be spoken in a contracted form.
- Model *See if you can solve it* with *can* in reduced form and *Many of us have worked on this* with *have* in reduced form.
- Then point out the difference between those initial sentences and the additions to them, where the auxiliary is stressed. (Note: When auxiliaries are coupled with *n't,* they receive stress, even in initial statements. *See if you can't solve it yourself. I'm afraid I really can't.)*

Chart 2
- Read the pairs of example sentences out loud and ask students to notice the use of contracted forms in the sentences in the Statement column.

- Now have students focus on the Addition column. Read the pairs again. This time have students mark the words that receive stress in each of the sentences there. They will hopefully have observed (or you can help them!) the fact that words *so, too, either,* and *neither,* in addition to the content words (in this case people's names), always receive emphasis.

Chart 3
- Model the first exchange for students, drawing attention to the change in stress between the initial statement and the addition.
*They're not **rich,** but they **are** successful. (Are* is stressed in the addition to show contrast.)
- Call on students to read the other examples, being sure they stress the appropriate words.

Chart 4
The example statements and their accompanying tags or short answers provide an excellent opportunity to observe the above generalization about contractions in action.
- Ask students what they notice about the use of contractions in the statements vs. tags and in the statements vs. short answers.
- Have students practice reading the pairs of sentences aloud. Another important feature of tag questions is that their meaning is conveyed by the type of intonation used. This will be treated in Note 6.

Grammar Notes

Note 1
- Ask students how many words they can think of that are used as auxiliaries. Have them write these on the board. If they are written at random, ask students how they could group them. Eventually the following categories should emerge:
  The verb *be: am, is, are, was, were*
  The verb *do: do, does, did*
  The verb *have: have, has, had*
  The modal verbs: *can, could, will, should, may, might, must*
- Ask students what they think the purpose of auxiliaries, or helping verbs is in English. Here is a partial list of functions:
  —They show time.
  —In some cases they reflect the person and/or number of the subject.
  —They are used in forming questions and in making sentences negative.
  —They are used for short answers, additions, contrasts, emphasis, and tag questions.

List on the board the functions students come up with (providing they are accurate), and help them to add others based on the examples they have been reading.

Note 2   *(Exercise 2)*
- Go over the examples with the class, having students read the sentences aloud and paying attention to the use of contractions and appropriate stress and intonation.
- Then have them work in pairs or small groups to generate some additional examples of each category.
- You might want to point out some special-case tag questions:

   I'm right, aren't I? (instead of <u>amn't</u>, which isn't used)

   Everybody came to the picnic, didn't they? (The informal, conversational tag question for sentences containing the -*one* or -*body* words has *they*, not *he* or *she*.)

Note 3   *(Exercises 2–3)*
The use of forms of *be* in additions when it is only implied in the initial statement is likely to be challenging.
- Expand the example to show how *be* was inferred:

   Frank seems like (he is) a good parent. In fact, he is.
- You may want to give students some additional practice.

   Many politicians sound like actors. (That's because they are.)
- Similarly, *do, does,* and *did* are often invisible in initial statements, and students may need additional practice pulling out those auxiliaries:

   Sometimes people have no idea what a candidate really stands for. (Many people really don't. [= They don't have any idea . . .])

Note 4   *(Exercises 2–4)*
Advanced-level students are often quite familiar with *too* and *either* but not with *so* and *neither*. Give your class plenty of practice on the latter two. We use *so* and *neither* when we want to emphasize the concept that comes last in the sentence.

Note 5   *(Exercises 2–4)*
- To clarify the first rule and accompanying note, write the first four examples on the board and get students to identify the affirmative and negative parts and the contrast words. For example:

   affirmative
   Some think all leaders are firstborns.

   negative   contrast word
   They aren't, though.
- Ask students to read the sentences aloud, paying attention to whether the auxiliaries used are stressed or not. For example:

   not stressed   stressed
   *They're not twins, but they **are** both firstborns.*
- Go over the remaining examples having students read them aloud with attention to stress.

Note 6
- Tag questions are a wonderful way to review all of the auxiliaries in affirmative and negative forms, and it can be fun as well as challenging for students to have some rapid-drill practice.
   —Start with the first example.
   The birth order theory makes sense, doesn't it?
   —Then make one change, requiring a different tag, which students then supply:
   The birth order theory doesn't make much sense, (does it)?
   —Now change a different word:
   The birth order theory made sense, (didn't it)?
- Intonation is crucial to conveying whether a tag question is meant to check or comment on information, and students will benefit from some practice in discriminating between and producing both versions.

   On the board write:
   checking

   doesn't it?
   commenting

   doesn't it?
   Say some tags with rising intonation, pointing to the first column and a few with rising-falling intonation, pointing to the second column.

   Then say them randomly, asking students to raise one or two fingers to indicate which meaning is intended.

   Now have individual students read some of the pairs from the Tag Question box on page 59 aloud, and you and the class indicate which meaning you understood.

→ For additional practice, see the Supplementary Activities on pages 98–99.

Note 7

To reinforce the concept that contractions cannot be used for affirmative short answers but can be for negative ones, you may want to do a short oral and/or written drill. You can do this conventionally or play a circle game:

• Student A gives a short answer and calls on Student B, who either says "No contraction" or gives the contracted form.

• Student B then creates a new, full-form short answer and turns to Student C, who then speaks to Student D, and so on.

• Ask students to use only those auxiliaries that have the possibility of being contracted with subject pronouns: *am, is, are, have, has.*

Student A	Student B	Student C
Yes, I am.	No contraction.	*No, I'm not.*
	No, I am not.	*Yes, they have.*
		Etc.

Focused Practice (pages 62–67)

Exercise 6

monitor: to carefully watch something over a period of time

Communication Practice (pages 68–71)

Exercise 7

If your students are not familiar with TV and radio talk shows, you may wish to record one to play in class. Ask the students if they ever listen to or watch such programs and why they think some people like to listen to talk shows and call in to them.

inheritance: money, property, etc. that you receive from someone after they have died

down payment: the first payment that you make on something expensive, which you will continue to pay for over a longer period of time

ethical: relating to principles of what is right and wrong

Exercise 8

• Before they begin reading, you might ask your students if they have any opinions about raising children, and in particular, about the way Americans raise their children.

• You may want to review some ways of agreeing and disagreeing, eliciting some from students.
I agree/disagree with you. I think so, too. I don't think so, either, etc. Remind students

that the grammar points they have practiced in this unit will be very useful here. For example,
American parents have lost their way. You're right. They <u>have</u>.
Children shouldn't be allowed to tell parents what to do. I agree. They <u>shouldn't</u>.

childrearing: raising children

It just so happens: said when one thing you are about to mention is related to what someone else has said

assumption: something that you think is true although you have no proof

bribe: to offer someone, especially a child, something special to persuade them to do something they don't want to do

Exercise 9

• Ask students to describe what is going on in the picture and write key vocabulary on the board.

• Have students work in pairs to compare the families and relate them to families in their own culture.

• Ask pairs to report their conclusions to the class.

Exercise 10

Questions to generate ideas and elicit vocabulary:

• Did you pay more attention to your parents than they did to you?

• Do you think children should listen to their parents?

• Do you think parents should listen to their children?

Further Practice

At the end of his article, "Asian Parents Differ on Child Rearing," John Rosemond says, "It's not too late . . . to save ourselves."

• What advice would he give to American parents today? Have students work in small groups to make a list of guidelines for parents.

• ⏱ Imagine an American family going to a family counselor with their child(ren) for advice. Have students work in small groups.

—Assign roles: family counselor, parent(s), child(ren)

—Think of:
  a situation the parents will describe to the counselor
  the questions the counselor will ask
  what the child(ren) will say
  what the parents will say
  what the counselor will advise

—Then role-play the scene.

GRAMMAR OUT OF THE BOX ......

Let's talk about famous people, shall we?
Bring in several pairs of biographies of famous people with the same jobs or professions—for example, two actors, two dancers, two painters. (You might find it more convenient to choose just two biographies and photocopy them for the whole class.) Have students work in pairs. Give each pair a set of biographies. Have each student read one of the biographies. Then have pairs comment on their biographies using additions and tag questions. Write these examples on the board:

A: Julia started acting when she was very young.

B: So did Kim. She was a teenager when she appeared in her first film.

A: Julia is a great actress.

B: She is. She starred in *Fear of Love*, didn't she?

A: Julia isn't beautiful, but she does have an appealing personality.

B: Kim is attractive. She isn't very pleasant, though.

 UNIT 5

Modals to Express Degrees of Necessity

Unit Overview

Ways to express degrees of necessity, ranging from obligation to no obligation, are the focus of this unit.

- Obligation (necessity) is expressed by *must*, *have to*, and *have got to*. If no obligation exists, we use *don't have to*.
- Advice is conveyed by *had better*, *should*, and *ought to*.
- Expectation is expressed by *supposed to*.
- Suggestions are formed with *could* and *might*.

Grammar in Context (pages 72–74)

Background Notes

In the United States, what do you bring to your hosts when you are invited to dinner? Some people bring nothing on the assumption that they will invite their hosts some time in the near future. But most Americans prefer to bring a gift, with flowers, wine, and sweets the most common choices. Sometimes people bring food, especially desserts, that they have prepared. But a CD or book would be appropriate, too, if you know the people well enough to know their tastes.

Vocabulary

pointer: a useful piece of advice or information that helps you do or understand something

branch office: an office in a particular area that is part of a large company

appropriate: correct or right for a particular time, situation, or purpose

relieved: feeling happy because you are no longer worried about something

rectify: to correct something that is wrong

it struck me: when a thought, idea, fact, etc., strikes you, you think of it, notice it, or realize that it is important, interesting, surprising, bad, etc.

gracious: behaving in a polite, kind, and generous way

chuckle: to laugh quietly

Comprehension Questions

- When the author and his wife went to Masayuki and Yukiko's home for dinner, they made a number of social (cultural) errors. What were they? *(They didn't leave their shoes pointing toward the door. They brought a gift that was both inappropriate and unwrapped. Helen took more food than she was able to finish. Helen offered to help in the kitchen. They accepted an additional drink instead of politely refusing.)*
- Feeling uncomfortable about aspects of the evening with their Japanese friends, what did the author do? *(He asked his friend Junichi about it because he had lived in the United States and Japan.)*
- The author writes, "But even though Masayuki and Yukiko were most polite and friendly and never gave any indication that anything was wrong, we felt a bit uncomfortable about the evening." What might this say about Japanese culture? *(Japanese are very polite and will not indicate when they are upset about something.)*

Discussion Topics

- What things do American travelers or business people do that offend people in other countries?
- Are students aware of any cultural "mistakes" foreign students sometimes make in the United States?

Grammar Presentation (pages 75–78)

Identify the Grammar

Now we know what we <u>should</u> and <u>shouldn't</u> have done.

. . . you<u>'re supposed to</u> take off your shoes when you enter a Japanese home

. . . you <u>could have</u> taken some flowers.

. . . you<u>'ve got to</u> eat everything that's offered to you?

You <u>don't have to</u>.

. . . visitors <u>aren't allowed to</u> go into the kitchen.

We<u>'d better</u> get going.

Grammar Charts

This unit will be partly review and consolidation. Focus on those modals or uses of modals that are likely to be new to your class.

- Ask a few questions to ensure that students understand the relationships between the different modals. For example:
  —Which words show necessity to do something?
  —Which words show necessity to <u>not</u> do something?
  —Which words show it is not necessary to do something?
- Focus attention on the past forms with questions like these:
  —Does *must* have a past form when it means obligation? (*No, but* had to *expresses the idea.*)
  —What is the past form of *can't*? (*couldn't*)
- Focus attention on negative forms with questions like these:
  —Which modals or modal-like expressions have negative forms that mean the opposite? (*must, had better, should, should have, be supposed to, be to*)
  —How do you say the opposite of *You ought to leave early*? (*You shouldn't leave early* OR *You don't have to leave early*.) (Note: *Ought not* is old and very rarely used.)
- Review subject-verb agreement:
  —Ask students what happens if the subject changes from *you* to *he*, e.g., *You should. He _____. Does the modal change? (No)*
  —Which modals are like this? (*must, ought to, could, might, can*)
  —What about *have to* and *have got to*? Elicit *He* <u>has to</u>/<u>has got to</u>.
  —What about *You* <u>are supposed to</u>/<u>are to</u>? Elicit: *I* <u>am supposed to</u> . . . *I* <u>am to</u> . . .

- Ask students to notice the verb forms following the modals and elicit from them that the base form is used after simple modals and the past participle is used after perfect modals.

→ For additional practice, see the Supplementary Activities on page 99.

- Explain that modals and modal-like structures are often reduced in conversational speech. Tell students that they do not have to pronounce modal structures in this way, but it's important to learn how native speakers reduce these words so that they will be able to understand them.
  —*have to* becomes *hafta*
  —*you'd better* becomes *you better*
  —*we're supposed to* becomes *we're sposta*
  —*going to* becomes *gonna*
  —*could have* becomes *coulda*
  —*we've got to* becomes *we gotta*
  —*have* becomes *'ve*, which is pronounced like *of* (but not written like that)

Grammar Notes

Notes 1–2
- The pronunciation work above leads nicely to a listening exercise in which students discriminate between the simple and perfect forms of *should, could,* and *might.* Write on the board:

Present	Past
should	*should have*

  Ask students to listen and point to the one they hear (or have them respond on paper, placing a check under the appropriate column) as you say a series of sentences at normal speed with reduced forms:
  We should invite him.
  We should have invited him.
  We should have called her.
  I could write them.
  I could have written them. Etc.
- Remind students that the formation of the perfect modal requires the past participle, which is often irregular. Elicit a few examples. (e.g., *should have* (write) <u>*written*</u>)
- Point out that some modals have multiple meanings, and the forms they can take vary accordingly.
- Ask students to make a list of the modals and modal-like expressions listed here that have a perfect form: (*could, may, might, must, ought to, should, would, have to, be supposed to*)
- Tell students that four of these modals, when combined with *have*, are used for a meaning

other than necessity. Ask if they can identify them. (*May have, might have, must have* are used <u>only</u> to express probability. *Could have* can be used both for suggestions and probability.)

Note 3 *(Exercises 2–3)*
- Ask students which expression they think is most often used to express strong necessity. (*have to*)
- Point out that *must* is very rarely used in speech to express necessity but is more commonly seen in signs. (*Employees must turn off lights before leaving.*)
- Have students work in pairs to generate sentences using the modals studied up to now—simple and perfect—to show obligation.

Notes 4 and 9 *(Exercises 2–3)*
- Go over both notes with students, drawing special attention to the Be Careful! explanation in Note 4.
- Have students paraphrase the modal expressions below:
    You must . . .
    You must not . . .
    You have to . . .
    You don't have to . . .
  Use these expressions:
    It is necessary that you . . .
    It is necessary that you not . . .
    It is not necessary that you . . .

Note 5
- Point out the forms of *had better*. It is sometimes used in the past: *You'd better not have scratched my car.* (You're in trouble if you did.) The question form is also worth mentioning: *Hadn't we better get going soon?*
- Explain to students that they need to be careful in using *had better*. It is a strong expression and can seem rude or impolite if not used correctly. It is usually used by people who have authority over other people or with people they know very well.

Note 6 *(Exercises 2–3)*
- Point out that *should* is more commonly used than *ought to*, particularly in past forms.
- You may also want to mention to students that *shall* used to be used as a form of *will*. North Americans still occasionally use *shall* for the future, but when they do, they are being very formal or trying to sound funny or different.

Note 7 *(Exercises 2–3)*
You may want to draw attention to the difference between *have to* and *supposed to*:
You have to have a license to drive. (It's a requirement.)
You're supposed to obey the speed limit. (This is the expectation and the law, but many people don't obey it.)

Note 8 *(Exercises 2–4)*
- Let your students know that these polite forms will be very useful to them. You could also point out that *could have* and *might have* referring to past opportunity are close in meaning. The form with *might have* is a little more polite, less direct.
- Have students work in pairs to practice polite forms of suggestion, both present and past.
    I've been invited to dinner at my friend's parents' home. What should I bring?
    You could bring some flowers.
    You needn't (need not) bother.
    He needn't have bothered.
    NOT *You need bother.*

Focused Practice (pages 78–83)

Exercise 2
rude: speaking or behaving in a way that is not polite and is likely to offend or annoy people

gesture: something that you do or say to show how you feel about someone or something

Communication Practice (pages 84–88)

Exercise 6
Ask these questions, and have the class discuss them: "Are surprise parties common in your countries?" "Have you participated in any in another country?" "If so, are they different?" "Do you like surprise parties?"

put . . . off: to arrange to do something at a later time, especially because there is a problem, difficulty, etc.

Exercise 7
be on a tight budget: to have very little extra money to spend

astonished: very surprised about something, especially because it is unusual or unexpected

grateful: feeling that you want to thank someone because of something kind that they have done

miserable: extremely unhappy

broadening: if an experience is broadening, it makes it easier for you to accept other people's beliefs, ways of doing things, etc.

Exercise 8

When groups have finished their work, you might want to have students from different countries summarize the information about their cultures.

Exercise 9

Questions to generate ideas and elicit vocabulary:
- Can you think of a situation you should have handled differently?
- Describe what happened and how you felt about it.
- What would you do now in a similar situation?
- What do you think the result would be?

Exercise 10

- Have students work in small groups to come up with at least eight questions they have about other cultures.
- Let each student be responsible for researching two of these and reporting back to class.

Further Practice

Any behavior can be misinterpreted across cultures. Even such apparently positive actions as expressing appreciation or admiration can lead to misunderstanding. For example, in some countries, if you say "Thank you" a lot as Americans typically do, you can be seen as cold, distant, or superior. Instead, you are supposed to say nice things about the person who did the kindness rather than thank the person for the kindness itself. Have students work in small groups to act out scenes demonstrating how people show appreciation in their cultures. Have them write short dialogues and act out the following scenarios: (1) A classmate invites you to dinner. (2) A friend gives you a book for your birthday. (3) A relative remembers your anniversary and offers congratulations. (4) Someone offers to show you the sights of their city. (5) An electrician, whom you will pay, fixes something in your house. (6) Your teacher shows you how to do something.

How culturally aware are you? Do a search on the Internet on cross-cultural etiquette and/or cultural awareness, and print out (part of) a test to find out how culturally aware you are. Have students take the test to find out how much they know about other cultures. Have students work in small groups to comment on the test and discuss what you must/should/are supposed to/are not allowed to do in other cultures. Also encourage students to use the test as the basis for a discussion of related experiences they might have had, which could also have happened within their own culture. As students share their experiences, encourage their classmates to give their opinion by saying what they think the person should/ought to have done, or could/might have done in the situations described.

UNIT 6 Modals to Express Degrees of Certainty

Unit Overview

The focus of Unit 6 is on ways that modals are used to express varying degrees of certainty when speculating about the past, present, and future. The modals include *must, have to, have got to, may, might, can, could, should, ought to,* and their negative forms. Among the challenges here are learning:
- which degrees of certainty are indicated by certain modals
- which modals cannot be used for questions and/or negatives
- which modals are the equivalent of others in negative statements and questions
- which modals can be contracted

Grammar in Context (pages 89–91)

Background Notes

This unit deals with mysteries in everyday life and in history, myth, and legend. The reading examines the question of who "discovered" America. In the past, American schoolchildren were taught that Columbus made the discovery, but that opinion has become extremely controversial as claims have been made that various Europeans and Asians preceded him. More importantly, many have criticized the old view for ignoring Native Americans, who were certainly the first to arrive in the New World. To best discuss these issues, teachers might bring world maps to class.

Vocabulary

artifact: an object that was made and used a long time ago, especially one that is studied by scientists

fragment: a small piece that has broken off or that comes from something larger

abbot: a man who is in charge of a monastery

pottery: objects made out of baked clay

monk: a man who is a member of a group of religious men who live together in a monastery

monastery: a building or group of buildings where monks live

candidate: a person, group, or idea that is a good choice for something

hemisphere: one of the halves of the earth

Comprehension Questions

- According to the reading, who are the best-known candidates for the title of "discoverers" of the New World? *(the Vikings)*
- What evidence is offered that the Vikings found the New World? *(Viking records and artifacts)*
- What evidence is offered that the Irish reached North America? *(a written account, religious artifacts, and stone carvings found in Virginia)*
- Who were the real discoverers of America? *(the Native Americans who migrated across the Bering Strait more than 10,000 years ago)*
- In what sense did Columbus "discover" America? *(in that he started two-way communication between the Old and New Worlds)*

Discussion Topics

- Why do you think there is so much interest in the Vikings, Japanese, Chinese, Egyptians, Hebrews, Portuguese, and Irish monks, who may or may not have sailed across the ocean to the "New World"? We know for a fact that none of them discovered America. And we know for a fact that it was as a result of Columbus's voyages that the New World was permanently connected to the Old, so why is there all this interest in these other explorers?
- What is the evidence offered to support the claim that the Japanese reached Ecuador 5,000 years ago—pottery fragments similar to those found in Japan from the same period? Is this enough evidence to support this claim? Why or why not?

Grammar Presentation (pages 91–93)

Identify the Grammar

. . . Columbus <u>may not have been</u> the first to visit the Western Hemisphere.
Scholars originally assumed Vinland <u>must have been</u> present-day Newfoundland.
Today the assumption is that Vinland <u>couldn't have been</u> Newfoundland.
<u>Could</u> the climate <u>have been</u> warmer in Erickson's day?
The pottery evidence <u>must</u> mean something.

Grammar Charts

Your students will already be familiar with the forms and sentence patterns of modals, so in general their attention will be more on the meaning than on form in this unit. However, an aspect of form and meaning regarding these modals that is quite challenging is that some modals are used only in affirmative statements. In these cases students will need to learn which other modals to use to form negatives and questions that convey the same meaning.

- Ask students to study the charts looking for examples where the negative is expressed in the usual way. (e.g., *must, mustn't; may, may not; might, might not*)
- Now have them look for examples where a modal doesn't have a negative counterpart using the same modal. *(have (got) to, had to, have, should, ought to)*
- Ask them for the opposites of:
  It must be true. *(It can't be true. / It couldn't be true. / It must not be true.)*
  It can't be true. *(It must be true.* NOT *It can be true.)*

Grammar Notes

Note 1 *(Exercise 2)*
- Your students will probably already have some ideas about using modals to show certainty. Draw a diagram like this on the board and ask them to tell you where they think the following words should be placed: *should, must.*

0% ←——→			Certainty	←——→	100%
			should	*must*	

- Point out that *may, might,* and *could* are fairly close in meaning and belong in the same place on the scale.

0% ← →		Certainty	← →	100%	
		could *may* *might*	*should*	*must*	

- Have students work in pairs. Ask them to use some of the above modals to speculate about what someone they know might be doing at the moment.
- Another good way to practice the use of modals to show certainty is to take a number of magazine pictures to class. Ask students to speculate about what is happening in the pictures. Have students work in groups and write as many sentences as they can.

Note 2   *(Exercise 2)*
- Ask students where they would place *have to* and *have got to* in the above diagram. *(with* must*)*
- Ask them if they think there is any difference in usage among them. Generalizing from what they have learned about *must* in Unit 5, they may think that *must* is formal and more restricted in speech than the others. Point out that, on the contrary, when *must* is used for probability, it is quite common in informal speech; in fact, it is probably the most usual way to express that something is almost certainly true. On the other hand, *have got to* is decidedly informal and is therefore somewhat less useful than the other two.
- Ask students how they would express the opposite of *It must be true.* They will probably say, *It must not be true.* Ask if they can think of other ways. *(It can't be true.)* Ask which of these shows stronger certainty. *(It can't be true.)*
- Point out that *must not* is actually less certain than *must.* On the other hand, *It can't be true* is as strong a negative statement as *It must be true* is in the affirmative.
- Some useful expressions with *must* and *can't* for probability that you might like to teach students are: *You must be kidding!* and *You can't be serious!*

Note 3   *(Exercises 2–3)*
- Point out that in expressing possibility:
  —In affirmative statements, *may* and *might* are more often used than *could.*

—In questions, *could* is more commonly used than *might,* and *may* cannot be used at all to form questions.
- Ask students if they can make a generalization like the ones above about negative formation with these modals. *(May and might can be used with not, but are not contracted.)*
- Have students work in small groups to make questions and statements, both affirmative and negative, using *may, might,* and *could* appropriately.

Note 4   *(Exercise 3)*
- Point out that *must have* + past participle and *had to have* + past participle are similar in meaning, but *had to have* shows a greater certainty:
    John must have gone home. (I'm almost certain that he did.)
    John had to have gone home. (It's almost impossible that he didn't.)
- As indicated in the Pronunciation Note in Unit 5 (page 26), in informal speech we commonly reduce *have* in combination with modals: *must have* sounds like *must've* or *musta. Could have* sounds like *could've* or *coulda,* and so on.
- Read the following and similar sentences at normal speed with appropriate reductions. Have students listen and identify the sentence they hear as affirmative or negative:

(+)	(–)
He could have *been there.*	*He couldn't have* *been there.*

- As you go over the notes with students, model the examples and have students practice saying them aloud, encouraging them to use appropriate reduced forms.

Note 5   *(Exercise 3)*
- Students will need some practice with the past modals. Go over the notes, model the examples, and have students say them, using reduced forms.
- Provide examples of the two meanings of *could have* + past participle:
    Mary could have left early. (It's possible that she left early.)
    Mary could have left early. (She didn't leave early, but she should have.)
  You may want to ask students which meaning was intended in the famous advertisement for V-8 juice: *I cuddahadda V-8!* (=*I could have had a V-8!*).
- Have students practice forming questions such as these:

Could the Chinese have come to America centuries before Columbus?
Might they have landed in North America?
Could Brendan and his associates have accomplished the voyage?

→ For additional practice, see the Supplementary Activities on page 99.

Notes 6–7 *(Exercises 2–4)*

• Review the "certainty diagram" with students. Ask them to place *should, ought to, may, might,* and *could* on it.

0%	← →	Certainty	← →	100%	
		could may might	should ought to	must	

• Ask students which modals they would use for the following situations:

  It's four o'clock. Their train _____ be here by now. *(should, ought to)*

  Did you hear the weather forecast? They said it _____ rain tomorrow. *(may, might, could)*

  What are you going to wear to the party? I don't know. I _____ wear my blue suit. *(might)*

  When will we see you again? I _____ be back on the East Coast next spring. There's a conference I'm planning to go to in April. *(should)*

• You may want to teach students this very useful phrase for "softening" the expression of an opinion: *I could / may / might be wrong, but . . .*

Focused Practice (pages 94–99)

Exercise 2
cherchez la femme: French expression for "look for the woman," meaning that a woman is somehow involved in the situation

retirement home: a building for old people to live in, where various services are provided for them such as food, social activities, and medical care

Exercise 3
dwelling: a house, apartment, etc. where people live

flourishing: growing or developing well

devastate: to damage something very badly or to destroy something completely

Exercise 5
hives: a condition in which someone's skin swells and becomes red, usually because they are allergic to something

rash: a lot of red spots on someone's skin, caused by an illness or an allergy

receptors: cells or groups of cells that receive stimuli

Hodgkin's disease: a type of cancer

tolerable: a situation that is not very good, but you are able to accept it

Communication Practice (pages 99–102)

Exercise 6
Before playing the audio program, have students look at the picture and guess what the discussion is going to be about.

I'd venture to say: said when you are about to say something although you are not sure of it

Let me see a show of hands: Raise your hands if you agree.

fidelity: faithfulness, accuracy

Exercise 7
Have students vote on which solutions are the most likely and which are the least likely, explaining why. *That can't have been the solution because . . .*

Exercise 8
• Have students look over the reading in Exercise 3 again. Tell them not to worry if they don't find enough information there for them to support an opinion—they can be playful and use their imagination.
• After students work in small groups, have them report to the class.
• Discussion topics:
  —Is Atlantis a myth?
  —Do students have other legends to share with the class?

Exercise 9
• To stimulate discussion you might want to offer some options, both serious and whimsical, regarding the purpose of Stonehenge: Stonehenge might have been used as:

  an enclosure for dinosaurs
  an athletic field by Martians
  a calendar
  a temple
  the foundation of a building
  a theater

• Students can find out more about Stonehenge on the Internet.

Exercise 10

Questions to generate ideas and elicit vocabulary:

• When were the pyramids built? How big are they? What technology was available?
• Does anyone in the class know what the crop circles in Britain are? Can you describe them? How many are there?
• Have you ever heard of the Loch Ness monster? Where does it "live"?
• Are you interested in any of these mysteries?
• Are there any other world mysteries that you would like to find out about?

Further Practice

As a rule, the lives of important figures are surrounded by myths and legends. When George Washington was a little boy and used his new hatchet to cut down a cherry tree, his angry father confronted him with the evidence. Little George, realizing he had done wrong, and understanding that he would be severely punished, said, "I cannot tell a lie. I did it with my hatchet." Many American school children have heard and believe this story. Yet it is totally false. Have students get into small groups and discuss similar legends that they know. Have them say whether they think each is true and tell why it is important, even if it is not true.

 **GRAMMAR OUT OF THE BOX ......**

Making up the news. Bring in several newspaper articles with headlines that lend themselves to discussion and speculation. Cut out the headlines to separate them from the articles. Have students work in groups. Give each group a headline, and have students make speculations about the present, the past, and the future—what could be happening, what could have happened, and what could happen next. (Encourage the use of a variety of modals to express degrees of certainty.) After students have finished discussing, hand out the matching articles so students can read them and confirm their guesses. You may want to follow up by having students write the headline they worked on on the board, and report to the class on their guesses and what actually happened.

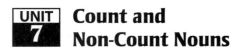 **UNIT 7 Count and Non-Count Nouns**

Unit Overview

Unit 7 focuses on count and non-count nouns, with emphasis given to using non-count nouns in countable ways. These include:
• adding phrases such as *a piece of*
• using the indefinite article to put nouns in countable use: *In Italy, I tasted a new pasta.*
• using the plural form to mean "varieties": *That shop has many different teas.*

Grammar in Context (pages 114–115)

Vocabulary

at someone's disposal: available for someone to use

glance at: to look quickly at someone or something

vending machine: a machine that you can get cigarettes, candy, drinks, etc. from by putting in money

empty calories: calories are units for measuring the amount of energy a food can produce; empty calories have no nutritional value

bland: food that is bland has very little taste

brisk: quick and full of energy

Comprehension Questions

• In what ways have supermarkets changed most in recent years? *(They now sell take-out meals and new products like packaged salad.)*
• What is the problem with vending machines in schools? *(Kids fill up on sodas and chips and do not want to eat nutritious food.)*
• Why do school districts allow vending machines in their schools? *(because the districts find it hard to turn down the money that the companies offer them to place vending machines in their schools)*
• What does the reading recommend about losing weight? *(Eat moderate quantities of regular food. Make sure to include five to eight servings a day of fruits and vegetables. Get exercise. Drink plenty of water and juice.)*
• What should dieters avoid? *(Avoid low-fat diets and sodas. Minimize sugar and salt.)*

Discussion Topics

• Everyone has a "diet story." Discuss the diets you have gone on. Why did you go on them? What restrictions did you observe? Were the diets successful? Why or why not?

• Junk Food, "The Food we Love to Hate": Compare notes. What junk food do you love to eat, even though you know it is not good for you? Have you tried to stop? What happened?

Grammar Presentation (pages 116–119)

Identify the Grammar

COUNT NOUNS
A low-fat diet . . .
We go to supermarkets . . .

NON-COUNT NOUNS
Everything revolves around speed and convenience.
They offer . . . packaged salad.

NON-COUNT NOUNS IN COUNTABLE FORM
Play a couple of games of tennis.

NON-COUNT NOUNS IN UNCOUNTABLE USE
Soda is loaded with sugar.

NON-COUNT NOUNS IN COUNTABLE USE
I'm worried the kids are filling up on sodas . . .

Grammar Charts

• How can you recognize a countable word? (*The singular is preceded by* a / an, *or one. The plural usually has* -s *at the end and can be preceded by a number.*)
• Some nouns have both count and non-count meanings. What are some examples? (*chicken, hair, light, noise,* and *work*)
• What are some examples of words that allow you to count non-count nouns? (*a cup of, a piece of, a game of*)
• In the sentence "Cheese is produced in France," does *cheese* refer to one kind of cheese or many kinds of cheese? (*many*)

Grammar Notes

Note 2
• Ask questions to elicit some examples of non-count nouns, such as *television* and *radio,* with their countable counterparts: "What do you watch in the evenings?" (*television*)
"What do you watch it on?" (*a television = a TV set*) "Which do you like better, television or radio?" " How many radios do you have?"
• Write the words on the board.
• Discuss whether each noun is count or non-count.

Note 3 (*Exercises 3, 5*)
• Give students a few minutes to read the categories and examples, and ask any vocabulary questions.
• Invite students to select a few words and write sentences on the board using them. Make any necessary corrections.
• Refer students to Appendix 5.
• Have students work in small groups. Assign each group two or three categories. Their task is to add five more non-count nouns to each category, writing them on the board. (Note: In Appendix 5, the "Miscellaneous" category, which corresponds to "Others" in this note, has only one additional item.)
   Allow students two minutes to look at the Appendix to find examples to fit their categories, after which they close their books and work with their group to compile their lists.
   Have representatives of each group present their words to the class.

Note 4 (*Exercises 2, 5*)
The main new grammar point in the unit is the use of non-count nouns in a count sense, and this is what students will need the most practice with.
• Model the phrases in the right column, drawing attention to the rhythm set up by the alternation of stressed and unstressed words (e.g., *a **piece** of **fur**niture*). Have students repeat them after you.
• Ask if they can think of other words they can make countable by preceding them with these phrases:
   a piece of _____ (e.g., *fruit, fish, cake, information, advice*)
   a grain of _____ (e.g., *sand, salt, truth*)
• Refer students to Appendix 6.
• Pair work for study of Appendix 6:
   Student A reads a phrase (e.g., *a piece of*) and Student B reads all the examples using it (e.g., *a piece of advice, a piece of equipment,* etc.). Student B then reads a phrase (e.g., *a matter of*) and Student A looks for examples (*choice*).
• Ask if students can think of other phrases outside of Appendix 6 (e.g., *a slice of, a head of, a stalk of, a bag of, a pound* [or any other measurement] *of, a pack of, a package of, a box of, a bottle of, a carton of, a tube of, a roll of*).
   Write the above phrases on the board or have students write them on cards.
   Write non-count nouns that can combine with the phrases, (e.g., *bread, pie, broccoli, lettuce, celery, oil*).

Alternatively, bring in pictures or have students bring in pictures.

Have students match up the phrases with the non-count nouns.

Note 5 *(Exercises 3–5)*
- Ask students, "Do you drink coffee?" What is a common way of asking for three orders of coffee? *(three coffees)*
- To clarify that in countable use, a given noun can usually be singular or plural, ask students to generate sentences using *TVs, chances,* and *a tea.* (Note: *a money,* on the other hand, is not possible.)

→ For additional practice, see the Supplementary Activities on page 100.

Note 6 *(Exercise 4)*
- *Some* is a very useful modifier in English. Point out that it is used with both count and non-count nouns, and it indicates an unspecified quantity of something.
- To get students comfortable using this structure, have the whole class or a few large groups play a memory game:

  Student A says: *I went to the store, and I bought some <u>apples</u>.*
  Student B adds: *(Student A's name) bought some apples, and I bought some <u>oranges</u>.*
  Student C continues: *(Student A's name) bought some apples, (Student B's name) bought some oranges, and I bought some <u>tea</u>.*

This game can also be used to integrate practice of non-count nouns preceded by phrases (e.g., *a roll of paper towels*).

Note 7 *(Exercise 4)*
- Elicit sentences using *criterion, phenomenon,* and *nucleus* in both the singular and plural.
- Ask students if they can think of other nouns ending in *-s* that are usually singular (e.g., *means, sports, linguistics*)
- Refer students to Appendix 4 for a list of irregular noun plurals and allow them to see how many more they can find.

Note 8 *(Exercises 4–5)*
The use of the word *people* is usually a particularly difficult thing to master. Elicit a number of sentences from the class in which the word is used both in a plural sense (= more than one person) and in a singular sense (= a particular group of human beings).

Focused Practice (pages 120–124)

Exercise 2
speck: a very small mark, spot, or piece of something

Exercise 4
remodeling: changing the shape or appearance of something, such as a house, room, building, etc.

Exercise 6
samba: a fast dance from Brazil

Communication Practice (pages 125–127)

Exercise 7
- Have students work in groups to create similar listening exercises based on favorite recipes.
- Invite one or two groups to then present their recipes to the class as a listening, ask follow-up comprehension questions.

lumpy: containing small solid pieces

Exercise 8
- Have students work in groups to construct similar information gap activities with other non-count nouns and the phrases used to make them countable. They can refer to the Appendices as well as any notes they have taken from work earlier in the unit.
- After checking their work and providing any corrections, photocopy one of these to be distributed at the next class meeting. Allow the originating group to play the teacher, handing out the pages to pairs of students and monitoring their performance.

Exercise 9
Questions to generate ideas and elicit vocabulary:
- Do you have a funny story to tell about a meal?
- Have you ever been in an embarrassing meal situation that involved spilling something, knocking over a platter of food, etc.?
- Have you ever been in a situation in which you were expected to eat something you didn't like or felt you couldn't eat? What did you do?

Further Practice
- Americans have a saying, "You can't be too rich or too thin." So, why are more and more Americans becoming obese? Form teams of three or four students. Pairs of teams debate the benefits of different eating habits. One

team argues for the benefits of eating right and staying thin, stressing the physical, social, and economic benefits of being thin (e.g., *health, attractiveness, economic benefit, longer life*). The other team argues for the benefits of people eating whatever they want, including convenience and junk food. These benefits can be psychological, practical (e.g., time), cultural, or economic.

- Getting kids to eat the right thing often means a fight. Childhood obesity is a big problem in the United States. Our children have never been so fat, and if the trend continues, their lifespans will be shorter than ours. Ask students (1) if this problem exists in their countries, and (2) if parents in their countries are concerned about getting children to "eat right" and, if so, how do they get their children to eat what they should?

 **GRAMMAR OUT OF THE BOX • • • • • •**

How do you think it'll taste? Bring in cookbooks or recipes from different sources. Have students work in small groups. Give each student a cookbook or a recipe. Have students choose a recipe to read, and then list the ingredients in two columns, *Count Nouns* and *Non-Count Nouns*. Encourage students to use a dictionary to look up words they might not know. Ask students to write a checkmark in front of all the ingredients they like. Have students discuss whether they would like to try the dish, and support their answer by saying which ingredients they like and which they don't. Point out that as students talk about the recipes, they can suggest replacing some of the ingredients with others they like better.

 UNIT 8 **Definite and Indefinite Articles**

Unit Overview

The article system in English, with its numerous rules and exceptions, is one of the more difficult areas to master. This unit builds on students' understanding of count and non-count nouns from the preceding unit and teaches article usage (*a/an, zero article, the*) in relation to nouns that are:

- countable vs. non-countable
- specific vs. non-specific
- definite vs. indefinite
- generic vs. specific
- unique
- geographical names

Grammar in Context (pages 128–130)

Background Notes

Many writers have dealt with the "mystery of Easter Island," asking who built and erected the gigantic statues there. This unit's reading, based on an article by a leading authority on the collapse of cultures, deals with a mystery that is perhaps more relevant today: What caused the island's environmental disaster? This unit's thematic focus is the impact of technology and science on the environment.

Vocabulary

drastically: strongly, suddenly, and often severely

topple over: to become unsteady and then fall over, or to make something do this

gigantic: extremely large

extraterrestrials: living creatures that people think may live on other planets

cranes: tall machines used by builders for lifting heavy things

assumption: something that you think is true although you have no proof

deforestation: the cutting or burning down of all the trees in an area

nutrients: chemicals or foods that provide what is needed for plants or animals to live and grow

scale: the size, level, or amount of something

shy away from: avoid doing or dealing with something because you are not confident enough or you are worried or nervous about it

Comprehension Questions

- What is the "real" mystery of Easter Island? *(Why did the ecology of Easter Island change so drastically?)*
- Who settled Easter Island? *(the Polynesians)*
- What caused the environmental catastrophe on Easter Island? *(the deforestation caused by human beings)*
- How did the decline of Easter Island happen? *(Nobody knows.)*
- What lesson does the decline of Easter Island hold for us? *(Will we fail to recognize that we are destroying our environment until it is too late?)*

Discussion Topics

- The reading itself provides an excellent discussion question: "Are future catastrophes in the works?" In other words, will our environmental carelessness lead to the collapse of our society?
- Discuss the environmental changes that have occurred in your lifetime. Are the air and water cleaner or dirtier? Has the temperature changed? Is the climate different? Has deforestation occurred? Has Arctic or Antarctic ice melted? Have deserts grown larger? How have these changes affected your life?

Grammar Presentation (pages 130–132)

Identify the Grammar

INDEFINITE ARTICLE

non-specific
Most of it was covered with <u>a subtropical forest</u>.

non-specific
We've become aware of <u>an even greater mystery</u>.

ZERO ARTICLE

non-specific
<u>Plural Count Nouns</u>: *On <u>roads</u> leading out*

non-specific
from Rano Raruku . . . <u>statues</u>.

<u>Non-Count Nouns</u>: *. . . a rather desolate place*

non-specific
covered . . . by <u>grassland</u>.

non-specific
The island was <u>home</u> to as many as 15,000 people.

<u>Proper Nouns</u>: *What happened to <u>Easter Island</u>? It was settled . . . by <u>Polynesians</u>.*

DEFINITE ARTICLE

generic
<u>Singular Count Noun</u>: *<u>The wheel</u> had been invented millennia before.*

specific
<u>Plural Count Noun</u>: *Who built <u>the statues</u>?*

(Note: There are no examples of the generic use of the indefinite or zero articles in the reading.)

Grammar Charts

- Choose one of the examples on the board illustrating the use of the indefinite article for non-specific nouns and add another to show generic use:

INDEFINITE ARTICLE

Non-specific: *Most of it was covered with <u>a subtropical forest</u>.*

Generic: *<u>A subtropical forest</u> is home to many different plants and animals.*

- Ask students why the article *a* is used in the above examples. (Forest *is a countable noun;* a *is used both for non-specific and generic reference.*)
- Ask them which of these sentences they think could be correct in English. *(a, c, d)*
  a. *<u>A forest</u> is home to many different plants.*
  b. *<u>Forest</u> is home to many different plants.*
  c. *<u>Forests</u> are home to many different plants.*
  d. *<u>The forest</u> is home to many different plants.*
- Why is *b* incorrect? (Forest *is countable and it needs an article, either* a *or* the.)
- Are the examples in the third chart specific or generic? *(generic)*
- What if we put *the* in front of forest? Does it change the meaning?
  a. *<u>The forest</u> is home to many animals. (Once again, this is a generic forest. So the meaning is the same.)*
  b. *<u>The forest</u> was his home. (Here the meaning is different. This forest is a specific one.)*
- Could both of these sentences be used as the first sentence of an article? *(No, only sentence* a, *because it is non-specific.)*
  a. *A few centuries ago <u>forests</u> covered most of North America.*
  b. *A few centuries ago <u>the forests</u> covered most of North America.*
- Ask students which articles proper nouns are used with. (zero or *the*). Have them supply some examples.

Grammar Notes

Note 1
The key to understanding the difference between the definite and indefinite article is the concept of definiteness. Cuisenaire rods or other similar objects of different colors and lengths can be used to demonstrate this concept clearly.

- Place a number of rods (or other items) on a table, making sure that you have more than one of certain colors.
- Give students commands like this: Take a yellow rod and a red rod.

- Write on the board: *Take a* _____ *rod*. Ask students which colors they can use *a/an* with. *(They should identify the colors for which there is more than one rod.)*
- Now write *Take the* _____ *rod*. Again, ask students which colors they can use with *the*. *(They should identify the colors for which there is only one rod.)*

Note 2 *(Exercises 2–3)*
The concept of a noun becoming definite after the first mention is, once again, nicely demonstrated with the use of cuisinaire rods or other objects in the classroom. Once a rod has been picked up, it is definite.
- Set up groups of rods on a table, with more than one each of various colors (or use groups of countable classroom objects such as books, pens, pencils, erasers, pads of paper).
- Give students commands like these: Pick up a yellow rod and a red rod. Give the yellow rod to Juan, and give the red rod to Anh.

Note 3 *(Exercise 3)*
- Have students work in pairs or small groups to label the examples with the five categories given for the zero article and then write three more sentences for each. You may want to point out a few more "habitual locations" (e.g., *church, prison*) since there are a limited number of these.
- Write the categories on the board and invite several students to add some of their own sentences under the appropriate heading.

Notes 4 and 7 *(Exercises 3–4)*
Since both of these notes deal with generic nouns, it may be helpful to teach them in succession.
- Have students work in pairs or small groups to label the examples in Note 4 with the categories a, b, and c. You might want to point out that plural count nouns (a) and non-count nouns (c) are the most common types of generic nouns in English.
- Write a number of generic nouns on the board, singular (count and non-count) and plural, and do a rapid drill, asking students to provide sentences, supplying the correct article.
- Then, moving to Note 4, introduce the use of *the* with generic nouns. Starting with singular nouns, point out that when generic reference is made to inventions or the names of musical instruments, it is more common to use *the* than *a/an*. In the expression *play* _____ *piano/violin*, etc., *the* is required.

- Regarding plural forms, note that while the definite article is possible with peoples and animal and plant species, it is actually more common to use the zero article for generic use. Note also that the definite article is not used with most other plural generic nouns.
- Write these sentences on the board.
  1. a. A computer is a machine that does calculations and processes information.
     b. The computer is a machine that does calculations and processes information.
     c. Computers are machines that do calculations and process information.
     d. The computers are machines that do calculations and process information.
  2. a. The guitar is an instrument with six strings.
     b. A guitar is an instrument with six strings.
     c. Guitars are instruments with six strings.
     d. The guitars are instruments with six strings.
  3. a. The Polynesian is an excellent navigator.
     b. A Polynesian is an excellent navigator.
     c. Polynesians are excellent navigators.
     d. The Polynesians are excellent navigators.
- Ask students which of the sentences on the board are correct in expressing generic meaning. *(1: a, b, c; 2: a, b, c; a is preferred; 3: c, d; c is most common)*

Note 5 *(Exercises 2–3)*
Once again, a classroom demonstration is useful to establish the concept of a noun being definite when both the speaker and listener know which particular person, place, or thing is being talked about.
- Set up groups of countable objects (books, pens, pencils, erasers, etc.) on a table (or use rods).
- Invite a student to take an object and then put it down. Have another student describe the action as you write on the board: *Tran took a yellow pencil and put it down.*
- Now write on the board: _____ *pencil that Tran took is yellow.* Elicit *The* from the students.
- Repeat Step 2 with several other students. Have the class watch carefully so that pairs of students can later describe who took what: Student 1: *Maria took a book.* Student 2: *The book she took is blue.*

Note 6 *(Exercises 2–3)*
- After reading the notes, elicit examples of other unique things and write them on the board—for example, *the sun, the sky, the moon, the Earth, the ozone layer, the atmosphere.*

- Have students work in pairs to compose five sentences using these words and five using adjectives that make nouns unique. Encourage them to be playful and come up with some amusing or outrageous sentences. Invite students to share their favorite ones and write these on the board.

Note 8   *(Exercise 4)*
- Point out that the definite article is used not only with public places but with services (e.g., *the doctor, the dentist, the hairdresser*) and things that are very familiar to the speaker (e.g., *the TV, the radio, the stereo, the oven, the computer*).
- Explain that the definite article is used for public places because the speaker and listener have a shared understanding about the place.
  a. Other public places commonly preceded by *the* include: *store, bakery,* and *drugstore.*
  b. Do a rapid fire drill in which students fill in the blank: *I have to go to _____.*
  c. Elicit more examples of public places that would require the definite article and continue the drill, changing the sentence to: *I'll meet you at _____.*
- There are some generalizations that can be made about *the* with geographic names: Most countries are not preceded by *the*. On the other hand, most bodies of water, mountains, and regional areas (e.g., the *Northeast*) are. Reassure students that help is on the way: They can find out which of these are preceded by the definite article in Appendices 7 and 9.
  a. Bring in a few world maps and ask students to fantasize and make a list of places they would like to visit.
  b. Have each student write down twenty geographical names including ten countries, and a few each of other geographical locations—regions, oceans, rivers, mountain ranges—using *the* where it is required. Have them refer to the Appendices as they do this.

→ For additional practice, see the Supplementary Activities on page 100.

Focused Practice (pages 133–137)

Exercise 2
unauthorized: without official approval or permission

evacuate: to move people from a dangerous place to a safe place

vicinity: the area around a particular place

defect: a fault or missing part that means that something is not perfect

first mate: the officer on a non-military ship who has the rank just below captain

vessel: a ship or large boat

Exercise 3
permafrost: a layer of soil, in very cold countries, that is always frozen

thaw: if ice or snow thaws it becomes warmer and turns into water

emission: the sending out of gas, heat, light, sound, etc.

Exercise 4
device: a machine or other small object that does a special job

woodwind: the group of musical instruments that you play by blowing and pressing keys

stringed instrument: a musical instrument, such as a violin, that produces sound from a set of strings

convert: to change from one form, system, or purpose to a different one, or to make something do this

Exercise 5
tamper with: to make changes to something in a way that is dangerous or has a bad effect

isolate: to separate a substance from other substances so that it can be studied

determined: having decided something

unpredictability: the quality of changing a lot, so that it is impossible to know what will happen

Communication Practice (pages 138–140)

Exercise 6
This passage is based on recent events involving the Makah Indian tribe in northwest Washington. United States courts have ruled that, based on treaties between the Makah and the United States government, the Makah have the right to hunt a limited number of whales each year. Ask your students what they think about this issue. Do they agree more with the wife or the husband? Should limited whaling be allowed anywhere in the world?

Exercise 7
- It is common practice in the United States for people to sell used things at yard sales such as the one depicted. Ask students if they are familiar with this custom and if they have anything comparable in their countries.
- Invite students to talk about how they dispose of things in their countries.
- Elicit additional ideas about how the items in the picture could be disposed of and write them on the board (e.g., *take them to*

the city dump, use for landfill, put out for garbage collection).

Exercise 8

Questions to generate ideas and elicit vocabulary:
• What are some reasons why animals are endangered?
• Do you know any specific animals that are threatened?
• Do you think it is important to save all endangered animals?
• What causes air/water pollution?
• What can be done to improve air/water quality?
• Are government regulatory agencies currently doing their job to protect the environment in the United States? In your country?
• Do you know some specific examples where pollution has been improved?
• Why is garbage becoming a problem?
• What is "garbage" in one culture may be a resource in another. Do people in your country throw out the same things that people in North America do?
• What do you think of recycling?

Further Practice

The composition "Genetic Engineering" that students edited on page 137 is written from a conservative point of view. The author and perhaps most Americans today believe that "we should leave genetic engineering to the Creator." Have a spirited debate about genetic engineering. Divide the class into two teams. Team A supports the author's positions: (1) Genetic engineering will upset the balance of nature. (2) Genetic engineering will take away people's control over their lives. (3) Chance will be removed from our lives. Team B challenges these positions: (1) Human beings have been upsetting the balance of nature since the dawn of time. (2) Humans have gained greater control over their lives by domesticating plants and animals—a form of genetic engineering. (3) Inoculating against smallpox is just another form of genetic engineering.

 **GRAMMAR OUT OF THE BOX** ......

Why not take action? Bring in leaflets from different kinds of environmental organizations. Alternatively, search environmental organizations on the Internet and print out information. Have students work in groups and give each group material about three environmental organizations. Have students read the material, discuss the aims of the organizations, and say whether they would like to join or contribute to any of them. Encourage students to support their views. Have each group write a brief report on what one of the organizations does. Have students pay particular attention to the use of articles as they write. Ask students to submit the reports to you for correction. Then have each group report to the class on the organizations they discussed. (Discourage students from reading the reports they wrote. Have them use their reports as a guide instead.) List the organizations on the board as they are brought up by students. Follow up by taking a poll to find out which environmental organization the class is most interested in.

 UNIT 9 Quantifiers

Unit Overview

Students will learn which quantifiers to use to express a range of meanings:
• with count and/or non-count nouns
• in affirmative statements vs. questions and negative statements
• in conversational and more formal styles
Semantic differences in pairs such as *a few/few* and *a little/little* are also highlighted in the unit.

Grammar in Context (pages 141–142)

Vocabulary

originate: to start to develop in a particular place or from a particular situation

"plastic": credit cards, debit cards, and bank cards

crisp: paper or cloth that is crisp is fresh, clean, and new

have little use for: dislike

balance: the amount of money that you have in your bank account

correspondingly: in a manner similar to something you have already mentioned

huh?: said at the end of a question to ask for agreement

deduction: the process of taking away an amount from a total

means: the money or income that you have

Comprehension Questions

- What gives paper money its value? *(trust in the government)*
- What is the most abstract type of money? *(e-money)*
- How does the transfer of e-money work? *(The balance in one account is increased, and the balance in the other account is correspondingly decreased.)*
- According to the reading, what are some advantages of cash? *(universal acceptability, convenience, and "personal connection")*
- What are some disadvantages of electronic money? *(It encourages people to spend more than they have. Mistakes are easily made and hard to correct.)*

Discussion Topics

- Do you pay any bills electronically? Why or why not?
- How often do you use credit cards? If you use them, what do you use them for? Do your credit cards encourage you to spend more money than you should? If so, under what circumstances do you buy things you do not have the money for?

Grammar Presentation (pages 143–146)

Identify the Grammar

QUANTIFIERS USED WITH COUNT NOUNS
. . . *few* flower vendors take checks
. . . getting *a couple of* hot dogs
. . . pull out *a few* bills

QUANTIFIERS USED WITH NON-COUNT NOUNS
It's inconvenient to take *a great deal* of money . . .
. . . the trend toward . . . *less* use of cash . . .
Some people have *little* use for credit cards.

Grammar Charts

- Ask students which words mean "all." *(each, every)*
- Which words mean a large number or amount? *(many, a great many, much, a great deal of, a lot of, lots of, plenty of, most)*
- In the sentence *They have few investments,* could *a few* be used with more or less the same meaning? *(No, it would have a more positive meaning.)*
- *A few* is used with count nouns. What is the equivalent for non-count nouns? *(little)*

- What is the non-count equivalent of *many?* *(much)*
- Are *a lot of* and *lots of* about the same in meaning? *(yes)*

Grammar Notes

Note 1

- Give students the opportunity to practice using quantifiers alone in response to a few questions (e.g., *How many friends have you made? Many. / A lot. / A few.*)
- Note that the following quantifiers cannot stand alone when answering a question, but would need to be followed by a pronoun: *each* of them, *every* one (e.g., *How many of the bills did you pay? Every one.*). The following quantifiers can stand alone if *of* is dropped: *a couple, a great deal, a lot, lots, plenty* (e.g., *I found some scarves on sale and bought a couple.*). And *no* becomes *none* (e.g., *How much time is left? None.*).

Note 2   *(Exercise 3)*

Many quantifiers can be used for both count and non-count nouns. But some are limited to one or the other. Which quantifiers can be used for count nouns only? Which for non-count?

- Put these two sentence frames on the board:
  I have _____ time.   I have _____ problems.
- Do a quick drill, supplying quantifiers and getting students to put them in the right sentence (e.g., *a great deal of, a couple of, several, both, many*).

Note 3   *(Exercises 2–3)*

- In general terms, we can say that *few* and *little* are negative in meaning, while *a few* and *a little* are positive.
- To provide practice making the distinction between *few* and *a few, little* and *a little,* have students work in pairs to write two sentences using each form.

Note 4   *(Exercises 2–4)*

- Write these sentence frames on the board and ask students which of the following quantifiers would work in each frame for informal, spoken English:
  much, many, a lot of, a great deal of, lots of, a great many.

  I have _____ time.
  (a lot of, lots of)

  I have _____ problems.
  (many, a lot of, lots of)

I don't have ＿＿
time.
(much, a lot of,
lots of)

I don't have ＿＿
problems.
(many, a lot of,
lots of)

Do you have ＿＿
time?
(much, a lot of,
lots of)

Do you have ＿＿
problems?
(many, a lot of,
lots of)

• You may want to point out that certain quantifiers are clearly informal: *a bunch of, a couple of, plenty of.* Most others are neutral as to formality.

Note 5   *(Exercises 2–5)*

• Point out that although *some* and *any* are both used in questions, *any* is neutral, while *some* conveys a more positive expectation. It is thus usually more polite to make offers with *some.*

• Have students illustrate the principles in the notes by working in pairs and writing four sentences: an affirmative statement, a negative statement, an offer, and a negative question.

• Invite several students to put their sentences on the board leaving a blank for *some* and *any.* Let them be "the teacher," asking the class to supply the quantifier and writing in the responses.

→ For additional practice, see the Supplementary Activities on page 101.

Note 6   *(Exercises 3–5)*

Have students work in pairs or groups to write sentences with *most/most of, many/many of, few/few of,* and *all/all of.*

Focused Practice (pages 146–150)

Exercise 2

Scandinavian: related to the area of northern Europe consisting of Norway, Sweden, Denmark, Finland, and Iceland

souvenirs: objects that you keep to remind yourself of a special occasion or a place you have visited

economical: using time, money, products, etc. without wasting any

Exercise 3

left over: remaining after all the rest has been used

premium cable channels: expensive, high-quality TV channels available only to those with cable connections

sack lunch: a lunch prepared at home and taken elsewhere

Exercise 4

gross domestic product (GDP): the total value of all the goods and services produced in a country, except for the income received from abroad

life expectancy: the length of time that a person or animal is expected to live

birth and death rate: the number of births and deaths for every 1,000 people

Exercise 6

measure: an official action that is intended to deal with a particular problem

loophole: a small mistake in a law or rule that makes it possible to legally avoid doing what the law is supposed to make you do

revenue: money that the government receives from tax

Communication Practice (pages 151–152)

Exercise 7

Discussion: If there had been no ATM machines nearby, what could they have done?

Exercise 8

Discussion: Ask students if any of the facts surprised them. Do they have any other facts to contribute?

Exercise 9

Questions to generate ideas and elicit vocabulary:

• Were you ever in a situation where you ran out of money? What did you do?

• Have you been in a situation where you gave the wrong tip? How did you feel?

• Did you ever lose your wallet? When did you find out? What did you do?

Further Practice

The article "What's Happening to Cash?" indicates that cash is now generally used only for small purchases like flowers, hot dogs, gifts, and tips. This is not the whole picture. Many businesses prefer cash even if they take credit cards as a service to their customers, and certain kinds of labor are most often paid in cash. Ask students why they think this is. In small groups have students (1) talk about this, and (2) put together a list of all of the situations they can think of where cash is preferred and the reasons why.

GRAMMAR OUT OF THE BOX......

Reviewing holiday resorts. Bring in descriptions of a variety of holiday resorts—for example, Cancún in Mexico or Saint Moritz in Switzerland—with information about attractions, shopping, restaurants, nightlife, currency, language, and so on. Have students work in small groups to discuss the places. Hand out material about several places to each group, and ask students to choose a holiday resort where they would like to go. Have students explain what they like/dislike about the different resorts using quantifiers. Write these examples on the board:

• What I don't like about Cancún is that in summer most of the hotels are crowded. Also, there are a lot of tourists and there are only a few natural beaches.
• What I like about it is that most hotels are first-rate. People who take a vacation in Cancún must spend a great deal of money!

After discussing in groups, you can ask students to write a brief review of one of the places.

UNIT 10 Modification of Nouns

Unit Overview

In this unit students will learn how to:
• modify nouns with adjectives or other nouns
• form compound modifiers (e.g., *computer-generated, 10-year-old*)
• use adjective modifiers in the correct order
• distinguish between participial adjectives ending in *-ing* (to describe who or what causes a feeling) and those ending in *-ed* (to describe who or what experiences a feeling)

Grammar in Context (pages 153–155)

Vocabulary

syndrome: a set of qualities, events, or behaviors that is typical of a particular type of problem

squad: an organized group of players that make up a sports team

sportscaster: someone whose job it is to speak on television or radio broadcasts of sports games

spontaneously: happening or being done without being planned or organized

film-buff: someone who is very interested in and knows a lot about film

rave: to talk in an excited way about something, saying how much you admire or enjoy it

special effects: unusual images or sounds in a movie or television program that have been produced artificially

profound: showing great knowledge and understanding

decade: a period of ten years

tedious: boring, tiring, and continuing for a long time

irony: a situation that is unusual or amusing because something strange happens, or the opposite of what is expected happens or is true

phenomenon: something that happens or exists in society, science, or nature, often something that people discuss or study because it is difficult to understand

immense: extremely large

Comprehension Questions

• Why did everyone expect the American team to lose? (*The Soviet team was apparently unbeatable.*)
• According to the reading, why did the Americans win? (*They had no expectations. They played spontaneously and energetically.*)
• What is the "expectation syndrome"? (*a condition in which events do not turn out as we feel they will or ought to*)
• What is "focal dystonia"? (*an abnormal muscle function caused by extreme concentration*)
• What is Stevens's recommendation about expectations? (*It is better to hope for things than to expect them.*)

Discussion Topics

• The reading states that the American squad "simply played spontaneously and energetically. The result: they won." Books have been written about the U.S. win over the Soviets, and many people would disagree with this analysis. They would say that spontaneous and energetic playing all by itself could not defeat the best team in the world.
—Look back at an important achievement in your life. What were the ingredients of that success?
—Consider things like personality, expectation, preparation, and help from others.
—In small groups, compare success stories. Then compile a list of the various

ingredients of success. Can successes like these be repeated throughout life?

- Most of us have had the experience of going to a movie that was highly recommended by a friend or reviewers, and finding that we didn't like it.
  —Has this happened to you? If so: (a) What was the name of the movie? (b) What didn't you like about it? (c) Do you think that your heightened expectations caused you to dislike the movie more than you would have otherwise?
  —On the other hand, haven't you also had the experience of liking a recommended movie? If so, what does this imply about the "expectation syndrome"?

Grammar Presentation (pages 155–157)

Identify the Grammar

    adj.   adj.   noun   head noun
 . . . the men's semifinal ice hockey match

             compound modifier
 . . . its fantastic computer-generated scenes of

compound modifier
strange-looking creatures

Grammar Charts

- Use the first of the above sentences to generate new ones. Erase one word at a time and get students to supply a new word of the same category. You might wind up with something like this: women's final skating competition. Then, for fun, erase the words from right to left and see what students can come up with!
- Have students compose group sentences following the Order of Adjective Modifiers Chart. The first few times have them start and end with the phrases given, changing only the adjectives.
- Looking at the third chart, ask students why there is only one sentence on the left and three on the right. (The order with different modifier categories is fixed, while the order with same categories is flexible.)
- Moving to the last chart, ask students what they notice about the second words in the modifiers in top row. (They are participles— past and present.) Have students generate a few other compound modifiers following the examples given.

Grammar Notes

Notes 1–2   *(Exercise 4)*

- *Milk chocolate* and *Chocolate milk* illustrate the importance of word order in English. In this amusing example, as the words are reversed, so is the meaning. Of course, it is not often that we find nouns and noun modifiers which are reversible, but there are some. Let your students have fun with these noun combinations and try to think up a few more. (e.g., *country home, piano player, family dog, animal party*)
- To practice using both adjective and noun modifiers: Ask students if they can think of other common phrases where one noun modifies another (e.g., *soccer player*). Have them work in pairs for a minute or two to generate as many as they can think of. (*piano student, tennis teacher*, etc.)
  Write this sentence on the board.
        adj.   noun   head
        mod.   mod.   noun
  Pele is a famous soccer player.
  Ask students if they think the word order can be changed. *(No.)* Have students generate new sentences with the same categories.

Note 3   *(Exercise 4)*
When using participial adjectives, students are often confused as to which form to use.

- It is worth spending some time to ensure they understand the principles that *-ing* causes and *-ed* experiences a feeling.
- Write these sentences from the book on the board, erasing the adjective, and have students supply the correct participial forms of the following words: *amaze, surprise, interest, frighten.*
      It was a _____   The viewers
      movie.   were _____.

Note 4   *(Exercises 2, 4)*

- As you go over the categories, elicit more examples of each from students. Point out that the "opinion" category also includes qualities.
- Please note that there are other adjectives based on participles that don't involve causing or experiencing feelings (e.g., *boiled, boiling, rolled, rolling, carved, carving, written, processed*). They can be placed in various locations but are usually located between colors and origins (e.g., *We bought a knife with a large, beautiful carved wooden handle.*)

- Have students work in pairs or small groups to create the longest descriptions they can think of. You can start them off with something like this:
  a beautiful, expensive antique, hand-finished 12-foot oak library table

Note 5 *(Exercise 2)*
- Another option for two modifiers in the same category is to combine them with *and* if the words have a similar function (e.g., *old and tired*); or with *but* if they are contrastive (e.g., *old but energetic*).
- This comma is reflected in speech by a pause between the adjectives. Read the example sentences in Note 5 aloud and have students repeat, pausing at the comma.

→ For additional practice, see the Supplementary Activities on page 101.

Note 6 *(Exercises 3, 4)*
- As students may be relatively unfamiliar with compound modifiers, it's a good idea to be sure they understand how they are formed. Provide sentences containing phrases and ask students to convert them to modifiers that precede the noun. For example:
  It's a program controlled by the government. → *It's a government-controlled program.*
  It's a bag that weighs 40 pounds. → *It's a 40-pound bag.*
- Have students work in small groups to generate sentences such as those on the left and then exchange them with other groups, who then transform them into sentences with compound modifiers.

Note 7
Writers of college composition and technical writing texts commonly ask students to avoid "stacking noun modifiers." Sentences with more than two noun modifiers together are often difficult to understand. Create a number of sentences with stacked noun modifiers and have the students unstack them so that no more than two nouns occur in succession. For example,
  I bought a student party idea book.
can be rewritten as:
  I bought a book containing ideas for student parties.
  OR
  I bought a book written by a student containing ideas for parties.

Focused Practice (pages 158–162)

Exercise 2
humor: to do what someone wants so they will not become angry or upset

Exercise 3
panic: to suddenly become so frightened that you cannot think clearly or behave sensibly
ordeal: a very bad or frightening experience
lisp: to speak, pronouncing "s" sounds as "th"

Communication Practice (pages 162–166)

Exercise 6
Discussion: After Part A, ask students what they think of the idea of distracting oneself or others to keep from excessive focusing on goals. Have they had any experience with this sort of thing? Does it work?

Exercise 7
After groups have discussed these questions, have someone from each group report to the class.

Exercise 8
Discussion: Would you choose to know the hour of your death?

Exercise 9
Discussion:
- Why did the Titanic sink? (It was believed to be unsinkable. Because of this, many things that could have saved lives were not done: There were insufficient lifeboats. Warning signals were ignored by staff. Distress signals were interpreted by a nearby ship as fireworks.)
- What are some other catastrophes that no one expected? Could people have been prepared for them?

Exercise 10
The examples given in the Student Book should activate students' memories of positive expectations that didn't turn out well. For those students who would like to write about negative expectations that were either fulfilled or happily reversed, here are some questions:
- Expectations can be positive or negative. Can you think of a time you had negative expectations of an outcome that in fact turned out positive for you?
- Why were your expectations negative?

- How did you feel when things turned out better than expected?
- Did it change your expectations for the future?

Further Practice

There is something special about the Olympics. Sports fans love them and so do people who are not particularly interested in sports.

- Have your class consider these questions: What is it about the Olympics that makes them different from all other sports events? Is it the sight of all those talented men and women from all around the world gathering together to compete in peace? Is it the fact that these Olympians have struggled and trained for years and nobody is paying them multi-million dollar salaries to compete? Is it the excitement of watching the human body and spirit striving to do things that have never been done before? What do you think?
- Have students meet in small groups to tell each other about their most exciting Olympic moment. What person or event was it that they found most thrilling? And why?

 **OUT OF THE BOX . . . . . .**

Words that sell. Bring in a wide variety of magazine advertisements for different kinds of products. Make sure the advertisements contain modifiers. Have students work in small groups; give each group four or five advertisements. Have students display the advertisements, discuss them, and identify the adjective, noun, and / or compound modifiers that are used to describe the products advertised. Set a time limit of approximately 2 minutes for students to memorize the phrases and sentences used to describe the products. Then ask students to put the advertisements facedown and write down the phrases / sentences they remember. Encourage students to try to be as accurate as possible. Have students put the advertisements faceup to check for accuracy.

 UNIT 11 **Adjective Clauses: Review and Expansion**

Unit Overview

Adjective clauses are dependent clauses that modify nouns. In Unit 11, students will learn to:

- identify nouns (with identifying, or essential, clauses) or to add extra information (with nonidentifying, or nonessential, clauses)
- position adjective clauses inside or after the main clause
- use relative pronouns as subjects *(who, which, that)*, objects *(whom, who, that)* or possessives *(whose)*
- begin clauses modifying times with *when* or *that* and places with *where*
- learn which relative pronouns can be omitted
- use *which* to refer to a previous idea
- recognize formal and informal usage

Grammar in Context (pages 180–182)

Background Notes

The theme of this unit is personality types, in particular those presented in one of the most famous personality tests, the Myers-Briggs test. The use of such tests for hiring and job assignment is so common in American businesses that important decisions affecting people's lives are often based on their performance on such tests. In this unit personality types are dealt with not only in the context of work, but also within the family and at school.

Vocabulary

resemble: to look like, or be similar to, someone or something

decade: a period of 10 years

correlation: a relationship between two ideas, facts, etc., especially when one may be the cause of the other

loan: an amount of money that you borrow from a bank, financial institution, etc.

insight: the ability to understand or realize what people or situations are really like

Comprehension Questions

- Out of whose work did the science of personality identification grow? *(Carl Jung, Katharine Briggs, and Isabel Briggs Myers)*
- How does the reading define introvert and extrovert? *(An introvert is a person whose energies are activated by being alone. An extrovert is a person whose energies are activated by being with others.)*
- What are the four categories of personality dimensions? *(extrovert or introvert, sensor or intuitive, thinker or feeler, judge or perceiver)*
- The reading asks, "What good is classifying people?" *(It can give insight, help us*

understand others better, perhaps minimize or reduce conflict, and help us understand ourselves.)

Discussion Topics

- Ask students whether they feel the categories of introvert and extrovert are useful and whether they see themselves fitting into one of these categories.
- Can students think of people (possibly themselves) who fit into the remaining categories: sensor / intuitive, thinker / feeler, and judger / perceiver.
- The Myers-Briggs test has been criticized for forcing choices between one or the other personality trait. Critics say that real personalities show more of a combination of traits. Another criticism is that Myers-Briggs assumes that personalities stay the same over time, whereas many of us would say that we're now this, now that. What do you think?

Grammar Presentation (pages 182–186)

Identify the Grammar

1. *The hosts have a new party game <u>that involves asking everyone to</u> . . .*
2. *. . . they developed a test, <u>which has been refined many times over the decades</u> . . .*
3. *This category has to do with the way <u>that people direct their energy</u>.*
4. *An introvert is . . . a person <u>whose energies are activated by being alone</u>.*
5. *She's the kind of person <u>whom others consider shy</u>.*
6. *He . . . is likely to be imagining a time <u>when he was hiking alone in the mountains</u>.*
7. *Sensors are practical people <u>who notice what is going on around them</u> . . .*
8. *. . . Jack, <u>whose parents own a sofa company</u>, notices that his hosts have bought a new sofa . . .*
9. *The loan officer, <u>who makes Gary feel criticized</u>, is only trying to do his job.*

Grammar Charts

- Write the sentences above on the board or make an enlarged photocopy of them to distribute to students in small groups.
- Ask students to look at the first two charts and then see if they can figure out which of the above sentences would go in the first chart (sentences 1–7) and which in the second (sentences 8–9).

- Now have them look at the next two charts and again identify which sentences would go into the first (relative pronouns used as subjects: 1, 2, 3, 7, 9) and which would go into the second (relative pronouns used as objects: 5). Ask students to underline the relative pronouns.
- Ask students to look over the remaining charts and identify the other words that can begin adjective clauses. *(whose, where, when)*
- Have students look at the two sentences above with *whose* (4 and 8) and notice that one of them has commas around the adjective clause. Ask, "Which one is an identifying clause?" *(4)* "And that makes the other one . . . ?" *(a nonidentifying clause)* "In which case could I erase the clause and still have a sentence that means more or less the same ?" *(the nonidentifying clause)*

Grammar Notes

Notes 1–2

- Working in small groups, have students identify and underline the nouns and pronouns that are modified by adjective clauses in the examples in the first two notes.
- Then have them write a sentence for each of the examples that follows the same pattern. (e.g., *John is a man <u>who works very hard</u>. → Maria is a friend <u>who lives nearby</u>*.)

Note 3   *(Exercises 2, 4)*

- Working in pairs or small groups, have students look at the examples, draw an arrow from the relative pronoun to the noun or pronoun it refers to, and then underline the verb that agrees with the noun or pronoun that the clause modifies.
- Again, have students write a sentence for each of the examples that follows the same pattern and uses the same relative pronoun.

Note 4   *(Exercises 4–5)*

- Your students may need some help seeing objects of verbs in adjective clauses. If so, break a few sentences apart. For example, write on the board: *Mr. Pitkin, whom I mentioned yesterday, is my boss*. It can be seen as a combination of two original thoughts: *Mr. Pitkin is my boss. I mentioned him yesterday.* Ask students if they see an object in the second sentence. *(him)* Ask where they think *him* went when the two thoughts were combined. *(It became* whom.*)*
- Point out that *whom* always stands for an object, and in formal writing it is the only

correct choice when referring to a person in the object position of an adjective clause. *Who* is actually a subject pronoun, but these days it is commonly used in informal writing and conversation in both subject and object positions.

- Ask students to look at the three example sentences about the test and say which one they think most English speakers would use. *(The test I took was difficult.)* Why? *(Because the relative pronouns are not necessary here, and people usually do what is easiest.)*

Note 5   *(Exercises 2, 4)*

- Following the first two examples, have students break down the third example into its two component thoughts: *(Harvey is a lawyer. We're renting his house.)* Ask students what happened to *his*. *(It became* whose.*)*
- Have students work in pairs to write five pairs of sentences and then combine them with *whose*.

Note 6   *(Exercises 2–5)*

- Have students write sentences using *where* about their home town, their native country, their first home, their first school, and their current residence.
- Have them exchange papers with a partner and ask each other questions, e.g., *Was the town where you grew up on the coast or in the interior of the country?*
- Have several students write their sentences on the board. Show them how *where* can be replaced by *that / which* + a preposition:

    Was the town that you grew up in on the coast . . . ?
    OR
    Was the town you grew up in on the coast . . . ?

- Point out that this simplified version with the preposition alone is very common in informal conversation.
- Have students work in pairs to transform five of their sentences in this way.

Note 8   *(Exercises 2, 3, 5)*
Have students label the example sentences as identifying or nonidentifying.

→ For additional practice, see the Supplementary Activities on pages 101–102.

Focused Practice (pages 187–192)

Exercise 3
promotion: a move to a more important job or rank in a company or organization

team player: someone who works well with other people so the whole group is successful

irritate: to make someone feel annoyed and impatient

recruit: to find new people to work in a company

congenial: nice, in a way that makes you feel comfortable and relaxed

mystify: to be impossible for someone to understand or explain

Exercise 4
remodel: to change the shape or appearance of something such as a house, room, building, etc.

run smoothly: if a planned event, piece of work, etc. runs smoothly, there are no problems

invaluable: extremely useful

telemarketing: a method of selling things in which you call people on the telephone and ask if they want to buy something

Exercise 5
even tempered: not becoming angry easily; calm

Exercise 6
tough: difficult to do or deal with, and needing a lot of effort and determination

dormitory: a large building at a college or university where students live

Communication Practice (pages 193–194)

Exercise 7
After they have completed the exercise in their books, have students listen a second time to identify the adjective clauses and what they modify. (Note: Five of the seven adjective clauses refer to the whole previous idea.)
(1) When they hear an adjective clause, students raise their hands. (2) Replay that portion of the tape, or read the tapescript as many times as needed. (3) Students write the sentence with the adjective clause. (4) Call on individual students to read the adjective clauses and identify what they refer to.

paper pusher: someone whose job involves completing paperwork

impulsive: tending to do things without thinking about the results

Exercise 8
Ask students to think about experiences they have had and share their stories with their partners. They can then draw on this to make generalizations about strategies they use when they don't get along with someone.

Exercise 9

To reinforce the distinction between identifying and nonidentifying clauses, dictate the sentences below from the listening, repeating them as many times as needed. (1) Remind students to use commas to set off nonidentifying clauses. (2) Ask students to pay attention to any pauses they hear. (3) Do the first one as an example. Ask students if they hear any pauses.

1. *The supervisor, who lives right down the hall from me, is really helpful.*
2. *I really like the one who's from Minnesota.*
3. *Well, my English course, which is really tough, is going to require a lot of writing.*
4. *So is the history class that's held in the morning.*
5. *The history class that I have in the afternoon looks like it's going to be the easiest.*
6. *The girls who live on the second floor eat with us at the cafeteria on our floor.*
7. *Well, my advisor, who is from Minneapolis, is wonderful.*

Exercise 10

Questions to generate ideas and elicit vocabulary:
• Do any of the categories fit you well?
• Do you see your personality as leaning strongly in one direction in any or all of the categories?
• Do you feel your personality moves between opposite categories, sometimes going one way and sometimes another way?
• What are the situations that bring out particular personality traits?

Further Practice

• Have students work in groups of four.
  —Each student identifies an animal to represent him or her but does not reveal this choice to the others.
  —Each student then chooses an animal that represents the personality of each of the other three members of the group.
  —One person at a time reveals his or her choices for Student A, explaining the reasons for the choice.
  —Finally, Student A reveals his or her own choice of animal and why.
  —Students go around the circle, repeating the third and fourth steps, until each person's personality has been discussed.
• Have students answer these questions:
  —Did you see yourself the way others did? Or were self-perceptions and the perceptions of others very different?

—Did you have any insights into your own personality or the personalities of others?

Definition hunt. Have pairs use a dictionary to find eight nouns with definitions that use adjective clauses. Encourage students to find definitions of interesting words and to make sure the definitions they choose cover a wide range of the relative pronouns taught in this unit. Have each pair join another pair. Students take turns reading out the definitions and guessing the words.

UNIT 12 Adjective Clauses with Prepositions; Adjective Phrases

Unit Overview

In Unit 12, students will learn to:
• use adjective clauses with prepositions
• use adjective clauses with quantifiers
• use adjective clauses with nouns
• reduce adjective clauses to adjective phrases
• change adjective clauses to adjective phrases

Grammar in Context (pages 195–197)

Vocabulary

dismiss: to refuse to consider something seriously because you think it is silly or not important

trilogy: a group of three related plays, books, movies, etc. about the same characters

corrupt: to encourage someone to start behaving in an immoral or dishonest way

addictive: if something is addictive, you want to have it all the time

wizard: a man who is believed to have magic powers

dwarf: an imaginary creature that looks like a small man

elf: a small imaginary person with pointed ears and magical powers

compelling: so interesting or exciting that you have to pay attention

appoint: to choose someone for a position or a job

inclined to: tending to behave in a particular way

prominent: well known and important

distinguish: to do something so well that people notice you, praise you, or remember you

prototype: a model for something new

Comprehension Questions

- Why did the author not want to take his children to see *The Return of the King? (He is not a fan of fantasy or science fiction.)*
- Why does the author recommend *The Return of the King* even to people who don't like fantasy? *(It has good acting, awesome special effects, interesting characters, and a compelling story and theme.)*
- What is the theme of the movie? *(the struggle between good and evil)*
- Why does the author refuse to reveal the ending? *(He doesn't want to destroy your pleasure.)*
- What rating does he give the movie? *(four stars out of four)*

Discussion Topics

- What is your favorite movie? Why? What kind of movie is it—a comedy, musical, drama? Is it an adventure movie, science fiction, or fantasy? Is it a romance or an epic? Is it a mixture of some of these types or altogether different? Do you usually like the same kinds of movies?
- Some people go to the movies to see a particular actor. They will see any movie their favorite star is in. Do you have a favorite star? Who is it? What is it about the person that you find so compelling?

Grammar Presentation (pages 197–200)

Identify the Grammar

1. *I've seen quite a few fantasy films, <u>most of which bored me silly</u>.*
2. *. . . I gave my wife several good reasons why she should take the kids and not I, <u>all of which she dismissed quickly</u>. . .*
3. *The movie (and the book <u>on which it is based</u>) is about the struggle between good and evil.*
4. *The forces of evil, <u>represented by the Dark Lord</u> . . . must get the ring back . . .*
5. *Anyone <u>interested in cinema</u> should see this film.*
6. *The Return of the King has many prominent actors, <u>all of whom distinguish themselves</u>.*

Grammar Charts

- Have students work in pairs or small groups to match the sentences on the board with the chart that shows their structures. *(1, 2, 6: Chart 2; 3: Chart 1; 4, 5: Chart 4)*
- Working with the first sentence on the board, erase *most* and elicit other words to fill that slot, e.g., *some, one, a couple.*
- Ask students if similar substitutions could be made in any other of the above sentences. *(2 and 6. However, in sentence 2, "all of which" might also refer to the entire concept rather than to the "several reasons," in which case the substitutions wouldn't work.)*
- Ask students in small groups to look through the reading, decide on their favorite sentence containing an adjective clause or phrase, write it on the board, and identify the chart that describes it. If they don't come up with this one, you might point it out: *Sometimes you hate the things <u>you expect to love</u> and love the ones <u>you expect to hate</u>.* This great example of the expressive power of adjective clauses would actually fit into Chart 4 in Unit 11, rather than the current unit, but focusing on it and examples like it provides an opportunity to integrate what students have learned before with the new material.

Grammar Notes

Note 1

- Have students work in pairs to label the example sentences as formal or informal. Then, so that they gain facility forming sentences such as these, have them transform the sentences from formal to informal and vice versa, omitting the relative pronoun where possible. (e.g., *formal → informal: Bill is the man I spoke to.*)
- Draw attention to the last two example sentences. Ask in which one of these it is possible to omit the relative pronoun and move the preposition to the end. *(only the identifying [essential] clause)*
- Review identifying and nonidentifying clauses if necessary.

Note 2 *(Exercises 2, 4, 5)*

- Ask students which of the relative pronouns can refer both to people and things *(whose)*, which refers only to people *(whom)*, and which only to things *(which)*.
- Write a few sentences with this pattern on the board, some with the clause in the middle, some with the clause at the end, leaving out the commas for students to supply. Then have

students expand the sentences into two sentences, for example, *The students in this class, most of whom are present today, are advanced.* → *The students in this class are advanced. Most of them are present today.*

→ For additional practice, see the Supplementary Activities on page 102.

Note 3 *(Exercises 4–5)*

• Point out that this structure is formal and is generally reserved for writing or formal speaking.

• Ask students to study the example sentences and notice the nouns that come before *of.* *(example, occurrences).* One is singular; the other is plural. Why? (Example *refers to* one musical. Occurrences *refers to* strikes.)

• Have students work in pairs or small groups to write sentences about (1) plants and animals using *example,* or (2) geographic features and weather using *occurrence.* Tell them to use both singular and plural forms as appropriate, and remind them to use commas, for example, *Citrus fruits, examples of which are lemons and oranges, have been cultivated for centuries. Citrus fruits, an example of which is the lemon, have . . .*

Notes 4–6 *(Exercises 3–5)*

• Ask students to look at the examples in the three notes and consider whether any information is lost when the adjective clause is shortened to a phrase.

• Divide your class into two teams. Teams A and B each prepare a number of statements containing adjective clauses about members of the other team. The opposing team converts each statement to a sentence containing an adjective phrase, for example:

A: *The woman who is wearing a red scarf is from Brazil.*

B: *The woman wearing a red scarf is from Brazil.*

Focused Practice (pages 200–204)

Exercise 2

trivia: detailed facts about past events, famous people, sports, etc.

animated: an animated cartoon, movie, etc. is made by photographing a series of pictures, clay models, etc., or by drawing a series of pictures with a computer

critical successes: art, movies, books, etc. liked by the critics

Exercise 4

sequel: a book, movie, play, etc., that continues the story of an earlier one, usually written by the same person

Exercise 6

cinematic: relating to movies

tram: a vehicle that has several cars connected together to carry a lot of people

Communication Practice (pages 205–206)

Exercise 7

buff: someone who is very interested in movies, cars, etc., and knows a lot about them

make a comeback: to become powerful, popular, or famous again after being unpopular or unknown for a long time

Discussion: If students have seen any of the movies mentioned by the reviewer, ask them whether they agree or disagree with the reviewer's opinion. You might then discuss the issue suggested in question 10: black-and-white vs. color movies. Some critics and movie fans feel that many of the world's greatest movies are in black and white and that movies in color make life look too pretty. How do students feel about this?

Exercise 8

Discussion: Ask if anyone in the class has seen the movie and what they thought about it. Did it deserve all of the awards it received? Why?

Exercise 9

Discussion: Ask students if there are movie rating systems in their countries. If so, how do they compare to those in the United States?

Exercise 10

An alternative or additional step that might be fun for Part A is to have Student A describe a person (or group of people) to Student B, who listens and locates that person in the picture, for example, *The woman who is walking down the aisle has just stepped on a piece of chewing gum.* Student B finds the woman described and then describes another part of the picture for Student A to locate, and so on.

Exercise 11

Questions to generate ideas and elicit vocabulary:
• What are the elements of a good movie?
• What kinds of movies do you like?

- Do you tend to like movies that are popular?
- Would you go to a movie just because you liked the actors?
- Can good acting alone make a movie worth seeing?
- What about scenery or special effects?

Further Practice

Have students work in small groups. Their task is to tell the others in the group about a movie they have seen, following the structure used in the reading:

- Tell why you went to the movie.
- Describe your expectations of the movie before you saw it.
- Give a brief summary of the plot (You don't have to tell the ending.)
- Describe three things that you liked or didn't like.
- Give your rating of the movie.

GRAMMAR OUT OF THE BOX . . . . . .

Sequel outdoes first hit. Bring in film reviews of big movie hits. Have students work in small groups. Give each group a review for students to read. (Note: You may want to have all groups work with photocopies of the same review.) Have students imagine that the sequel to the movie has been released and turned out to be an even more successful film. Have students decide on the plot, main actors, director, and so on, of the sequel, and write its imaginary review, which should contain (some of) the information below. Students should complete the reviews with their own ideas and make any changes they might deem necessary.

[name of the film], directed by _____, _____.
It's an excellent movie based on _____.
The sequel, released in _____, _____.
It's a fascinating movie starring _____.
It's a suspense / love / crime story that takes place _____.
It is about a _____ who _____.
The movie has many famous actors, _____ of whom _____.
It was nominated for ten Oscars, _____ of which _____.
It has lots of special effects, _____ of which _____.
The ending, which _____, _____.
This top-earning film, which _____, _____.

Follow up by having students share their imaginary reviews with the class.

UNIT 13 The Passive: Review and Expansion

Unit Overview

The passive voice in all of its forms (using *be, get* and modals with *be*) and the passive causative with *have* and *get* are taught for the following uses:
- when the agent is unknown or unimportant
- when we want to avoid mentioning the agent
- when we want to focus on the receiver of the action with a *by* phrase
- to introduce new information about the agent
- to credit someone who did something
- when the agent is surprising

Grammar in Context (pages 220–222)

Background Notes

In many cultures we find folk heroes who might normally be called criminals, such as Robin Hood and Sinbad. One such figure from the recent American past is Dan Cooper, who disappeared after hijacking a plane and parachuting into the wilderness with $200,000. The mystery of Cooper's disappearance, presented in the reading, leads to the treatment of other current "mysteries" such as UFOs and crop circles.

Vocabulary

get away with: to not be noticed, caught, or punished when you have done something wrong

advance: an attempt to start a sexual relationship with someone

alias: false name, usually used by a criminal

parachute: a piece of equipment fastened to the back of people who jump out of airplanes which makes them fall slowly and safely to the ground

proceed: to move in a particular direction

cockpit: the part of an airplane in which the pilot sits

patron: someone who uses a particular store, restaurant, or hotel

Comprehension Questions

- When "Dan Cooper" first handed the flight attendant a note, what did she think it was? (*a romantic advance*)

- Cooper threatened to blow up the plane unless he received three things. What were they? *($200,000, four parachutes, and a plane that would fly to Mexico)*
- What did the bills look like after eight and a half years of being buried in the ground? *(They had decayed so much that only the picture and serial numbers were visible.)*
- Why do people think Cooper could not have survived the jump? *(a combination of the weather conditions and the impact of his fall: the temperature was too cold—7 degrees below zero—and he wore no survival gear)*
- Why did Cooper become a legend? *(His story has been told in books, articles, and a movie, and it is believed that he got away with the crime.)*

Discussion Topics

- The reading does not mention why one man would need four parachutes. Why do you think Cooper demanded that many?
- What do you think happened to Dan Cooper? Do you think he survived the jump out of the plane and the landing? Did he get away with it? Which of the explanations in the reading seems most reasonable to you?

Grammar Presentation (pages 222–226)

Identify the Grammar

1. *The flight attendant was handed a note by a mysterious middle-aged man.*
2. *The plane proceeded to Seattle with none of the other passengers even aware that it was being hijacked.*
3. *Cooper has not been seen or heard from since that night.*
4. *. . . was he killed trying to commit the perfect crime?*
5. *He received $200,000, all in twenty-dollar bills that had been photocopied by FBI agents so that they could easily be found.*
6. *. . . the area has been searched but no trace of Cooper has been found.*
7. *. . . Cooper had to have been killed by the combination of the weather conditions and the impact of his fall.*
8. *. . . the cash must have been deposited there before the bands fell apart.*
9. *Jerry Thomas thinks that . . . eventually his body will be found.*
10. *Did he have the $5,800 buried by an associate . . . ?*

Grammar Charts

- Write the sentences above on the board or make photocopies and distribute them to students in pairs or small groups. Have students use the chart of Passive Verb Forms to identify examples above of the passive used in different tenses. *(1, 4: simple past; 2: past progressive; 3, 6: present perfect; 5: past perfect; 9: future)*
- Have students look at the charts showing the Passive with Modals and identify examples of these in the sentences. *(5: could be found; 7: had to have been killed; 8: must have been deposited)*
- Ask students which chart sentence 10 fits into. *(The Passive Causative)* Spend a few minutes going over the examples in that chart and ask students to come up with a few of their own.

Grammar Notes

Notes 1–2   *(Exercises 2–4, 6)*
- Draw attention to the examples in Note 1 showing how active sentences are transformed into passive ones.
- In Note 2 ask students to identify the tenses used in the examples. Elicit transformations of a few of them into the active voice using *they*, and, again, ask students to identify the tense, being sure that they see the parallel, for example:
  Cooper has not been caught. (present perfect)
  They have not caught Cooper. (present perfect)
- Then let students practice transforming active sentences into passive ones. Have them work in pairs to look through the reading for ideas, for example, *Cooper ordered the flight attendant to go to the cockpit. → The flight attendant was ordered to go to the cockpit by Cooper.*
- Have several students write their examples on the board and review them with the class.

Note 3   *(Exercise 6)*
- Point out that in most cases, the active voice is considered stronger than the passive, and it is generally preferred. However, there are occasions when the passive is needed. Go over the three categories listed in the note.
- Perhaps the most interesting of the three uses is to avoid mentioning the performer when it is inappropriate to do so, for example, *We were told not to use the photocopy machine for personal use. (The speaker doesn't want to say who told them this.)*

- Ask students if they have been in situations in which they have wanted to say something without mentioning the agent. Have them work in pairs and generate some examples of passive sentences for each of the three reasons described in Note 3.

Note 4   *(Exercise 6)*

- After working through Note 3, where the focus was on avoiding mention of the agent, students may find Note 4 contradictory. If so, ask them which of the uses of the passive pointed out in Note 3 apply here. *(c)*
- *By* phrases occur quite naturally in the context of books / plays *written by,* music *sung / written / composed by,* paintings *painted by,* inventions *invented by,* etc.
  - —Have students work in small groups to make up "quiz material"—one group for art, one for music, one for literature, one for inventions.
  - —Each group lists titles and agents on a sheet of paper, or on the board, without connecting them.
  - —They then quiz another group about the items on their list, and the other group quizzes them. Examples of resulting sentences: *The lightbulb was invented by Thomas Edison. Don Quixote was written by Cervantes.*

Note 5

- Here is a demonstration you can stage to familiarize students with both direct and indirect objects as subjects: Place an object on each of several students' desks when the class is out of the room. When they return, have the students make two types of sentences, for example:
  Maria was given a set of keys.
  A set of keys was given to Maria.
- Ask students to transform the above sentences into the active voice and identify the parts of the sentence:

        indirect   direct
  subject   object   object
  <u>Someone</u> gave <u>Maria</u> <u>a set of keys</u>.

- Then ask them to notice where those sentence parts went in the two sentences above. *(Maria, the indirect object, became the subject in the first sentence. A set of keys, the direct object, became the subject in the second one.)*
- Have students work with a partner to generate pairs of sentences such as those above about the other objects placed on students' desks.

Note 6   *(Exercise 4)*

- Encourage students to explore the use of modals in the passive by having them work in small groups to test out which modals can be used in each of the example sentences in the note.
- Divide up the sample sentences among the groups and have representatives of each group write their list of possibilities on the board.
- As a class, consider which ones could be expressed in the past and write those forms.

→ For additional practice, see the Supplementary Activities on pages 102–103.

Note 7

- Point out that the *get* passive is often used to emphasize action and to suggest that someone or something is subjected to another force. Write two sentences like these on the board:
  The boy <u>was hit</u> by a car.
  The boy <u>got hit</u> by a car.
  The first sentence is a relatively neutral factual statement, while the second emphasizes the action and takes on a more dramatic meaning.
- To give students practice forming the *get* passive, do a quick oral drill, calling on individuals to substitute the appropriate form of *get* for *be* in the example sentences in Note 6.

Notes 8–9   *(Exercise 5)*

- For some rapid oral practice with the forms, do a circle drill with students in which they play with the example sentences in Notes 8–9.
  - —Begin by substituting *get* for *have.* Sit in a circle with the students. Address one student, saying, for example, *Tomiko, you should <u>get</u> your car serviced.*
  Tomiko then addresses another student with her sentence: *José, I just <u>had</u> my car serviced.*
  - —Continue around the circle, alternating between *get* and *have.*
  - —When they have finished this round, continue the drill, this time transforming the sentences to reflect a different time period. For example, *We had the windows washed* becomes *We <u>are going to have</u> the windows <u>washed</u>.*
- Have students work in pairs or small groups to personalize the practice by asking each other questions such as the following:
  Where do you get your photographs developed?
  Do you cut your own hair or have it cut?

Focused Practice (pages 226–231)

Exercise 2
the authorities: the people or organizations that are in charge of a particular country or area; sometimes the police

locale: the place where an event happens

accomplice: a person who helps someone such as a criminal to do something wrong

Exercise 3
vault: a room with thick walls and a strong door where money, jewels, etc. are kept to prevent them from being stolen or damaged

undisclosed: undisclosed information has not been made available to people in general

Exercise 4
sight: to see something from a long distance away or for a short time

in order: if things are in order, they are correctly arranged

perplexing: if something is perplexing, it makes you feel worried and confused because it is difficult to understand

Exercise 6
late-model: recent type design

paramedic: someone who has been trained to help people who are hurt or to do medical work, but who is not a doctor or nurse

Exercise 7
extraterrestrial: a living creature that people think may live on another planet

speculation: the act of guessing without knowing all the facts about something, or the guesses that you make

Communication Practice (pages 232–234)

Exercise 8
Students' ability to understand this listening exercise and to answer the questions correctly depends on their understanding of the meaning conveyed by the passive voice. It thus provides an excellent opportunity both to demonstrate to students the importance of learning the grammatical content of this unit and to diagnose their command of it.
- Before doing the listening, go over the vocabulary below with students.
- Ask students if they enjoy going to the zoo, if they have ever seen a koala bear, what they think a keeper in a zoo does.

janitor: someone whose job it is to clean and take care of a large building

reference: information about you that is written by someone who knows you well, usually to a new employer

black market: the system by which people illegally buy and sell foreign money, goods that are difficult to obtain, etc.

underworld: the criminals in a particular place and the criminal activities they are involved in

koala: an Australian animal like a small bear with no tail that climbs trees and eats leaves

keeper: someone who cares for or protects animals

Exercise 9
Discussion: Ask students to describe their favorite sandwiches.
Activity: Divide the class into small groups and have each group construct a similar exercise about another mystery to give to a different group.

Exercise 10
- Before breaking up into small groups, have a class discussion. Ask students if they have any stories to share about UFOs or aliens.
- ⏱ Invite students to close their eyes and imagine what a UFO or alien might look like and then describe these to their partner. Encourage them to draw pictures.

Exercise 11
Questions to generate ideas and elicit vocabulary:
- Do mysteries interest you?
- Do you ever read mystery stories? Do most of them have solutions?
- Do you know of any unsolved mysteries?
- What kind are they? Do they involve crimes? Someone's disappearance? Geography?

Further Practice
Have a whole-class discussion. Ask students if anyone knows of a person who committed a crime and got away with it. What was the nature of the crime? How did that person escape punishment? Was it intelligence, luck, or both?

Discussing a criminal case. Bring in articles about unsolved criminal cases. Have students work in pairs. Give each pair an article. Have students read the article and underline the passive forms. Have students study some of the passive forms in the article and ask, "Why was the passive voice preferred? Why do you think the agent was mentioned in some of the passive statements?" (You may want to refer students to Notes 3 and 4 in the Grammar Presentation.) Then have each pair join another pair. Students take turns retelling the stories they read paying particular attention to passive forms. Encourage students to share what they might already know about the stories and make speculations about what might happen next.

 You may want to record on a videotape a TV news report of a criminal case and play it in class. After discussing the report, have students listen again and write down a couple of passive sentences. Follow up by calling on a few students to read out the passive sentences they wrote.

UNIT 14 — The Passive to Describe Situations and to Report Opinions

Unit Overview

This unit focuses on ways that the passive is used in many everyday contexts as well as in academic discourse to:
- Describe situations or states: *The country is composed of two regions.*
- Report opinions or ideas
  —with *to* phrases: *The people are alleged to have come from the East.*
  —with *it + that* clauses: *It is alleged (by some) that the people came from the East.*

Grammar in Context (pages 235–237)

Background Notes

Although the literature of anthropology is usually associated with remote and "primitive" cultures, this unit's reading offers a humorous "anthropological" look at a more familiar society and offers students a new perspective on the contrast between the "primitive" and the "advanced." The theme of cultures and cultural differences is expanded to include great figures from history worldwide.

Vocabulary

expend: to use money, time, etc. to do something

herd: a group of animals of one kind that lives and feeds together

drawback: a disadvantage of a situation, product, etc.

ailment: an illness that is not very serious

tendency: a probability that a person or thing will develop, think, or behave in a certain way

apparel: a word meaning "clothing," used especially by stores or the clothing industry

excrement: the solid waste material from a person's or animal's bowels

alleged: an alleged fact, quality, etc. is supposed to be true, but has not been proven

Comprehension Questions

- Where do the Asu live? *(between Mexico and Canada)*
- What is the name of the Asu's sacred creature? *(the rac)*
- What is the connection between rac ownership and social status in Asu society? *(The more racs a family has, the higher its social status.)*
- What is the most common rac ailment? *(the tendency for its shoes to deteriorate rapidly)*
- What is the average lifespan of the rac? *(five to seven years)*

Discussion Topics

- At what point in the reading did you realize that the author was talking about the importance of the car in American society? What clues gave it away?
- Why do you think the author pretended to be an anthropologist studying some primitive society?

Grammar Presentation (pages 237–239)

Identify the Grammar

1. *The territory of the Asu is located . . . between . . . Mexico and . . . Canada.*
2. *On the southeast, their territory is bordered by the Caribbean.*
3. *Relatively little is known of the origin of this people, though they are said to be from somewhere in the East.*
4. *. . . the cow is regarded as a sacred animal and is treated with great respect . . .*
5. *. . . it is felt that the more racs a family has the higher its social status is.*
6. *Those not possessing at least one rac are considered to be of low social status.*
7. *In some large Asu cities, citizens are surrounded by their racs . . .*
8. *. . . merchants that provide rac food are sometimes alleged to be profiting excessively . . .*

Grammar Charts

- Write the sentences above on the board or make photocopies and distribute them to students in pairs or small groups. Have students use the charts to answer the following questions:
  —Which of the above sentences describe situations or states? *(1, 2, 7)*
  —Which report opinions or ideas? *(3, 4, 5, 6, 8)* Can you find more in the reading?
  —Which are followed by prepositional phrases? *(2, 7)* (You may wish to point out that in #4 *regarded* is followed by *as* + a noun phrase.)
  —Which are followed by *that* clauses? *(5)*
  —Which are followed by *to* phrases? *(3, 6, 8)*
- Ask students to notice how active sentences with *that* clauses and *to* phrases are converted to passive ones, and to do the same for the sentences above (that *clause: 5;* to *phrase: 3, 6, 8)*
- Ask students if they see a passive construction in the above sentences that doesn't fit the charts in this unit. *(4: . . . is treated . . .)*

→ For additional practice, see the Supplementary Activities on page 103.

Grammar Notes

Notes 1–2   *(Exercise 2)*
Have students look at the examples in Note 1 and identify which could be rewritten:
- with a *by* phrase
- in the active voice

Note 3   *(Exercise 2)*
- Working in small groups have students describe their home towns and / or countries using the stative passives exemplified in this note.
- Refer students to Appendix 11 for a list of Common Stative Passive Verbs and Prepositions. Have students write five sentences, being sure to use some of the verbs they haven't used before. (You may want to point out that *be listed* is commonly used in the context of telephone and other directories.) Share these sentences with the class.

Note 4
- A simple substitution drill will help students become comfortable with the *it* + *be* + past participle + *that* construction. Write on the board:
  It is assumed that this culture is very old.
  Erase *assumed* and elicit another verb from a student, who then says, e.g., *It is <u>alleged</u> that*

this culture is very old. This student selects the next student, who substitutes a third verb, and so on, until all the verbs have been used.
- Now invite students to have some fun with this construction. Write on the board:
  It is _____ that _____.
  Have students work in pairs to generate five sentences, which can be serious or amusing. Have them share their favorite ones with the class.
- Ask students to look at the examples in the note and notice the way the passive sentence that they practiced has been transformed into an active one *(Scholars assume . . .).* Have them similarly transform the other example sentences into active ones.
- Have students look at Appendix 10, Verbs Used in the Passive Followed by a *That* Clause. At this point only a few of these will be new. Go over any vocabulary questions.
- Ask students if they have some ideas about which of these words are "<u>all-purpose</u>," used both in informal conversation and in all kinds of writing, and which are generally limited to more formal speech or <u>written or academic use</u>. Set up two columns on the board and ask students to tell you which column they think each word belongs in. *(all-purpose: assume, believe, claim, feel, say, think; <u>written, academic:</u> fear, hold, postulate, theorize)*

Note 5   *(Exercises 3–4)*
- Have students look at the first two examples and notice how the first sentence has been transformed from the active into the passive voice in the second one. Ask them to do the same for the four other examples in the note. In the first sentence the word *scholars* is used as the subject. Ask students if, in addition to *scholars*, they can think of some other words to use as subjects in sentences when they don't know who the agent really is. (*For academic writing, possibilities are* historians *and* students of this period. *In conversation or informal writing,* they *is very commonly used;* people *can also be used informally. Some* is a convenient, all-purpose word which can stand for some people, some historians, etc.)
- Draw attention to the note about the use of *consider.* Ask students if there are any examples of the passive in this note where *consider* could be used in place of the existing verb. *(all of them)* Ask if there are any sentences where the infinitive phrase could be dropped after *consider. (He is <u>considered</u> [to be] the author.)*

- Point out the note about the need to follow *regard* by *as*. Ask students to try using *regard* in as many of the examples in Note 5 as possible and to write the resulting sentences. *(He is regarded as the author. Native Americans are regarded as the real discoverers.)*

Note 6   *(Exercise 3)*

- By now students should have some facility with the two constructions reviewed in this note. If you think they need further practice manipulating these structures, you could have them transform the example sentences into different passive constructions.
- Knowing when to use passive constructions is as important as knowing how to form them, and the information presented in this note about achieving formality and distance through the use of these particular grammatical forms will be of value to students in their academic work. Another point that you might want to make is that an element of good writing is sentence variety. Even in settings that call for the use of the passive, students will need to vary their writing to include active sentences as well; in fact, as a rule they will want to use considerably more active than passive sentences in their writing.
- Examine the use of active and passive sentences in the reading. As there are seven paragraphs in the reading, to the extent possible, have students work in groups of six or seven, with one student in each group taking responsibility for a particular paragraph (since paragraphs 1 and 2 are short, they can be combined).

Have students:
—scan their paragraphs, looking for examples of active and passive sentences, writing *A* for every active sentence and *P* for the passive ones
—look at the resulting pattern
—count up the number of active and passive sentences, and share the information with their group

Meet as a whole class to discuss observations.

Focused Practice (pages 240–244)

Exercise 3
circle: a group of people who know each other

Exercise 5
conclusive: showing without any doubt that something is true

dismiss: to refuse to consider someone or something seriously because you think they are silly or unimportant

Communication Practice (pages 245–247)

Exercise 6
Ask if any students have ever experienced an earthquake. Have them talk about their experiences. Before playing the audio program, go over the vocabulary below. After the listening ask students where this earthquake took place. (Hopefully, they will recognize Atlantis as the fictional place they have read about in previous units.)

register: to automatically record or display an amount on a machine or instrument

Richter scale: a scale that shows how strong an earthquake is, with 1 being very weak and 10 being the strongest

epicenter: a place on the Earth's surface that is above the point where an earthquake begins

inland: in a direction away from the coast and toward the center of a country

loot: to steal things, especially from stores or homes that have been damaged in a war, riot, or natural disaster

grave: very serious and worrying

Exercise 7
Discussion Topics
- Ask students if they found the reading amusing. What were the some of their favorite lines?
- Do Asu or people like them live in the students' home countries, too? Do they also worship racs? If not, how are things different in their countries?

Exercise 8
Discussion: Anastasia Romanova. Some students may have seen the Disney film and some may even have seen the 1954 film with Ingrid Bergman and Helen Hayes. Most Russian citizens seem to think that Anastasia could not have escaped assassination, and recent DNA evidence seems to support this belief. Nevertheless, the story has been featured on *Unsolved Mysteries* and continues to have considerable appeal. What do your students think? Are there any similar mysteries or legends in their own country?

You could also use the transcript to do a dictation focused on passive constructions.

behead: to cut off someone's head as a punishment

monarch: a king or queen

Bolshevik: someone who supported the Communist party at the time of the Russian Revolution

Exercise 9

Before forming small groups, do a whole-class brainstorming activity to generate ideas and vocabulary. Ask students to look at the pictures and call on volunteers to say whatever comes to mind. Write some key words on the board.

Exercise 10

Questions to generate ideas and elicit vocabulary:

- What are myths and legends?
- Do you have any favorite ones?
- Are you aware of any legends that are specific to your culture?
- When you were young did you hear or read stories about certain heroes or legendary characters?
- Did you have any favorite characters? What were they like?
- Can you think of any movies that portray legends?

Further Practice

- Have your students meet in small groups to discuss these questions: What was the author's motive in writing "Sacred Beasts"? How do you know? What evidence does the author provide to support her criticism of the car culture? Do you agree or disagree with the author's criticism? Are there any real alternatives to the automobile in modern American society?
- Meet as a whole class to share ideas about alternatives to the automobile.

 **OUT OF THE BOX** . . . . .

Unraveling a mystery. Bring in information about the Nazca lines in Peru from different sources—for example, books about archaeological mysteries, encyclopedias, travel magazines, or websites. Have students work in small groups. Hand out the material and have students read about this mystery of pre-Colombian archaeology. As students discuss, encourage them to express their views about the Nazca lines. After discussing in groups, have students share their findings with

the class. Encourage the use of the passive to describe situations and report opinions. You may want to write the following on the board to prompt students:

The Nazca lines are	located in . . . found in . . . considered . . . regarded as . . .

It is	believed alleged said thought	that . . .

The Nazca people The Nazca lines	are	believed to . . . alleged to . . . said to . . . thought . . .

UNIT 15 Gerunds

Unit Overview

In this unit students will learn how to use gerunds:

- in every situation that nouns are used in: subject, object, subject complement, object complement, object of preposition
- after possessives
- in both active and passive constructions
- in present and past forms

Grammar in Context (pages 258–260)

Vocabulary

perceive: to think of someone or something in a particular way

simplistic: treating difficult subjects in a way that is too simple

long since: if something has long since happened, it happened a long time ago

catch up on: to do something that needs to be done, that you have not had time to do before

counterpart: someone or something that has the same job or purpose as someone or something else in a different place

spare someone's feelings: to avoid doing something that would upset someone

awfully: very

Comprehension Questions

- Why doesn't the author like the traditional description of friends as either true or false? *(He recognizes at least six types.)*
- What are the author's six types of friends? *(convenience friends, special-interest friends, long-time friends, cross-generational friends, part-of-a-couple friends, "best" friends)*
- Why is Bill important to the author? *(He is a father figure and mentor.)*
- Who are Amanda and Gretta? *(the author's wife and the wife of a friend)*
- Who is Ken? *(one of the author's two "best" friends)*

Discussion Topics

- Do you think it's possible to have a true friendship with a person of the opposite sex?
- Is it possible to be "friends" with your children? Or, if you are still living at home, can you be friends with your parents? What about being friends with a teacher or boss?

Grammar Presentation (pages 260–263)

Identify the Grammar

1. *I was having difficulty <u>finding</u> a subject for this month's column.*
2. *I also remembered <u>learning</u> . . . a rhyme . . .*
3. *. . . I see that my <u>perceiving</u> friendship in this way was pretty simplistic.*
4. *I tried <u>taking</u> the bus . . .*
5. *My brother's passion is <u>kayaking</u>.*
6. *We can go for months or years without <u>contacting</u> each other . . .*
7. *We enjoy just <u>catching</u> up on each other's activities.*
8. *It's someone who doesn't . . . avoid <u>telling</u> you what you need to hear . . .*
9. *Other times we just like <u>being</u> together without saying much of anything.*

Grammar Charts

- Write the sentences above on the board or photocopy and distribute to students in pairs or small groups. Have students categorize these sentences according to which patterns they represent in the charts. *(1: gerund as object complement; 2, 4, 7, 8, 9: gerund as object; 3: possessive + gerund; 5: gerund as subject complement; 6: gerund as object of a preposition)*

- Ask students to look at the charts and notice how the negative is formed. How would they make sentences 3 and 4 above negative?

Grammar Notes

Note 1 *(Exercises 2, 6)*
Have students make lists of their hobbies and what they like to do in their free time and then talk about this in small groups. Gerunds are likely to come up naturally in this context. After the small groups talk, take a class survey: How many of their sentences included gerunds?

Note 2 *(Exercises 2, 5, 6)*
- Ask students to interview their partners to find out what they enjoy doing and how much time they spend in an average week or month practicing or doing what they like. Then have them report to the class using these verbs followed by gerunds: *enjoy, spend time, practice.*
- Refer students to Appendix 12. Have them spend a few minutes looking through the list of verbs followed by gerunds and then choose five to base sentences on. Have students write sentences and exchange them with their partner. Call on individuals to share with the class a favorite sentence from among those their partner has written.
- Have students work in small groups to:
  —categorize as many of the words in Appendix 12 as they can into groups that are useful to them (Examples of categories might be: verbs expressing positive feelings, negative feelings, communication, mental activity)
  —find pairs or groups of words that mean (a) (almost) the same thing and (b) (almost) the opposite
- Have students generate sentences for each of these categories to share with the class.
- Ask the class if they *had difficulty doing* the activity and if they thought it was *worth doing!*

Note 3 *(Exercises 2, 6)*
- Working in pairs, have students make up new sentences using the verb and preposition combinations shown in the examples.
- Refer students to Appendix 13, and have them scan the list of adjective + preposition expressions. Tell them they will be making use of these words in the next activity, and give them a few minutes to ask any questions they may have about them.

- Ask each student to make a list of five or six of the expressions in Appendix 13 that they think might be most useful to them. On a separate, small piece of paper have them write a gerund. Now do a drill using the "wheels" system (described on page 12 of the Introduction). Have half the class stand in a circle facing outward and the other half stand in a circle around them, facing inward. The students in the inner circle show their gerund card (e.g., *dancing*) to the students in the outer circle facing them. The students in the outer circle, referring to their list of useful adjectives + prepositions, respond with an appropriate sentence (e.g., *I'm not accustomed to dancing.*).

  Then the students in the outer circle show their gerund card to the students facing them, and again, elicit a sentence. After this, the students in the outer circle move to the right, where they face a new partner with a new gerund. Continue until everyone has gone around once.
- The Be Careful! Note points out a problematic area. One of the more challenging areas of English is knowing which verbs take prepositions and which ones they take. Assure students that this knowledge comes over time as they have more and more exposure to English. When in doubt, they should refer to their dictionaries.

Note 4   *(Exercises 3, 5, 6)*
- To get students to feel comfortable with the use of the possessive before a gerund, do a quick drill, eliciting substitutions for the nouns, pronouns and gerunds in the example: *Pete's dominating . . .* → *Maria's dominating . . .* → *her dominating . . .* → *their dominating . . .* → *their controlling . . .*
- Elicit a few personal examples from the class, using the same sentence frame or a variation.

Note 5   *(Exercise 4)*
- To clarify that past gerunds are used to show an action earlier in time, have students break down the second example sentence into two sentences and label them to show the sequence:

  1

  I met Jane in my first week of college.

  2

  This helped me throughout my college career.
- Write the example sentence on the board *(Having met Jane . . .)*. Then erase all but the

following to elicit some examples of past gerunds from students:

  Having _____ helped me _____.

Another good way to practice this structure is to have students create their own sentences with the verb *remember,* for example, *I remember having heard that . . .*
- To practice gerunds in passive constructions, you might write structures such as these on the board and elicit others from the students, encouraging them to use other verbs:

  I hate / dislike being . . . / I hate getting . . .
  I like / enjoy being . . . / I like getting . . .
- If you want to give students some practice with the past passive, elicit sentences in which they talk about their personal experience, using a frame such as this:

  Having been (past participle) *is one of the best things that ever happened to me.*

→ For additional practice, see the Supplementary Activities on page 103.

Focused Practice (pages 263–269)

Exercise 1
engage in: to take part or become involved in an activity

pursue: to continue doing an activity or trying to achieve something over a long period of time

Exercise 2
collapse: to suddenly sit or lie down, especially because you are very tired

punch a time clock: to record the time that you start or finish work by putting a card into a special machine

put in: to spend time or use energy working or practicing something

karaoke: the activity of singing to specially recorded music for fun

Exercise 7
jerk: someone who is stupid or who does things that annoy or hurt other people

wilderness: a large area of land that has never been built on or changed by humans

chauffer: to drive someone in your car

Communication Practice (pages 270–271)

Exercise 8
Discussion: Ask students if they have ever heard of orienteering. Does it sound interesting to them?

cross-country skiing: the sport of moving across fields, through woods, etc. on skis *carpooling:* if a group of people carpool, they travel together to work, school, etc., in one car and share the costs

Exercise 9
To facilitate the reporting of results to the class, write the items added by students on the board and take a vote to see how many students would add those to their list and how they would rank them.

Exercise 10
Questions to generate ideas and elicit vocabulary:
• How did you meet some of your friends?
• How long have you known them?
• How often do you see or talk to them?
• What do you do when you are together?
• What are some interesting experiences you have had with them?

Further Practice
• In "Friends" we saw one middle-class American man's ideas about the different kinds of friendships we have. It's probable that every person sees friendship differently. How would you categorize the different kinds of friendships you have? Have students meet in small groups to discuss their categories. Are there any types of friendship everyone agrees on? Share your findings with the class.
• Some people have imaginary friends. Do you? Imaginary friends are common among children. What function do they serve? Have students meet in small groups to discuss these questions and then share their ideas with the class.

 **OUT OF THE BOX ......**

More on friendship. Bring in a self-help audiocassette or CD about making and keeping friends. Have students listen to an excerpt and take notes about main ideas. Discuss the main tips. Then have students complete sentences expressing their own views about friendship.

   Write the following examples on the board to prompt students:

A good friend should be grateful for _____.
Appreciating _____ is very important.
It is worth _____.
_____ with a friend is very enjoyable.
Not _____ is a big mistake.
A good friend looks forward to _____.
It's important not to get angry at _____.
A good friend doesn't mind _____.

 Bring in a short story that deals with friendship. Have students read it and discuss it. You may want to make up some questions using the grammar in this unit for students to use as a guide when discussing the story.

Unit Overview

Infinitives are used as nouns in many situations—as subjects, objects, subject complements, and adjective complements. This unit presents them in a wide range of functions and forms:
• *it* + infinitive phrase: *It's advisable (for a student) to take good notes in class.*
• *too/enough* with infinitives: *The project is too complicated to finish on time. He didn't call quickly enough to get the job.*
• Simple and past forms: *You seem to have forgotten.*
• Active and passive: *The work is supposed to be finished by tomorrow.*
• Elliptical use of *to*: *Steve knew he had to go to work but he didn't want to.*
One of the challenges presented by infinitives and gerunds is learning which verbs are followed by one or the other or both, the most memorable ones being those where there is a significant difference in meaning. Another challenge is learning which verbs can be followed by a noun/pronoun+ infinitive. Infinitives also follow adjectives and nouns. The content of this unit connects to Appendices 14–18, the study of which becomes an integral part of the work of this unit. The Appendices are listed at the end of the Grammar Notes.

Grammar in Context (pages 272–274)

Vocabulary
syndrome: a set of physical or mental problems considered together as a disease

subconscious: feelings, desires, etc. that are hidden in your mind, and you do not know that you have them

Comprehension Questions
• What is the difference between *procrastinate* and *postpone?* (*To postpone means to reschedule for a later time. To procrastinate means to avoid doing something.* Postpone *has a neutral sense.* Procrastinate *has a negative connotation.*)

- According to the author, what is the reason for procrastination? *(fear of failure)*
- What three principles does Dr. Stevens recommend for his clients who want to stop procrastinating? *((1) Never put things off. (2) Do not avoid painful or difficult things. (3) Carpe diem: Do not put off living.)*

Discussion Topics

- Reread the short dialogue at the beginning of the reading. If you were Steve, what would you have said?
- In the discussion about Blanche's procrastination, which led to a "failed" party, Blanche "expects to fail" and so delays calling her friends until failure is assured. A dinner party with friends should not fail unless you try hard to make it fail. Why do people cause their own failure? What does Blanche get out of having a failed party?

Grammar Presentation (pages 274–278)

Identify the Grammar

1. *I can't stop to type your paper now.*
2. *Today I want to ask you if there's such as thing as a procrastination syndrome.*
3. *To procrastinate is literally to put things off until tomorrow.*
4. *There are occasionally good reasons to postpone things . . .*
5. *They're afraid to make mistakes.*
6. *. . . she expects to fail . . .*
7. *Her friends . . . expected her to have called them.*
8. *It's too short notice for most of them to be able to come.*
9. *Blanche's fear has caused things to turn out like this.*
10. *What would you advise that person to do?*
11. *The first is never to put off until tomorrow what needs to be done today.*
12. *Not to avoid painful or difficult things is the second.*

Grammar Charts

- Write the sentences above on the board or make photocopies and distribute them to students in pairs or small groups. After students have read through the charts, ask them to find examples of the following patterns among the twelve sentences: infinitive as subject *(3, 12)*; infinitive as object *(2, 6)*; infinitive as subject complement *(3, 11)*; verbs followed directly by infinitives *(1, 2, 6, 11)*;

verbs followed by nouns / pronouns + infinitives *(7, 9, 10)*; adjectives followed by infinitives *(5)*; nouns followed by infinitives *(4, 9)*; too / enough with infinitives *(8)*; past infinitive *(7)*.
- Ask students which of the 12 sentences show negative infinitives. *(12).*
- Ask students to notice the verbs that precede infinitives in these sentences and make a list of them. *(stop, want, expect, advise, need)*
- Have students look at the charts and notice how the negative of an infinitive is formed. How would they make sentences 3 and 4 above negative?
- Draw attention to the *it* + infinitive construction. Ask students why parentheses are used around the words for *Alice / her*. *(because they are optional)* Elicit several sentences from students following the examples given, some with *for / of* + noun / pronoun and some without.
- Have students look at the Verbs Followed by Infinitives chart. Ask them what they think the difference is between the second and third lines. *(The verbs on the second line— convinced, told, urged, etc.—require a noun or pronoun before the infinitive. For those on the third line, the noun or pronoun is optional.)*
- Have students look at the Active and Passive Infinitives chart. Ask students why only infinitives can be used in the examples. *(Plan and expect are verbs that take infinitives; glad and happy are adjectives that are followed by infinitives.)*
- Have students work in pairs to generate active and passive sentences similar to those in the chart.

Grammar Notes

Note 1

- The *it* + infinitive structure is used a great deal in English and it's worth taking the time to help students develop some fluency with it.
  —Ask them to identify all of the grammatical elements in the structure. *(it + be + adjective [for / of + noun / pronoun] + infinitive)*
  —Put a few sentences such as the following on the board and have students transform them into *it* + infinitive structures:
    Smoking is bad for your health. →
    It's bad for your health to smoke.
- To practice forming negatives, put a few infinitive phrases such as the following on the board, then have students make them negative and complete the sentence, for example, *to graduate from college* → *Not to graduate from college was unthinkable.*

Note 2 *(Exercise 2)*
- Have students look at Appendix 17.
  —Ask them to make one list of the verbs that require a noun or pronoun before the infinitive.
  —Have them write an example sentence at the top of that list.
  —Have them write a list of the verbs after which an object is optional. Have them write two example sentences at the top of that list.
- Have students work in pairs, taking turns at being teacher and student. Student A, looking at his/her lists, gives Student B, who is not looking at the lists, a verb, and Student B makes a sentence. If it is a verb that does not require a pronoun/noun object, Student B says, "optional." Student A tells student B if he or she is right.

→ For additional practice, see the Supplementary Activities on page 103.

Note 3 *(Exercises 2, 6)*
- Have students look at the example sentences, and ask which of the "common adjectives followed by infinitives" listed in the note could replace the ones in the examples.
- Have students read through Appendix 18 and ask them if they have any questions.
- To practice using these adjectives with infinitives, do a whole-class substitution drill, with students sitting in a circle. Write the example sentence on the board. Call on a student to change the adjective, for example, *I was amazed to hear about that.* Go around the room for a much longer list of adjectives.

Note 4 *(Exercise 6)*
Invite students to make up sentences similar to the ones in the example:
  —about their school or other local places
  —about English, for example:
  English is a ____ language to ____.

Note 5 *(Exercise 6)*
- Have students explore verbs followed by both gerunds and infinitives to learn in which cases there is a difference in meaning.
  —Working in pairs, have students look at Appendix 15.
  —Have each student choose three verbs and write two sentences for each, one followed by an infinitive and one followed by a gerund.
  —While both gerunds and infinitives can be used after these verbs, there is sometimes a stylistic reason to prefer one or the other.

⏱ Have students share their papers with their partners and together consider if they have a preference for the gerund or infinitive form with each sentence.
- In contrast to the verbs listed in Appendix 15, there are a small number that will convey dramatically different meanings depending on whether they are followed by an infinitive or a gerund. Point out the examples with *stop* and *quit* in Note 5, and ask students if they can think of a few more examples using *stop*. *(I stopped smoking/to smoke.)*
- Have students turn to Appendix 16 and study the examples there. Working in pairs or small groups have students:
  —generate sentences using these verbs followed by gerunds and infinitives
  —write explanations similar to the ones in the book about the meaning of each.
  Ask students to share some of these sentences with the class.

→ For additional practice, see the Supplementary Activities on pages 103–104.

Note 6 *(Exercise 5)*
Go over the examples and elicit sentences from the class using the same patterns. For fun you might suggest they talk about what they think about English or gerunds and infinitives in particular! For example:
  English is too ____ to ____.
  There are too many ____ to ____.

Note 7 *(Exercises 3, 6)*
- Have students practice infinitives in the past form by adding past participles and completing sentences such as these:
  When I started high school I was expected to have . . .
  By the time people are twenty-one years old, they are supposed to have . . .
- For practice of the passive, write the example sentence on the board and have students substitute other content, for example:
  The work is supposed to be handed in next week/completed this semester, etc.

Note 8 *(Exercise 4)*
- The elliptical use of *to* is a very useful structure. Give students practice with it by asking questions that will elicit answers that use it. Write examples on the board:
  A: Are you going to the party?
  B: I'm planning to.
  A: Why did you take a second job?
  B: I had to. I've got a lot of expenses.

- Have students work in pairs to ask and answer questions requiring the elliptical use of *to*.

Focused Practice (pages 279–283)

Exercise 2
demon: an evil spirit

Exercise 3
tornado: an extremely violent storm consisting of air that spins very quickly and causes a lot of damage

Exercise 7
reluctant: slow and unwilling

fiancé: the man whom a woman is going to marry

Communication Practice (pages 284–286)

Exercise 8
Students will probably need some time to form the complete sentences that are asked for. Allow them to concentrate first on the content of their answers by just jotting down key words. Then they can go back and construct full sentences using passive infinitives.

head: to go in a particular direction

sheriff: the highest-ranking law officer of a county in the U.S.

inmate: someone who is kept in a prison or mental hospital

break: an escape from prison

install: to put a piece of equipment somewhere and connect it so that it is ready to be used

Exercise 9
Ask students if they can think of any other sayings to share with the class.

err: to make a mistake

divine: coming from God

seek: to look for something (in this case, something spiritual) you need

Exercise 10
Discussion: Do you think a messy desk is always a sign of procrastination? What does your desk look like?

Exercise 11
Questions to generate ideas and elicit vocabulary:
- Do you think most people procrastinate?
- Do you tend to procrastinate?
- What kinds of things do you generally put off doing?
- What are the consequences?
- Did your procrastination ever lead to something good?
- Did it ever have a very dramatic consequence?

Further Practice
- Discuss with the class: Why do you procrastinate? Some people say laziness is the reason. Dr. Robert Stevens claims it is fear of failure. He also says it is related to the expectation syndrome. Often people will procrastinate for different reasons. Sometimes it is fear of failure. Sometimes it is just laziness. But often it is because of resentment that we are expected to do something. It is not a question of failure. Often the jobs are not difficult at all, and the possibility of failure is not an issue, but because of resentment we just don't get around to doing things that we are expected to do. What about you? Why do you procrastinate?
- Have students sit in small groups of three or four, tell a story about a time they procrastinated, and why they think they did.

Change your life forever. Bring in the movie *Dead Poets Society.* Have students watch the part of the film in which Professor John Keating (Robin Williams) encourages his students to live their lives to the fullest, and says, among other things, *"Carpe diem,* lads! Seize the day. Make your lives extraordinary!"* Have students discuss Professor Keating's advice. On the board, write the questions below as a guide.
- What does Professor Keating advise his students to do?
- What does he advise them not to do?
- What are some good reasons to "Seize the day"?
- How do the students react? Are Professor Keating's ideas too revolutionary for them to understand? Are they reluctant or willing to follow his advice? Why?
- Do you think Professor Keating expects to be admired by his students? What motivates him to talk to his students the way he does?

After discussing as a class, you may want to have students write a paragraph about the movie scene they watched, using the questions as a guide. Point out that students should pay particular attention to their use of infinitives.

Adverbs: Functions, Types, Placement, and Meaning

UNIT 17

In this unit, particular emphasis is given to:
- Sentence or viewpoint adverbs (e.g., *actually, clearly, hopefully*)
- Focus adverbs: Changing the position of a focus adverb often changes the meaning of a sentence (e.g., *Only teenagers can attend. Teenagers can only attend.*).
- Negative and other adverbs requiring inversion (e.g., *Rarely do people make a career of the military.*)

Grammar in Context (pages 296–298)

Background Notes

Call-in radio and TV programs are very popular in the United States and often give listeners or viewers the chance to express opinions on controversial issues. In the reading, the theme of discussing divisive topics focuses on military service; in particular, the reading explores questions concerning the draft (the system in which people must join the military) and women in the military and in combat.

Vocabulary

controversial: causing a lot of disagreement, because many people have strong opinions about the subject being discussed

voluntary: done willingly, without being forced or without being paid

combat: organized fighting, especially in a war

stereotype: an idea of what a particular group of people is like that many people have, especially one that is wrong or unfair

spirited: having energy and determination or showing this quality

adopt: to formally approve a proposal, especially by voting

Comprehension Questions

- What is Mike Burns' opinion of the military in general? *(Service should be voluntary. A lot of evil things have been done by military forces. Maybe we shouldn't even have them.)*
- Does Burns think that women are too weak to serve? *(No, he doesn't think fighting is feminine.)*

- What does Sarah Lopez think about voluntary military service? *(She thinks military service should be required.)*
- What is Lopez' reason for supporting required military service? *(It's the only way to ensure fair treatment for all.)*
- Does Sarah Lopez believe that combat is feminine? *(Yes.)*

Discussion Topics

- What are the advantages and disadvantages of a volunteer army?
- If military service is not required, should young people do some kind of national service?

Grammar Presentation (pages 298–302)

Identify the Grammar

1. *A related issue that has recently become controversial is whether women should join the military and if they do, should they fight alongside men in combat?*
2. *. . . I'm definitely not in favor of women being in combat.*
3. *Mainly because young people are not all made the same.*
4. *Maybe we shouldn't even have them.*
5. *I'm a pretty accepting guy, but even I find that suggestion extreme.*
6. *Women just aren't suited for combat.*
7. *Is he on target, or is this just fuzzy thinking?*
8. *He made his point clearly, but I just don't agree with him.*
9. *Actually, I'd go further.*
10. *It wouldn't have to be only military.*
11. *National service has been started in a few countries, and it will hopefully be adopted in a lot more.*
12. *. . . I totally disagree with the way Jerry characterizes women.*
13. *No way is combat nonfeminine!*
14. *. . . if I'm ever called to combat, I'll go willingly.*

Grammar Charts

- Write the sentences above on the board or make photocopies and distribute them to students in pairs or small groups. After students have read through the charts, ask them to name or underline all the adverbs in these fourteen sentences.

- Draw attention to the first chart. Then have students identify the adverbs in the above sentences that modify entire sentences. *(3: mainly, 4: maybe, 9: actually, 11: hopefully)*
- Ask them to look at sentence 8. What does *clearly* modify—the verb or the whole sentence? *(the verb—how he made his point)* What are some other adverbs that modify verbs in the above sentences? *(2: definitely, 12: totally, 14: willingly)*
- Ask if students can find an example of an adverb of place. *(1: alongside)*
- Have students look at the chart on Focus Adverbs and then find examples of them in the above sentences. *(4, 5: even; 6, 7: just; 10: only)*
- Have students look at the chart on Negative Adverbs and then see if they can find an example of inversion in the above sentences. *(13)*
- Draw attention to the chart showing Adverbs and Adverbials. Ask if students can find an example of an adverbial phrase in the above sentences. *(1: in combat, 11: in a few countries)*

Grammar Notes

Notes 1–2
- Have students practice using the different kinds of adverbs by:
  —brainstorming and writing several adverbs of each catgegory on the board
  —eliciting substitutions for the adverbs in each of the example sentences
- Draw attention to the different positions possible for adverbs of frequency. Write these adverbs on the board and next to them the three example sentences with *sometimes*. Do a quick drill in which students substitute different adverbs of frequency for *sometimes*, in each of the positions possible. For example, point to *always*, eliciting the only sentence possible: She *always* disagrees with me. Then point to *often*, which should elicit all three sentence patterns in which *sometimes* appears.

→ For additional practice, see the Supplementary Activities on page 104.

Note 3   *(Exercises 2, 5, 6)*
- Draw attention to the explanation of sentence adverbs and to the paraphrase of *clearly* as *It is clear that. . . .* Explain that sentences with viewpoint adverbs derived from adjectives can often be restated that way, using *I am* + adjective + *that . . .* or *It is* + adjective + *that . . .*

Write the following sentences on the board and ask students to restate the sentence adverbs:

> <u>Sadly</u>, Mary was unable to do anything.
>   (= <u>It is sad / I am sad that</u> she was unable to do anything.)
> <u>Luckily</u>, Jerry wasn't hurt in the accident.
>   (= <u>It is lucky that</u> Jerry wasn't hurt in the accident.)

- Give students some practice recognizing when adverbs modify only the verb in contrast to the whole sentence. Go over the examples with *clearly* provided in the note. Then write these sentences on the board and see if students can identify the one with the sentence adverb:

> He acted mercifully.   Mercifully, he acted.

Hopefully, they will see the value of commas in helping to identify sentence adverbs!

- Have students look at the list of sentence adverbs in Appendix 19 and work in pairs to write five or six sentences using some of these words, being sure to use commas appropriately.

Note 4   *(Exercises 3, 5, 6)*
- Focus adverbs are very useful in creating the emphasis a speaker intends. In speech this emphasis is expressed not only by the use of the focus word but, as indicated in the note, with stress on the word it highlights. Go over the examples in the note, having students repeat the sentences after you with appropriate stress.
- Write the following sentences on the board:

> <u>Just</u> John came to the dinner.
> John came <u>just</u> to the dinner.
> John <u>just</u> came to the dinner.

  —Ask students which one means "John was the only one who came?" *(the first)*
  —What does the second sentence mean? *(He came only to the dinner—not to anything else.)*
  —And the third? *(He came to the dinner. He didn't do anything else.)*
- Now ask students where they would place the focus adverb *just* in the following sentence to convey each of the meanings below: *Helen doesn't like me.*
  1. *She doesn't like me. It's that simple. (Helen <u>just</u> doesn't like me.)*
  2. *It's far more than like. She loves me. (Helen doesn't <u>just</u> like me.)*
  3. *She likes other people, too. (Helen doesn't like <u>just</u> me.)*

Ask students which words are stressed in these sentences (*1: like, 2: like, 3: me*) and have them say the sentences, stressing these words. Note: Sentence 1 has normal rising-falling intonation. In sentence 2, where the emphasis is contrastive, the pitch rises higher on the stressed word, *like*, than in 1, and there is also a slight rise in intonation at the end of the sentence, on *me*, as if to suggest, "there is more to this story."

- Using the adverb *even* correctly is often difficult to master. Explain that *even* is used to talk about things that are not expected, for example:

  Mary seems to like everyone. She likes her teachers. She likes her boss at the fast food restaurant where she works. She likes her younger brothers and sisters. She <u>even</u> likes the new principal at school.

  (This is unexpected: No one else likes the new principal. We would expect Mary to have a similar view.)

  Steve is the opposite. He seems angry at everyone. He doesn't like his teacher. He doesn't like his parents. He doesn't like the new principal. He doesn't <u>even</u> care for his girlfriend.

  (This is unexpected: Although Steve doesn't seem to like many people, we would expect him at least to care for his girlfriend.)

Note 5   *(Exercises 4–6)*

- Your students should already be familiar with the concept of negative adverbs that force the inversion of the subject and the auxiliary when the adverb comes first in the sentence. This occurs in sentences such as *Neither do I* and *Neither does Ali,* so you may want to begin with simple sentences like these and then do a quick substitution drill with the other negative adverbs.
- The challenge here is that, in affirmative sentences, *do, does,* and *did* are often not present, so students will need extra practice with the simple present and past of verbs other than *be.* Help students to generate sentences involving *do, does,* and *did* starting with these cues:

  Only in ____ (country) ____.
  Only on one day of the year ____.
  Never / Rarely / Seldom / ____.
  Not only ____ but ____. (Point out that while the first half of this structure is inverted, the second half follows normal sentence order.)

- Now have students complete these sentences:
  Never in the history of the world have ____.
  Little did he know that ____.
  Hardly had he entered the room when ____.
- Note: Some of the adverbs listed are used in very specific ways, many of them somewhat formal and stylized. Some tend to be used as ready-made phrases (e.g., *little did he know / imagine . . .*). Students should not be expected to use these actively but to be aware that these forms exist. They will undoubtedly encounter them in reading, where, hopefully, they will be appreciated as "old friends."
- Point out that while *in no way* is formal, *No way* is quite informal. Most of the time it occurs alone, either as an indication of surprise or as a strong negative.

→ For additional practice, see the Supplementary Activities on page 104.

Note 6   *(Exercise 5)*

In contrast to most of the adverbs discussed in Note 5, the ones presented in Note 6 are very commonly used in speech. These structures may be new to your students, and it is worth helping them develop some fluency with them.

- Ask students to read the Be Careful! note and read aloud the examples where the subjects are nouns and then those where the subjects are pronouns, noticing the inversion in the case of the former and normal sentence order in the latter.
- Put several objects on your desk, some referred to by singular, some by plural nouns.
  —Ask a student to go to the board and to write the sentences you say.
  —Call another student to the front of the room, and as you hand these items to him / her, say, for example, "Here is my book." "Here are my keys." "Here is my pen."
  —Ask students what pronouns they would use to replace *my book (it)* and *my keys (they),* and elicit *Here it is / they are,* to make the point.
- Ask students to make sentences starting with *here* and *there* to describe taxis, buses, trains, and planes coming and going, for example, *Here comes the bus. There goes the train.*

Note 7

Ask students if they can think of other examples of adverbials—both single words and phrases. Write these on the board and have students use them in sentences.

Focused Practice (pages 302–307)

Exercise 2

vaccine: a substance which contains a weak form of the bacteria or virus that causes a disease and is used to protect people from that disease

Exercise 3

gambling: the practice of risking money or possessions because you might win a lot more if a card game, race, etc. has the result you want

lottery: a game used to make money for a state or a charity in which people buy numbered tickets, so that if their number is picked by chance, they win money or a prize

dam: a special wall built across a river, stream, etc. to stop the water from flowing

military recruiter: someone who finds new people to join the military

Exercise 5

cloning: making an exact copy of a plant or animal by taking a cell from it and developing it artificially

Exercise 7

stomp: to walk with heavy steps or to put your foot down very hard, especially because you are angry

roam around: to go around with no clear purpose or direction

Communication Practice (pages 308–309)

Exercise 8

Discussion: Do you think women should be in combat? If so, are there certain conditions you would propose?

Exercise 9

Questions to generate ideas and elicit vocabulary:
- Do you believe in capital punishment? Why or why not?
- Do you have any opinions about the way income tax is structured in the U.S./in your country?
- Should taxes be raised or lowered? Why?
- What do you think of the health care system in the U.S./in your country?
- Why do you think there are so many homeless people? What can be done about them?
- Have you seen any electric powered cars? What do you think about them?

Further Practice

Have a whole-class discussion in answer to these questions: What are the pros and cons of

required non-military national service? Who would serve? For how long? What would they do? Who would pay for it? How much would it cost?

Make your point. On a videotape, record part of a documentary that deals with a controversial issue. Have students watch the material and then encourage a friendly debate on the topic. Write the following language on the board to remind students of some of the adverbs they can use as they discuss:

I'm <u>definitely</u> (not) in favor of . . . <u>mainly</u>
  because . . .
<u>Basically</u>, I'm (not) in favor of . . .
I'd go <u>even</u> further: . . .
I <u>just</u> don't agree with . . .
I <u>even</u> believe that . . .
<u>Even</u> I believe that . . .
<u>Not only</u> should . . . , <u>but</u> [they] should <u>also</u> . . .
<u>Only</u> . . . should . . .
I'm a <u>pretty</u> conservative/accepting person,
  but . . .
<u>No way</u> is . . .
<u>Hopefully</u>, . . .
<u>Unfortunately</u>, . . .
<u>Obviously</u>, . . .

UNIT 18 Adverb Clauses

Unit Overview

The focus of the unit is adverb clauses and their placement, punctuation, and types:
- Time: *Whenever I exercise, I feel good.*
- Place: *Professional sports are played <u>where there are big stadiums</u>.*
- Reason: *She won the medal <u>because she had practiced tirelessly</u>.*
- Condition: *You'll improve <u>if you practice daily</u>.*
- Contrast: *<u>Even though he is quite young</u>, he was selected for the team.*

Grammar in Context (pages 310–312)

Vocabulary

commentator: someone who describes an event as it is happening on television or radio *synchronized swimming:* a sport in which swimmers move in patterns in the water to music

arena: usually a building with a large flat central area surrounded by seats, where sports or entertainment take place; but here = all the activities and people connected with a particular enterprise

excessive: much more than is reasonable or necessary

javelin: a sports event in which competitors throw a javelin, or light spear, to see who can throw it the farthest

stamina: physical or mental strength that lets you continue doing something for a long time without getting tired

rival: a person, group, or organization that you compete with in sports, business, a fight, etc.

also-ran: someone who has failed to win a competition or an election

excesses: actions that are socially or morally unacceptable because they are too harmful or too extreme

endorsement: saying in an advertisement that people should buy a particular product

ponder: to spend time thinking carefully and seriously about a problem

inevitable: certain to happen and impossible to avoid

off course: in the wrong direction

Comprehension Questions

- What is the writer's problem with new Olympic sports like badminton and synchronized swimming? *(They're silly.)*
- What were the original Olympic games related to? *(war)*
- What were the modern Olympic games designed to promote? *(peace)*
- What is the emphasis of the most recent Olympic games? *(breaking records and the achievement of fame)*
- What are two excesses of modern sports? *(cost and violence)*

Discussion Topics

- Many people, like the author, complain about high salaries and violence in sports. Why are the players' salaries so high? Why is violence in sports tolerated?
- Why are sports so important to people? What do sports give to the participant? What do they give to the spectator? Not everybody is interested in sports. What are some reasons for lack of interest?

Grammar Presentation (pages 312–315)

Identify the Grammar

- *If you added to that the cost of parking and eating, the cost was up to at least $75.*
- *For a moment I wondered why tickets have gotten so expensive until I remembered the key factor in the equation . . .*
- *We see it wherever we look, and it's certainly not decreasing.*
- *. . . Steve Moore had to be hospitalized because another player hit him in the head . . .*
- *Once we accept violence as inevitable, it will be almost impossible to stop.*

Grammar Charts

- Write the sentences above on the board (or make photocopies and distribute them to students in pairs or small groups). After students have read through the charts, ask them to identify (or underline) the adverbial clauses in these five sentences and say what kind of clauses they are.
- Ask students what they notice about the placement of adverbial clauses in the charts. *(They can come before or after the main clause.)* Ask if they think a change in position results in a change in meaning. *(No.)*

Grammar Notes

Notes 1–2

- Ask students to identify the subordinating conjunctions in the example sentences in these notes.
- Point out that in most cases, it is the presence of the subordinating word that makes the clause dependent. If you removed that word, the clause would become independent.
- Ask students to notice which of the example sentences have commas. Ask them why they have commas. *(because the dependent clause comes first)* Have them apply this rule by writing the first complex sentence in Note 1, reversing the order of the clauses:

  If you practice enough, you could win a medal.

Note 3 *(Exercises 2–6)*

- Three of the example sentences deal with future time. Ask students to notice the verbs used in both the main and subordinate clauses. In which clause is *will* used? *(the main clause)* What if the order of the clauses is changed? *(Will is still used only in the main clause.)* What about *be going to*—can it be used in a dependent clause? *(No.)*

- Have students say the example sentences as they are written and then reverse the order of the clauses.
- Ask students if there other subordinating conjunctions that could replace *as soon as* in the first example? *(when)*

Note 4   *(Exercise 4)*
Have students work in pairs to talk about places they have visited. Ask volunteers to describe some of their experiences using adverb clauses of place, for example, *Everywhere we went, people were so nice to us.*

Note 5   *(Exercises 2–6)*
- Point out that in conversation *because* or *since* are more commonly used than *as* to express reason. In writing, however, *as* is used a great deal.
- Go over the examples with *as* used to express both time and reason. Have students write a few sentences using *as* each way and exchange papers with a partner, whose task it is to identify the kind of clause.
- There are a few more conjunctions that express reason listed in Appendix 20. Give students a few minutes to scan the Appendix and see if they can find them. *(because of / due to / on account of the fact that / inasmuch as)*

Note 6   *(Exercises 2–6)*
- To be sure students understand the distinction between *even if* and *only if,* ask them which would be appropriate to combine the following sentences:
  We are taking this trip no matter what. _____ it rains, we are going. (even if)
  I'll give you my cell number for emergencies. Use it _____ you need to. (only if)
- To clarify the meaning of *unless,* ask students if they can express the idea conveyed by the fourth example sentence using *if. (If you don't train a great deal, you won't be a champion.)*
- You may want to point out that it is possible to have a sentence like this with *will* used to indicate volition or willingness, not future: *If you help me with my math, I'll help you with your English essay.*

→ For additional practice, see the Supplementary Activities on page 105.

Note 7   *(Exercises 2, 4–6)*
- It may be helpful to point out that clauses of contrast that show unexpected results can be seen as the opposite of clauses of reason, which have a predictable cause and effect relationship.
- Have students work in pairs or small groups to generate some sentences that show an unexpected result, and write some of these on the board. (e.g., *I stayed up very late. I wasn't tired.*) Ask students to combine these sentences using adverbial clauses. (e.g., *Though I stayed up very late, I wasn't tired.*)
- Ask students to look through Appendix 20 once again, this time to find additional conjunctions that can introduce clauses of contrast. *(in spite of / despite the fact that)*

Focused Practice (pages 316–322)

Exercise 2
the marathon: a long race in which competitors run 26 miles and 385 yards

puck: a hard, flat circular piece of rubber that you hit with the stick in the game of ice hockey

free throw: a chance for one player on a basketball team to throw the ball without any opposition because a player on the other team did something wrong

fouled: if a sports player is fouled, a player on the opposing team does something to them that is not allowed by the rules of the sport

bat: to hit the ball with the bat in baseball

touchdown: an act of moving the ball across the opposing team's goal line in American football

Exercise 3
revive: to bring something back into existence or popularity

Exercise 4
unleashed: if a strong force, feeling, etc., is unleashed, it is suddenly allowed to have its full effect

ego: the opinion that you have about yourself—if you have a big ego, you think you are very smart and important

strides: improvements in a situation or in the development of something

Exercise 5
fan: someone who likes a particular sport, kind of music, etc. very much or who admires a famous person

Exercise 7
deficiency: a lack of something that is necessary

Communication Practice (pages 323–325)

Exercise 8

Discussion: Discuss the reasons given by Lillian Swanson for her success. How important was family support in her achieving athletic success? How important were discipline and dealing with adversity/difficulties? Can you think of other ingredients for success?

charmed: always lucky, as if protected by magic

stick to (something): to continue to work or study in a very determined way in order to achieve something

Exercise 9

Discussion Topic: Raise this question with the whole class: Do you know anyone who practices an extreme sport? Why do they do it? What do they get out of it?

Exercise 10

Sports-related violence happens often enough in the United States and Canada, but it also happens elsewhere.
- Ask students to tell about other examples they've heard of.
- Is it realistic to think that sports can be played without violence?

Exercise 11, page 325

Questions to generate ideas and elicit vocabulary:
- What do people get out of participating in sports?
- What do people get out of watching sports?
- Should sports celebrities get the kinds of salaries they do?
- Why are sports violent? Are they more violent today than at other periods?

Further Practice

"It's not whether you win or lose that's important; it's how you play the game." The author of "Are Sports Still Sporting?" wants us to get back to this idea. Share this history with the class: This concept is a late 19th and early 20th century upper-class ideal of the gentleman amateur sportsman. The ancient Greek contests were fought for fame and glory, and the only thing that counted was winning. The loser was disgraced. Given the roots of the Olympic games in war, can you understand the ancient Greek attitude?

Have students consider this question in small groups and then report back to class: Which ideal provides a better guiding principle for modern sports: (1) "The only thing that matters is winning" or (2) "The important thing is how you play the game."

Advertising power. Bring in advertisements for sports equipment or any other kind of item that is suitable for people who practice sports. Have students work in small groups. Hand out several advertisements to each group. Have students study the advertisements and discuss the message behind each one. Encourage students to use adverb clauses of reason, condition, and contrast as they describe the messages. Write these examples on the board to prompt students:

> *You will beat your opponent only if you wear [brand].*
> *Since our equipment is the best, you won't be able to reach the top without it.*
> *Although it's expensive, you can't afford not to have it.*
> *If you drink [brand], you will have more energy.*

Follow up by having students share with the class their views about the advertisements and their messages.

You may want to write the following on the board to remind students of the language they learned:

REASON	CONDITION	CONTRAST
since	if	though
as	even if	although
now that	only if	even though
because	unless	whereas

 Record a couple of TV commercials directed to sportspeople on a videotape and bring into class for students to discuss.

UNIT 19 Adverb and Adverbial Phrases

Unit Overview

In this unit students will learn how to form adverb and adverbial phrases by:
- reducing adverb clauses of time to adverb phrases: *While in Italy, they had trouble.*
- changing adverb clauses of time to adverb phrases: *Before leaving, we visited Rome.*

- changing adverb clauses of time to adverbial phrases: *Waiting at the hospital, they were deeply troubled.*
- changing adverb clauses of reason to adverbial phrases: *Having been to Bari, I hope to return.*

It is important for students to recognize that transforming an adverb clause into a phrase is only possible when the subjects in the subordinate and main clauses are the same, thus avoiding the "dangling modifier."

Grammar in Context (pages 326–327)

Background Notes

The theme of compassion is represented in the reading by the story of a couple that donated their son's organs for transplant after the boy had been shot and killed. Offering one's own organs or those of a loved one for transplant is perhaps more common in America than in some other cultures, which may or may not indicate something about cultural differences related to compassion and grieving. In addition to cultural comparisons, this unit looks at comparisons of species by dealing with the possibility of grieving in animals.

Vocabulary

ruins: the parts of buildings that are left after the rest have been destroyed

bandanna: a large, brightly covered piece of cloth you wear around your head or neck

floor (the gas pedal): to make a car go as fast as possible by pressing the accelerator all the way down

shatter: to break suddenly into very small pieces or to make something break this way

outdistance: to run, ride, etc. faster than other people, especially in a race so that you are far ahead

alert: to officially warn someone of a problem or danger, so that they can be ready to deal with it

coma: a state in which someone is not conscious for a long time, usually after a serious accident or illness

transplant: the operation of moving an organ, piece of skin, etc., from one person's body to another

civility: here, a high level of civilized behavior

irony: a situation that is unusual or amusing because something strange happens or the opposite of what is expected happens or is true

cornea: the transparent protective covering on the outer surface of your eye

pledge: to make a formal, usually public, promise to do something or to give money to an organization, country, etc.

dawn on (someone): if a fact or idea dawns on you, you realize it or think of it for the first time

a blow was struck for organ donation: the cause of organ donation was helped

Comprehension Questions

- Why did the Greens try to escape from the criminals? *(They thought their new car could outrun them.)*
- Why were the Greens attacked? *(The criminals thought they were carrying precious stones.)*
- Why did Nicholas's parents offer to donate his organs to Italians in need of them? *(to return good for evil and so that someone could have the future he lost)*
- What happened to the Greens after their return to the United States? *(They began to receive requests to speak about their son and the importance of organ donation.)*
- How did they react to these requests? *(They realized that they had found their life's work.)*

Discussion Topics

- The final paragraph of "Compassion" asks a question. Given the circumstances of Nicholas Green's death, how many people would act as compassionately as his parents did? Would you?
- When the Italian talk show host said, "You have given us a lesson in civility," what did he mean to convey? What are the elements of civility in the sense that he used the word?

Grammar Presentation (pages 328–331)

Identify the Grammar

Please note: The following examples of target grammar points from the reading exclude phrases with subordinating conjunctions and those with having + *past participle, since students are asked to find all of those in the Discover the Grammar activity immediately following the notes. Write these sentences on the board.*

1. *Reg and Maggie Green were driving south . . . , their children Nicholas and Eleanor sleeping peacefully in the back seat.*
2. *Not knowing what to do, Reg carefully weighed the options . . .*
3. *Guessing that their newer-model car could probably get away from the old car the criminals were driving, Reg floored the gas pedal.*
4. *Shots rang out, shattering both windows on the driver's side of the car.*

(continued)

5. *The Greens' car took off, easily outdistancing the bandits' car.*
6. *Checking the children, Reg and Maggie found them still sleeping peacefully in the back seat.*
7. *Realizing that it would be far better to return good for evil than to seek revenge, they offered Nicholas's organs for transplant.*
8. *Profoundly moved by the gesture, Italians poured out their emotions.*
9. *Maurizio Costanzo . . . summed up the common feeling by saying, "You have . . . shown us how to react in the face of pain and sorrow."*

Grammar Charts

• Draw attention to the spaces marked Ø. Why are no adverb phrases possible here? *(Because the subjects of the two clauses are not the same.)*
• Have students look over the first two charts. Ask them to notice the words that the adverb phrases begin with. *(While, When, Before, After, On / Upon)*
• What is the difference between adverb phrases and adverbial phrases? *(Adverb phrases begin with the subordinating conjunctions* while, when, before, after, *and* since.)
• Write the nine sentences above on the board (or make photocopies and distribute them to students in pairs or small groups). After students have read through the charts, ask them to identify (or underline) the adverbial phrases in these sentences.
• If the phrases identified in the above sentences were clauses, which could begin with *because*? *(2, 3, 7, 8)* Which, if they were clauses, could begin with *while, as,* or *when*? *(1, 4, 5, 6, 9)*
• Which adverbial phrase is introduced by the preposition *by*? *(9)*
• Which adverbial phrase is negative? *(2)*

Grammar Notes

Notes 1–2 *(Exercises 2–3)*
• Ask students to notice, in Note 1, which words in the adverb clause of the third example sentence have been deleted to produce the adverb phrase shown in the fourth example sentence. *(we were)*
• Have them look at the next two example sentences beginning with *After we fixed . . .* and say which words have been deleted. *(we)* Which words changed? *(fixed → fixing)*

• Now have them look at the first two examples in Note 2 and say what has been deleted to change the clause to the phrase? *(they were)*
• Look back at the second sentence in the reading. *Reg and Maggie Green were driving south . . . their children Nicholas and Eleanor sleeping peacefully in the back seat.* Ask students to transform the adverbial phrase to a clause: *while their children, Nicholas and Eleanor, were sleeping . . .*
• Go over the Be Careful! note with students and then have them look at the example sentences in Notes 1 and 2, identifying the subjects in the main clauses and the adverb clauses that were reduced or changed to adverb phrases.
• Ask students if the information about commas in Note 2 reminds them of another rule about commas they recently learned. *(commas with adverb clauses)* Note that after adverb clauses in an initial position the comma is required, while it is often a matter of choice when it comes to phrases. For now it is better that they get accustomed to using the comma after phrases as well as clauses in the initial position.
• Have students read through the example sentences in Notes 1–2 to notice the use of commas.

Note 3 *(Exercises 2–4)*
• Note: While the examples show verbs other than *be,* it is also possible to derive adverb phrases in the same way from clauses with forms of *be,* for example:
> *After they were in Paestum for the day →*
> *After being in Paestum for the day, the Greens drove south.*
• In pairs have students talk about some of their recent activities using as many adverb phrases as possible, for example, *Yesterday before leaving work / school, I ran into a friend. We decided to go shopping. After shopping we were hungry, so we . . .*

→ For additional practice, see the Supplementary Activities on page 105.

Notes 4–6 *(Exercises 3–4)*
• Have students work in pairs to think of some past actions where it is important to show that one action preceded another and then express the ideas using an adverb phrase, for example, *(After) having paid my electric bill, I was surprised to come home and see the electricity turned off!* Encourage students to come up with humorous or dramatic contexts. Share some of these with the class.

- Note: Phrases beginning with *upon* or *on* are more common in writing than in speech. *Upon* has a distinctly formal feeling.
- Write several main clauses on the board and have students work in small groups to add time- or reason-related adverb or adverbial phrases to them, for example, *I wanted to be an actor. I was fascinated by the theater. I began to take classes.* Let them add other sentences as needed, including some without adverb phrases, to create a story, which one member of the group records. Share the results with the class. It will be fun to see how many different directions the stories take.

Notes 7–8 *(Exercises 3–4)*
- Write some sentences on the board and have students combine them, for example:
  > *The president was elected by a small majority. He didn't have the support to make major changes.* → *Elected by a small majority, he didn't have the support to . . .*
- Go over the Be Careful! note and write several sentences with adverb clauses on the board for students to transform into phrases, for example:
  > *Before he was elected, he had made many promises.* → *Before being elected, he had made many promises.*

Focused Practice (pages 331–337)

Exercise 3
bed sore: a sore place on your skin caused by lying in bed in one position for a long time

inseparable: people (or in this case, animals) who are inseparable are always together and are very friendly with each other

bond: a special relationship that makes people (or in this case, animals) loyal to each other

discount: to regard something as unlikely to be true or important

stillborn: born dead

calf: the baby of a cow or some other large animal, such as the elephant

nibble: to eat small amounts of food by taking very small bites

droop: to hang or bend down or to make something do this

Exercise 5
appeal: an urgent request for something important such as money or help, especially to help someone in a bad situation

tune out: to ignore or stop listening to something

numb: to make someone unable to think, feel, or react in a normal way

limp: to walk with a limp is to walk slowly and with difficulty because one leg is hurt or injured

Communication Practice (pages 338–339)

Exercise 6
- When they have finished answering the questions in their books, ask students if they think this newscast is real or fictitious. Ask at what point they realized it was fictitious.
- Point out that adverb (and adjective) phrases are very commonly used in news media because they allow a lot of information to be packed into a small space very efficiently. Play the audio program again. This time have students notice how adverb or adverbial phrases are used.
- Replay the audio program and have students write down the adverb and adverbial phrases they hear. Pause and replay the program as many times as necessary.

rebel: someone who opposes or fights against people in authority

good-faith: showing honest and sincere intentions

off the record: if something you tell someone is off the record, you do not want them to officially report that you said it

viable: a viable plan or system can work successfully

cease fire: an agreement to stop fighting for a period of time, especially so that a more permanent agreement can be made

Exercise 7
Discussion Topic: If you had been Damini's keeper, what would you have done to try to save her?

Exercise 8
Questions to generate ideas and elicit vocabulary:
- Who are some people known for their compassion?
- What are some examples of compassionate acts?
- Who deserves compassion?
- What are some situations that inspire compassion in you?

Further Practice
Given the outpouring of sorrow and the reactions of shame on the part of Italians, not to mention the Greens' being given Italy's highest honor by the Prime Minister, we can

assume that organ donation was rare, or at least very unusual in Italy at that time. Discuss as a whole class or in small groups: What are the attitudes toward organ donation in your nation or region? Are you a registered organ donor? Would you be if you were asked? What are the arguments for and against organ donation in your culture? Have attitudes toward organ donation changed in your lifetime?

Stories that teach a lesson. Bring in stories that deal with love and compassion. They can be fictional stories or fables such as "Androcles and the Lion," or true stories from magazines, newspapers, or organizations that help people in need, such as UNICEF. Have students read and discuss the stories. Then ask students to look at the grammar charts again and use ideas from the stories to write sentences using adverbial phrases.

You might want to write this example on the board:

Having run away from his master, Androcles made for the woods. On seeing the lion in pain, Androcles grew bold and decided to help.

UNIT 20 Connectors

Unit Overview

Connectors are used within sentences, to mark transitions between sentences, and to connect blocks of texts. The unit focuses on coordinating conjunctions, subordinating conjunctions, and transitions used to convey:

- Addition: *and, not, or; besides, furthermore, indeed, in addition, moreover*
- Condition: *or; if, even if, only if, unless; otherwise*
- Contrast: *but, or, yet; although, though, even though, whereas, while; however, nevertheless, nonetheless, on the contrary, on the other hand*
- Cause / Reason: *for; as, because, since*
- Effect / Result: *so; as, because, since; consequently, otherwise, therefore, thus*
- Time: *after, before, when, while; afterwards, meanwhile, next*

Transitions that connect blocks of text are used for:

- Listing ideas in order of time / importance: *First of all . . .*
- Giving examples: *For example . . .*
- Summarizing: *To summarize . . .*
- Adding a conclusion: *In conclusion . . .*

Grammar in Context (pages 340–342)

Vocabulary

worrisome: making you anxious

considerable: large enough to be noticeable or to have noticeable effects

frontal lobes: rounded parts of the brain in the front

glucose: a natural form of sugar that exists in fruit

deterioration: the state of becoming worse or developing into a bad situation

peg: a short piece of wood, metal, etc. that fits into a hole or is fastened to a wall, used especially for hanging things on

vivid: vivid memories, dreams, descriptions, etc. are so clear that they seem real

the real trick: the best way to solve a problem or to get a good result

tap: to make as much use as possible of the ideas, experience, knowledge, etc. that someone or a group of people has

Comprehension Questions

- What are the two types of memory that the author distinguishes between? *(long-term and short-term)*
- As we grow older, which type of memory do we lose first? *(short-term)*
- Where do short-term memory operations occur? *(the frontal lobes of the brain)*
- As we age, how much mass do the frontal lobes lose per decade? *(as much as 5–10%)*
- According to the author, what things can we do to slow memory decline? *(Eat several small meals each day instead of two or three big ones. Stay mentally active.)*

Discussion Topics

- The author of "Try to Remember" seems to be saying that memory loss in old age can be reduced with the right diet and hard work. Do you think she is right? Do you think her advice is practical? Are there other ways of dealing with memory loss or a poor memory?
- The reading discusses memory and "normal" memory loss. The unspoken problem is abnormal memory loss, Alzheimer's disease. Alzheimer's has become a political problem in the United States because presently the most promising cures for this disease involve stem-cell research, which uses human embryos in

the process. Some Americans feel that the use and subsequent destruction of human embryos, even those which are going to be discarded, is unethical. Most Americans, however, feel that the potential benefits of stem-cell research outweigh the ethical costs, if any. What do you think?

Grammar Presentation (pages 342–346)

Identify the Grammar

Please note: The following examples of target grammar points from the reading exclude the transitions identified in Charts 2–4 since students are asked to find all of those in the Discover the Grammar activity immediately following the notes.

- *I wouldn't be too concerned, though, for it's also very common.*
- *How does memory work, and what can we do to improve it?*
- *Memory courses can work, of course, but they depend on techniques that we can create and perform for ourselves.*

Grammar Charts

- Have students look at the examples in the first chart. Ask students if they think the meaning expressed by the different sentences is the same or different. *(pretty much the same)* Ask them why they think a speaker or writer would choose one form over another. *(Each form has a slightly different emphasis, allowing the speaker or writer to choose the best one to connect with what came before.)*
- Have students read through the remaining charts. Write the three sentences above on the board. Tell students that these sentences show examples of only one of the structures presented in the charts. Ask them to identify which. *(coordinating conjunctions)*
- Small Group Puzzle Activity: Photocopy the first and second charts *(Connectors: Placement and Punctuation and Connectors: Functions)*, enlarging them and making copies for each of the groups. Cut up the second chart as follows: Cut an L-shape so that the top row with the headings and the leftmost column with the functions are in one piece. Then cut along the dividing lines so that all the other boxes are in separate pieces. Give each group one copy of the first chart to use as reference and one of the second, cut up. Have students work in small groups with their books closed to reassemble the

Connectors: Functions chart.
- Ask students to look at Chart 2 and tell you if they remember which words they studied recently in Unit 18. *(all the subordinating conjunctions)*
- Have students look at the last two charts. Ask them what they notice about punctuation. *(Transition words are set off by commas or colons.)*

Grammar Notes

Notes 1–2   *(Exercises 2–4)*
- Ask students if they can name the coordinating conjunctions from memory. If not, let them consult the charts. *(and, but, for, or, nor, so, and yet)*
- As indicated in Note 2, these conjunctions are preceded by a comma when they connect two independent clauses. Remind students that an independent clause has a subject and a verb. Ask them to identify the subjects and verbs in the first two example sentences *(I forget / I write. I heard / you did mean?)*
- Write the following example on the board and ask students (1) to find the subjects and verbs *(I / think. Ø write)* and (2) if there are two independent clauses here. *(No.)*
  I think about things and write them down. Point out that in sentences like this, where a conjunction joins an independent clause with a verb phrase, or predicate, a comma is generally not used before the conjunction.
- For practice with coordinating conjunctions, create several pairs of sentences and ask students to join the sentences, using an appropriate coordinating conjunction.
- If students have difficulty with the conjunction *nor*, explain that it basically does the same thing as *and* but occurs in negative sentences. Make it clear that it functions in the same way as *neither* at the beginning of a sentence or clause.
  You will probably also want to point out that the conjunction *for* has roughly the same meaning as *because* or *since*, and that it is rare in conversation but common in writing, especially formal writing.
- Having recently completed the unit on adverb clauses, students should be quite familiar with the subordinating conjunctions and the comma rules.
  You might want to establish the connection between these and other connectors by having students transform the first two examples in Note 1. Ask them to:

—Change the structure of the first sentence to a complex sentence using a subordinating conjunction. (*Although I try hard, I can never remember new people's names.*)

—Change the second sentence to two independent clauses joined by a coordinating conjunction. (*I can't remember her name, <u>but</u> I can remember her face.*)

Notes 3–4 *(Exercises 2–4)*
• Some transitions, such as *however,* can be used comfortably in all sentence positions indicated. Others are more restricted. Tell students when in doubt, initial position is always safe.
• Appendix 21 lists sentence connectors by category. Working in small groups, have students look through the Appendix and identify words that they think might be able to replace each of the transition words in the example sentences used in Notes 3–4. Go over their choices as a class.
• Create controlled cloze exercises by taking short newspaper or magazine passages and deleting all the transitions. Have students work in small groups to fill in the blanks with transitions they consider appropriate.

→ For additional practice, see the Supplementary Activities on pages 105–106.

Note 5 *(Exercises 2–3)*
• Point out that all sentence connectors help us to better understand what we read or listen to because they allow us to anticipate the kind of information that is coming next. The transitions that connect blocks of text are particularly useful in that they show us the broad outlines of a writer or speaker's overall plan.
• Have students reread "Try to Remember," noticing the transitions that connect blocks of text. This will lead in nicely to the next activity, Discover the Grammar, where they look for specific kinds of transitions that connect sentences to each other.
• Refer students to Appendix 22 for a list of transitions to connect blocks of text.

Focused Practice (pages 346–350)

Exercise 3
aftermath: the period of time after something bad such as a war, storm, or accident has happened when people are still dealing with the results

caution: to warn someone that something might be dangerous, difficult, etc.

allocation: an official decision to devote a particular amount of money, time, etc. to a particular purpose

drag on: if an event drags on, it seems to continue for longer than is necessary

Exercise 5
the last straw: the last problem in a series of problems that finally makes you give up, get angry, etc.

stalled: to be stalled in your car is to be stopped or to be moving very slowly

vandalize: to damage or destroy things deliberately

tram: a streetcar

Communication Practice (pages 351–353)

Exercise 6
After students have answered the questions, play the audio program again. This time have them listen to the leader's first and last segments and identify the connectors she uses to:
• Connect blocks of text (*First segment:* First . . . Second . . . *Last segment:* Let's just sum up the point here. Most importantly . . .)
• To signal that examples are coming (*First segment:* For example, suppose . . . And suppose . . .)

crucial: something that is extremely important because everything else depends on it

Exercise 7
Teams score a point:
• for making a statement using connectors correctly
• for reproducing the statements of the other team accurately
You should be the judge of whether the initial statement is correct. However, if class size permits, it's a good idea to give each team the opportunity to review their members' statements in advance. Let the team that originated the statement be the judge of whether the opposing team has reproduced it accurately.

Exercise 8
Questions to generate ideas and elicit vocabulary:
• What makes a memory significant?
• Is there a particular time of your life that you remember most vividly?
• What do you remember best—emotions, thoughts, sights, sounds, smells, tastes, touch?
• Do photographs, pieces of music, or smells bring back certain memories?

Exercise 9

Details are easier to remember (as well as to describe!) if they are organized in some way. Begin by asking students how they would go about organizing a description of a painting. Would they do it spatially? If so, what vocabulary would they need to do this? (*on the left, on the right, in the foreground, in the background, going diagonally across,* etc.)

Further Practice

The author of "My Car Is Moving to the Suburbs" is clearly a young man who is not experiencing the memory loss of old age. He forgets where he puts his car, and he is worried about being able to remember which bus to take. Have you ever walked into a room and forgotten why you went there? Have you ever put something down and forgotten where you put it? Have you ever left the house without your keys? The answer to these questions for most of us is yes. In small groups, discuss similar "memory problems" in your life and what you do or did to overcome them. If someone in your group or someone you know is always forgetting things, ask other members of the group for advice.

GRAMMAR OUT OF THE BOX . . . . . .

Improve your memory. Do a search on the Internet on tips for improving your memory. Print out material and bring it in to class. Have students read the material, underline the connectors they come across, and then discuss it in groups. As students discuss, encourage the use of connectors. Then have students write a paragraph about one of the methods to improve memory that they discussed. Point out that they should use connectors to explain how the method works. Have students finish their paragraph expressing their views on the method.

What would you have done? Have students watch relevant parts of the movie *50 First Dates*, a romantic comedy about a veterinarian Henry Roth (Adam Sandler), who falls in love with Lucy Whitmore (Drew Barrymore). Lucy never remembers that she is dating Henry because she suffers from short-term memory loss, a disorder which wipes her memory clean every night. Encourage a light-hearted discussion about what students would have

done if they had been in Henry's situation. Also have them discuss the different ways in which Henry's father and Lucy's father behave.

UNIT 21 Noun Clauses: Subjects, Objects, and Complements

Unit Overview

Noun clauses are used in every way that individual nouns are: as subjects, direct or indirect objects, and objects of prepositions. In addition, they can function as subject and adjective complements; and with the addition of question words (e.g., *whether* or *if*) they become embedded questions. In this unit students will learn to:
- form noun clauses using *that* (stated or implied), *the fact that, Wh-* question words, *if,* and *whether (or not)*
- use noun clauses in many contexts, including *It's* + adjective + noun clause (*It's funny you should say that.*)
- form embedded questions and learn the value of using them

Grammar in Context (pages 364–365)

Vocabulary

outdo: to be better or more successful than someone else at doing something

mansion: a very large house

afterthought: something thought of, mentioned, or added later, especially something that was not part of the original plan

stroll: to walk somewhere in a slow, relaxed way

Comprehension Questions

- Did the mother have a favorite son? (*No, she loved each one for his own uniqueness.*)
- Why was the sibling rivalry so intense? (*Each brother wanted to be number one in his mother's affection.*)
- Even though the brothers spent a lot of money buying their mother lavish gifts, what did the mother need? (*Nothing.*)
- What did the mother suggest doing with the mansion and the chauffered car? (*selling them*)
- Why did she appreciate the trained parrot? (*She thought it was a delicious chicken.*)

Discussion Topics

- Do you think that most brothers and sisters want to outdo each other for their parents' love? Use examples from your experience.
- One of the interesting little details of the parable of "The Three Brothers" is that the chauffer Joe hires for his mother doesn't speak English. What do you think about the expectation that many people have that if you live and work in a country, you have an obligation to learn the language and customs of that country?

Grammar Presentation (pages 366–369)

Identify the Grammar

1. . . . *she didn't know what to do about it.*
2. *Joe . . . felt that he had to outdo his first brother . . .*
3. *Joe thought that he would certainly win his mother's approval with this gift.*
4. *Curly . . . was in a dilemma, wondering what he could do to top the gifts of the other two brothers.*
5. *The store owner told him this was a specially trained parrot that had memorized the* Encyclopedia Britannica.
6. *. . . the fact that the chauffeur doesn't speak English is a problem.*
7. *Curly was pleased that he had finally risen to the number one spot in his mother's affections.*
8. *All I know is that the chicken you gave me was delicious.*

Grammar Charts

- Looking at the first chart showing clauses used as objects, ask students why the word *that* is in parentheses. *(because its use is optional)* Have students say the two example sentences in that chart with and without the word *that*.
- Write the sentences above on the board (or make photocopies and distribute them to students in pairs or small groups). After students have read through the charts, ask them to:

    identify (underline) the noun clauses
    identify (circle) the word that begins each noun clause *(what: 1, 4) (that: 2, 3, 5, 6, 7, 8)* (Note that in 5 *that* is implied.)
- Have students work in small groups or pairs to determine in which of the eight sentences the noun clause functions as subject, object,

and complement. *(subject: 6, 8; object: 1, 2, 3, 4, 5; adjective complement: 7)*
- Ask students which of the above sentences contain questions. *(1, 4)*

Grammar Notes

Notes 1–2   *(Exercise 4)*
- Have students cover the left side of Note 1 and identify the function of each example sentence on the right.
- Have individual students read aloud the examples in Note 2. Where *that* is optional, have them read the sentences with and without the word *that*.
- Have students return to the examples in Note 1 and, working in pairs, identify in which sentences *that* is optional.

Note 3   *(Exercise 4)*
The fact that and *It's* + adjective + noun clause are very convenient structures in English, and it is worth spending some time to help students develop fluency with them.
- Have students find example sentences in Note 2 where *The fact that* could be used, and say these aloud: "The fact that she was a funny person was apparent. The fact that Joe has a good sense of humor is obvious." Point out that *the fact that* is less formal than the word *that* to introduce the clause.
- Write on the board: *It's funny that you should say that.* Erase *funny*, eliciting other adjectives from students, each time writing the new word in and erasing it. Then erase the noun clause and elicit several substitutions for it. For example, *It's interesting (that) you should ask that question.*

→ For additional practice, see the Supplementary Activities on page 106.

Notes 4–6   *(Exercises 2–3)*
- Embedded questions are extremely useful, and as indicated in Note 4, they are more polite than direct questions. Point out that we use embedded questions for a wide range of purposes—when we really don't know the answer, when we are unsure of the answer, when we want to say something without being very direct about it, and when we want to be polite. When approaching a stranger, for example, with a request for information, embedded questions are expected, for example, *Excuse me, do you know / could you tell me / I wonder if you could tell me* (note double embedded question!) *where the post office is.*

- Look at the example sentences in Note 4, and ask students to tell you what the original questions were and write them on the board.
   1. *Is she from around here?*
   2. *Who is she?*
   3. *What does* incongruous *mean?*
   4. *How far is it to the nearest town?*
- Ask students to identify the *Wh-* questions from the above list. (*2, 3, 4*).
   Write on the board *I'm not sure. Who is she?*
   And ask students to make an embedded question out of that. (*I'm not sure who she is.*) Ask them what has changed in the question. (*the word order and punctuation*)
- Returning to the above list of questions, write on the board:
   Is she from around here? and *I don't know.* Again, ask students to make an embedded question. (*I don't know if/whether she is from around here.*) Ask them what has changed. (*word order, punctuation, and the addition of* if *or* whether)
- Draw attention to the punctuation of examples in Note 5. Ask students why there is a question mark after the first one. (*because the embedded question is embedded in a question*)
- Write some *Wh-* and *Yes/No* questions with *do, does,* or *did.* For example: *Where does she live? Does she live nearby?* Ask students to make embedded questions starting with *Do you know.* (*Do you know where she lives? Do you know if she lives nearby?*) Once again, ask students what has changed from the original question. (*As with the preceding examples, word order and punctuation. However, in these examples, as the word order is changed,* does *disappears.*)
- Have students work in pairs to look through Notes 4–6 to find the expressions that are used to introduce embedded questions. Have volunteers write these on the board. (*I don't know, Do you know, I'm not sure, I'm not certain, I have no idea, Who knows, I wonder, Who knows, It is difficult to say.*) Ask if they can think of any others. (e.g., *Could you [please] tell me, Do you happen to know, It's hard to say/see, I can't imagine, Can you guess*)
- To practice making embedded questions, have each student select one of the introductory expressions and write it on a small piece of paper. On another small piece of paper have them write a regular question. Then do a "wheels" drill as described on page 00 of this Teacher's Manual: Half the class stands in a circle facing outward, and the other half stands in an outer circle facing inward; the outer circle revolves in a clockwise direction, and the inner circle revolves in a counterclockwise direction. When you tell them to stop, students work with the person facing them. Students on the inside circle present their questions to the students facing them, and the students in the outer circle use their introductory expressions to make embedded questions. Students in the outer circle then present their questions to the ones in the inner circle, and so on.

Note 7   *(Exercise 2)*
- Point out that when *whether* is used, the position of the word *not* can also be as follows: "We don't know whether or not she got the job." However, when *if* is used, the only position for *or not* is at the end of the sentence.
- Write on the board: <u>Whether</u> *she received it isn't known.* Ask students if *or not* can be added. (*Yes, but only after* whether: <u>Whether or not</u> *she received it isn't known.*)

Focused Practice (pages 369–374)

Exercise 2
tow: to pull a vehicle or ship along behind another vehicle using a rope or chain

Exercise 4
inevitable: certain to happen and impossible to avoid

eschew: to deliberately avoid doing, using, or having something

obfuscation: deliberately making something unclear or difficult to understand

Exercise 5
vulgar: dealing with or talking about sex and body wastes in a way people think is disgusting and not socially acceptable

punch line: the last few words of a joke or story that make it funny or surprising

animated: showing a lot of interest and energy

Communication Practice (pages 375–377)

Exercise 6
Discussion: Do you agree with Greg's position regarding jokes? Have you had similar experiences?

Exercise 7

There is one noun clause in the reading. Ask students if they can find it. *(par. 3: He was finally satisfied with the explanation that it was a very fast airplane.)*

aviation: the science or practice of flying aircraft

controller: someone at an airport who gives instructions to pilots by radio about where and when they can leave the ground or come down to the ground

cargo: the goods being carried in a ship, airplane, truck, etc.

cargo hold: the part of a ship or a plane where goods are stored

pound: a place where dogs and cats that are found on the street are kept until someone comes to get them

handler: someone whose job it is to deal with a particular type of object, especially to move it or lift it

cockpit: the part of an airplane in which the pilot sits

gauge: an instrument for measuring the amount, size, or speed of something

Exercise 8

Questions to generate ideas and elicit vocabulary:
- Do you tend to laugh easily?
- What makes you laugh?
- Can you think of a funny situation you were part of?
- Can you think of a joke you like?

Further Practice

Most of us have funny sibling rivalry stories. Sitting in a circle tell such a story to the class. (The story of Cain and Able is a sibling rivalry story, but it is not at all funny.)
- Discuss what these stories tell about human nature.
- Take a poll of your class. What percentage of the class:
  —has warm or supportive feelings toward their own siblings?
  —has difficult or strained relations with their siblings?
  —gets along well with some siblings but not others?

 **OUT OF THE BOX . . . . . .**

Time for a laugh. Bring in newspaper cartoons, jokes from *Reader's Digest* magazine, or jokes from websites on laughter and humor. In small groups, have students discuss the jokes/cartoons you bring in. Here is some language that you can encourage students to use:

- What I like/don't like about this joke is . . .
- What I think is funny is . . .
- What isn't so funny . . .
- It's amusing what . . .
- It's silly what . . .
- What I don't understand about this joke is . . .
- I don't understand what/why . . .
- Can you explain what/why . . .
- I wonder why . . .
- What makes me laugh is . . .
- I don't know whether to laugh or cry.
- Whether this is a good joke or not . . .

 Direct and Indirect Speech

UNIT 22

Unit Overview

Speech can be reported in two ways: direct, (quoted) speech, and indirect (reported) speech. This unit addresses both, with emphasis on the conversion of direct to indirect speech, building on the understanding of noun clauses and embedded questions students have gained from the previous unit, and adding the new challenge of making the changes in verb forms, pronouns, etc. required by the change in perspective that occurs when speech is reported.
- Direct speech: use of punctuation; use of reporting verbs *say* and *tell* (and others in Appendix 23)
- Indirect speech: statements, questions, verb changes, other changes (pronouns, possessives, *this, here, ago, now, today, yesterday, tomorrow*)

Grammar in Context (pages 378–380)

Vocabulary

poll: the process of finding out what people think about something by asking many people the same question

margin of error: the degree to which a calculation can be wrong without affecting the final results

statistically significant: if numbers are statistically significant, they are large enough to be meaningful

momentum: the ability to keep increasing, developing, or being more successful

Comprehension Questions

- Where do most of us get our news? *(television)*
- What kinds of journalistic mistakes are of most concern to the author? *(mistakes with numbers)*

- Which statement is true? "More than 100 million Americans breathe polluted air" or "On most days, the air in most American cities is healthy." *(both)*
- In the Legislature the Blues hold 40 seats and the Reds hold 46. How many seats do the Blues have to win to take control? *(four)*
- According to the article, what do we need to do to avoid drawing the wrong conclusions from statistics? *(educate ourselves, be careful, and think about what the numbers really mean)*

Discussion Topics

- The author of "Is News Reporting Accurate?" raises the question as to how much of news reporting can be trusted, particularly when numbers are involved. Putting aside the problems with numbers for a moment, what about the larger question: How much can you trust the accuracy of anything you see or hear on commercial radio and television?
- The article ends in a question: "Are we thinking for ourselves or letting others tell us what to think?" This is an important question because it is directly related to the success or even survival of democratic government, which depends on the participation of informed voters. What can we do to ensure fairness and accuracy in our news media?

Grammar Presentation (pages 380–385)

Identify the Grammar

In this unit examples of the target structures are not listed here since students will be finding all of the examples of indirect speech in the reading as part of the Discover the Grammar activity on page 386, part of which is previewed in Note 5.

Grammar Charts

- Ask students to look at the first two charts. Ask them if the verb *said* in the first chart could be replaced by *told*. *(No.)* Why not? *(The verb* tell *is followed by a person. You* tell *someone something.)* (Note: This usage is not to be confused with *tell a story / tell a lie*, which are ready-made expressions.) Ask if the word *that* is required. *(No.)*
- Have students look at Charts 3–6, showing indirect question formation. In the examples in Chart 4, are the words *if / whether* required? *(Yes)* What about Chart 6—are the

Wh- question words needed? *(Yes.)* Are the names of the people needed? *(No.)*
- Ask students if these first four charts remind them of anything they have recently studied. This should all look very familiar because changing direct to indirect speech is essentially forming noun clauses and embedded questions, which they have already practiced doing. However, there are some additional complications with reported speech, as shown in the last two charts!
- Have pairs of students read aloud the direct and indirect versions of each sentence in Chart 7. Ask students what is different in the indirect version. *(The pronoun is changed. The verb expresses an earlier time.)*
- Look at the last chart. Ask students what other words change. *(pronouns, possessives,* this, here, ago, now, today, yesterday, *and* tomorrow.)
- As a motivating "pre-test" have pairs of students test each other to see if they can transform the sentences in this last chart from direct to indirect speech. The student being tested covers the indirect speech column and tries to form the sentence. As this student makes mistakes, the "teacher" partner provides helpful feedback, giving the student opportunities to self-correct.

Grammar Notes

Notes 1–2

- Write the first two example sentences on the board without punctuation and invite volunteers to punctuate them properly. Point out that the final punctuation goes inside the closing quotation marks, a detail that many native speakers of English get wrong.
- Note that while *tell* is the preferred verb when mentioning the listener, it is possible to use *say* when preceded by *to* in some cases: *Andy said to Freda that she shouldn't worry.* But not *Frank said to us to pay attention.*
- Have students look at the list of reporting verbs in Appendix 23. Ask if they can think of any other words to add. *(state, proclaim, scream, whisper, inquire, answer, explain, assert, boast, complain)* Which reporting verbs would make the direct quotations in Notes 1–2 more dramatic? Invite students to try out a few substitutions.
- Ask students to look through some news articles, magazine interviews, or a piece of literature involving dialogue, and notice the variety of reporting verbs used. Have them

take notes on some of the ones they found most interesting and share this with the class.

- Point out that except for *tell* and *ask*, the other reporting verbs follow the pattern of *say*—that is, they are followed directly by the direct or indirect speech.
- Ask students to compare examples of the direct and indirect speech in Notes 1–2 and to underline the changes in the verbs, pronouns, and other words. Review these as a class.

Notes 3–4   *(Exercises 3–4)*

Most of the information in Notes 3–4 is a review of what students learned in the last unit on noun clauses. However, they will need considerable practice observing these rules in action as they combine them with the changes in verbs, pronouns, etc. involved in reported speech.

- Ask students to look at the first two example sentences of Note 3. What were the original questions? *(Are you going to vote? Have you heard the speech?)*
- Have students work in pairs to compare the examples of direct and indirect speech, underlining changes in verbs and circling changes in pronouns and other words. Review these as a class.

→ For additional practice, see the Supplementary Activities on page 106.

Note 5   *(Exercises 2, 4, 5)*

- Have students cover the left column of Note 5 and name the verb forms used in each example as direct speech is converted to indirect.
- The unit reading provides a good opportunity for students to see the transformation of direct to indirect speech in context. Have students turn to page 386 in their books and do Part A of Discover the Grammar. Review the answers as a class.

Note 6   *(Exercises 2, 4)*

- Elicit some examples of questions about general truths, write them on the board (e.g., *Kwan asked, "How cold does it get in northern Maine?"*), and have students convert them to indirect speech, remembering that the verb in the noun clause stays in the present. *(Kwan asked how cold it gets in northern Maine.)*
- Write the last example sentence on the board, underlining the reporting verb: *Bruce says he's going to vote.* Ask students what other forms that verb could take without requiring a change in the form of the verb in the main

clause. *(is saying, has said, will say, is going to say)*

→ For additional practice, see the Supplementary Activities on page 107.

Note 7   *(Exercises 2, 4, 5)*

- Have students work in pairs to compare the examples of direct and indirect speech, underlining changes in verbs and circling changes in pronouns and other words. Review these as a class.
- To give students practice discriminating among modals that change and those that don't change in reported speech, write the following sentence on the board and ask a volunteer to transform it into indirect speech:
  Ana said, "We'll go to the movies." → Ana said they would go to the movies.
  Replace the *'ll* with *could* and elicit the indirect version. *(Ana said they could . . . [no change].)* Continue with other modals.

Note 8   *(Exercise 5)*

- Have students read the example sentences aloud in pairs, noticing the changes.
- Write some sentences on the board with words that change in indirect speech and elicit indirect speech. For example:
  Tomiko asked, "Have you seen these pictures?" → Tomiko asked if I had seen those pictures.
  She said, "I took them three days ago." → She said she had taken them three days before.
  "I brought them with me yesterday." → She said she had brought them with her the day before.

Focused Practice (pages 386–391)

Exercise 3

Rosetta Stone: a large ancient stone that was found in Egypt in 1799, which had the same piece of writing on it in three different writing systems: Greek letters, Egyptian letters, and ancient Egyptian hieroglyphics

the Union: the United States

Boston Tea Party: an incident in 1773 when colonial Americans dumped a British cargo of tea into Boston Harbor to protest a tea tax

electoral votes: votes in the Electoral College, a group of people who come together to elect the U.S. President and Vice-President, based on the votes of people in each state

Communication Practice (pages 392–394)

Exercise 7

Play the audio program and allow students to write down key facts the reporter says as direct quotations, using correct punctuation. Divide up the quotations according to topic. For example, the reporter said, "Mt. St. Andrea erupted at 5:34. . . . There have been no deaths reported so far."

Exercise 8

If your class is large you might want to do this in three or four groups so that students are more involved. At the end have the directors of each group write the original messages on the board next to the final messages and, if there was a change, explain how it occurred.

Exercise 9

Discussion: Have you ever been in an accident? Did you report it? Do you remember what you said? Did the driver of the other car report the accident as well? Did he or she have a different story? Were there any onlookers? If so, how did they report the accident?

Exercise 10

Questions to generate ideas and elicit vocabulary:
- Do you read newspapers and/or news magazines?
- What kinds of stories interest you the most?
- What makes a good story?
- Has anything you read caught your attention recently?

Further Practice

Raise these concerns with the class: Fewer and fewer people have time to read the newspaper. They watch the news on TV for a few minutes while they eat breakfast or catch the headlines on the car radio on the way to work. As the government becomes more complex, fewer people feel capable of making decisions about it. In America, a president can be elected by fewer than half of the eligible voters.

Have students discuss these questions in small groups and report back to the class: What does this mean for democracy? Do you imagine that this condition will get better or worse? Why?

Reporting an interview. Bring in magazine interviews with famous people. Have students work in small groups. Give each group an interview to read and discuss. Then have students in each group underline interesting pieces of information and select some things they would like to share with the class. Have each group tell the class whose interview they read, and share the information they selected. Point out that for each piece of information, students should report both the question and the answer. Write these examples on the board:

We read an interview with . . .
What we found interesting was what she or he said about . . .
The reporter asked . . . , to which he or she answered that . . .
She also claimed that . . .

UNIT 23 Conditionals; Other Ways to Express Unreality

Unit Overview

Conditionals are presented in all forms: real conditionals for present and future, and unreal conditionals in past, present, and future. In addition, *wish* and *if only* statements offer additional ways to express unreality.
- Present real conditionals: *Water boils if it reaches 100°C.*
- Future real conditionals: *If it rains, we will close the windows.*
- Present unreal conditionals: *If I were you, I wouldn't accept the offer. I'd buy a new car if I had the money.*
- Past unreal conditionals: *I would have lent you money if I had known you were in financial difficulty.*
- "Mixed" conditionals: *If I hadn't gone to college, I'd still be working at the hardware store.*
- *Wish / If only* statements: *I wish I had a better job. If only I weren't so busy.*

Grammar in Context (pages 406–408)

Vocabulary

sweltering: too hot, making you feel uncomfortable
beastly: very

weirdo: someone who behaves strangely, wears unusual clothes, etc.

chest of drawers: a piece of furniture with drawers, used for storing clothes

mutilate: to severely and violently damage someone's body

serial killer: someone who has killed several people, one after the other, often in the same way

curb: the edge of a street, between where people can walk and cars can drive

insulin: a substance produced naturally in your body that allows sugar to be used for energy

token: something that represents a feeling, fact, event, etc.

flutter: to wave or move gently in the air

Comprehension Questions

- On what kind of day did the story take place? *(very hot)*
- In American culture, which sex is supposed to have intuition? *(females)*
- Where were Donna and Thain going when they met Mr. Wilkerson? *(to a yard sale)*
- Why was Donna unhappy about stopping to help Mr. Wilkerson? *(At first, she was afraid he might do harm to them. Then she was also concerned that by the time they got to the yard sale, all the good merchandise would be gone.)*
- What disease did Mr. Wilkerson suffer from? *(diabetes)*

Discussion Topics

- Why do you think the envelope containing the $50,000 check had no return address?
- Some people have commented that this story is too far-fetched, could never happen, etc. However, it is based on a documented happening in which a mysterious benefactor left a married couple a considerable amount of money after they had shown kindness to him. Ask students what they think. Have they heard of any happenings of this type?

Grammar Presentation (pages 408–412)

Identify the Grammar

Examples of the target structures are not listed here since in this unit students will be finding all the examples of conditionals in the reading as part of the Discover the Grammar activity on page 412. In conjunction with this activity, recommendations are made in each of the notes below for having students find examples from the reading relevant to the content being presented.

Grammar Charts

- Have students compare the first two charts. Both talk about present situations. Do both use present verb forms? *(No, the verb forms in the unreal conditionals are past.)*
- What about subject-verb agreement in Charts 1–2? *(Subject-verb agreement is normal with the real conditionals. For the present unreal conditional, instead of* It was(n't), *we see* It were(n't), *which is subjunctive.)*
- In Chart 3, Past Unreal Conditionals, what verb forms are used? *(In the* if *clause, the past perfect is used. In the result clause,* would have + *past participle is used.)*
- In the last chart, which deals with *wish / if only* statements, what verb forms are used for the present and future? *(would, could)* Which form is used for the past? *(past perfect)*

Grammar Notes

Notes 1–2   *(Exercises 2–3)*
- Ask students what verb forms are used in the first example sentence of real conditionals. (Water boils / reaches: *simple present / simple present*) Elicit some similar examples. For example, *Babies cry if they get tired.*
- Ask what verb forms are used in the second example. *(simple present /* will *future)* Elicit some examples of situations that are likely or possible in the future. For example, *If it rains, we'll postpone our picnic.*
- Have students look through the examples in Note 2 and identify which are about general truths or repeated actions *(the first three)* and which are about future ones *(the last three).*
- Now students will look through the reading to find examples of both types of real conditional. Have students turn to page 412 in their books and do the first two tasks in Discover the Grammar.

Note 3   *(Exercise 3)*
- Write on the board: *If I _____, I _____.* Have students tell you what can go into the blanks, and write these words under the blanks on the board:

  If I _____, I _____.
     were   *could*
              might + base form
    simple past *would*

- Have students find examples of the present unreal conditional in the reading, following the directions for Task 4 of Discover the Grammar on page 412.
- Ask students to think about three things they wish were true, at least one involving being

something and one involving having something. Write these as sentences and share them in small groups, for example:

> If I were president of the country, I'd / I wouldn't . . .
> If I had ten thousand extra dollars, I'd . . .
> If I could talk to one famous person in history, I'd talk to . . .

Note 4   *(Exercise 5)*
- Once again, write the following sentence frame on the board. Ask students to supply the verb forms, and write them below the blanks:

> If I _____,   I _____.
>   had +   could   have +
>   past   might   past participle
>   participle   would

- Have students find examples of the past unreal conditional in the reading, following the directions for Task 5 of Discover the Grammar on page 412.
- Ask students to write about a significant past event that happened to them or someone close to them. Have them then read their sentences aloud. Take one or two of the examples, and ask students to speculate as to what would or might have happened if events had proceeded differently. For example:

> My parents met at a party. My mother's best friend invited her to go to the party. My mother didn't want to go, but her friend insisted. She met my father at the party. (If my mother's friend <u>hadn't insisted</u>, my mother <u>wouldn't have gone</u> to the party. She probably <u>wouldn't have met</u> my father.)

- Once students are conversant with this structure, have them construct sentences using prompts like these:

> If I had grown up in a different town . . .
> If I had moved to a different city ten years ago . . .
> If I hadn't (gotten married / taken piano lessons, etc.) . . .

Note 5   *(Exercise 5)*
- Have students find examples of mixed conditionals in the reading, following the directions for Task 6 of Discover the Grammar on page 412.
- Write a sentence on the board and ask students to identify the past action and present result, for example:

> If my parents <u>hadn't moved</u> to this town, <u>I wouldn't be attending</u> this school.

- Write a sentence on the board to to show the present result of a past conditional situation, for example:

> If computers <u>hadn't been invented</u>, the world <u>would be</u> very different today.

Erase the present result clause and replace *computers* with *the cell phone* to elicit a new sentence. Invite students to make up sentences of their own based on other inventions or ideas of their own.

→ For additional practice, see the Supplementary Activities on page 107.

Notes 6–7   *(Exercise 4)*
- The structure that students may struggle with the most in this unit is the use of *wish*, particularly wishes about the present and future. Remind them that the central meaning of *wish* is a desire that a situation be different from what it is. That is, a wish involves a contrary-to-fact situation.
- Ask students to compare the notes about *wish* and *if only* and to identify what is the same and what is different in the patterns for their use. (*The only difference is that the clause following* wish *can be introduced by* that. *Otherwise, they follow the same pattern regarding verb forms.*)
- Have students look through the reading with a partner for examples of *wish* and *if only* statements, and identify the time frame each expresses:

> I wish I had an ice tea right now. (present)
> . . . I wish you would stop taking pity on every weirdo you see. (present)
> If only that chest of drawers would still be there! (future)
> If only I weren't so forgetful . . . (present)
> I wish there had been more time for us to get to know one another. (past)

- As pointed out in Note 6, *hope* expresses a desire about events that are possible, and normal verb forms are used. Ask students to find the one sentence with *hope* in the reading to confirm this. (. . . I just hope we <u>don't end up</u> in the newspaper headlines.)
- Ask students to write down three general situations (not actions) that they want to be different. Then have them make a *wish* or *if only* statement about each and share these with a partner. For example:

> **Situation**
> 1. *My husband works about 60 hours a week, and I don't get to see him very much.*
> 2. *I don't earn enough money.*
> 3. *I'm always tired.*

Wish statement

1. *I wish he had a different job.*
2. *I wish I earned/could earn more money.*
3. *If only I weren't tired all the time.*

Next, ask them to write a sentence with *wish + would/could* + base form expressing a single action that would change each situation wished about, for example:

> *I* <u>*wish*</u> *my husband* <u>*would look for*</u> *a better job with fewer hours.*

→ For additional practice, see the Supplementary Activities on page 107.

Focused Practice (pages 412–417)

Exercise 2
Venus fly trap: a plant that catches and eats insects

Exercise 3
Shoot: start speaking (informal, used in the imperative)

Exercise 6
The world owes (someone) a living: If the world owes you a living, you are unwilling to work in order to get things and expect them to be provided for you.

give in: to agree to something you were unwilling to agree to before, especially after a long argument

Communication Practice (pages 418–420)

Exercise 7
After students have answered the questions, play the audio program again and let them listen for examples of real and unreal conditionals and *wish* statements. As they hear one of these, let them raise their hands. Pause the audio program, replaying it as necessary, and have students repeat the sentence, saying whether it describes a real or unreal situation. Following are examples of targeted structures from the listening (all unreal except for sentence 5):

1. *I wish Bob and I weren't going together.*
2. *I wish you hadn't done that.*
3. *I thought he'd break up with me if I refused.*
4. *What would you have done?*
5. *If the teacher finds out, she'll fail both of us.*
6. *If I were you, I'd call him up and tell him I'd changed my mind.*

go together: to have a romantic relationship with someone

break up: to end a marriage or romantic relationship

Exercise 8
The team that asks the question should be responsible for knowing the answers to their questions. To this end, it would be useful to have some research tools on hand—such as an atlas or world map and an encyclopedia—so that teams can refer to them as needed. Alternatively, as each team is preparing their questions, you can be available as a resource, perhaps establishing the ground rule that you are available to provide any information they need as long as they form their question correctly!

Exercise 9
Discussion: Have you ever received a gift that you thought was too generous? How did it make you feel?

Exercise 10
Questions to generate ideas and elicit vocabulary:
• Do you use your intuition, or inner voice?
• Do you tend to trust your feelings about things as much as your thoughts?
• Do you pay attention to your dreams? Do you sometimes get answers to your questions from them?
• What are your decisions usually based on—how you feel, what you think, or both factors?
• What do you think they should be based on?

Further Practice
Have students work in small groups to outline a biography of Quentin Wilkerson, the generous old man who left the young couple $50,000 in "Intuition." Have them use what little information is given about his life in the story and invent more about him: How old is he? Why is he traveling around the country? Why is he traveling alone? Why does he travel by bus? How did he make his money? Why doesn't he have any children? Why won't he be traveling around any more? Have each group share their "roughly sketched" biography with the class.

GRAMMAR OUT OF THE BOX ......

No regrets. Bring in a magazine or newspaper story that ended well because someone made the right decision at the right time. Have students read the story and discuss what would have happened if the person had reacted differently, what they think the person wished at that moment, and what they would have done themselves if they had been in that situation.

⏱ You can also choose to work on fictional stories such as "The Truth About Pyecraft" by H. G. Wells, in which Pyecraft, a fat man obsessed with losing weight, makes a decision which he then regrets, or "The Honest Man and The Devil," by Hilaire Belloc, in which a man decides to have nothing to do with the devil and is then surprised by the consequences of his decision. In relation to these stories, have students discuss questions similar to the ones suggested above.

| UNIT 24 | **More Conditions; The Subjunctive** |

Unit Overview

Additional ways of using the conditional—implied and inverted conditions—build on the unreal conditionals that were presented in the last unit. The subjunctive is introduced with verbs and adjectives of advice, necessity, and urgency.

- Nonstandard conditions: *Without your help I wouldn't have succeeded.* (= If you hadn't helped.)
- Inverted conditions: *Had I seen her, I would have called you.*
- Verbs followed by the subjunctive: *The doctor suggested (that) Frank switch medications.*
- Adjectives followed by the subjunctive: *It is urgent that she get to the hospital.*
- Gerund and infinitive phrases as alternatives to the subjunctive: *We suggest getting a second opinion. It's important for her to understand her options.*

Grammar in Context (pages 421–423)

Background Notes

This unit's reading looks at a problem that is an urgent matter in industrialized nations—the care of the elderly. As is well known, many older Americans spend their final years apart from their families in homes or communities for the aged. Other issues connected with aging, such as conflict within families and older people finding homes and work on their own, broaden the theme of how to live one's "golden years."

Vocabulary

be at your wit's end: to be very upset because you have not been able to solve a problem even though you have tried very hard

at a moment's notice: without being given much time to prepare

nursing home: a place where people who are too old or sick to take care of themselves can live

life expectancy: the length of time that a person or animal is expected to live

cruise: a vacation in which you travel on a large ship

senior: someone who is over sixty years old

Comprehension Questions

- Where is the woman's mother living now? *(in her own house)*
- When the doctor asks, "What if she moved in with you and your husband?" what does the woman reply? *(She says her husband and she have their own life, and it's important for her mother to keep her independence.)*
- Why doesn't the woman like the nursing home option? *(She's heard bad things about nursing homes.)*
- What is the woman's concern about both retirement and assisted living centers? *(They are expensive.)*
- Which country mentioned has the highest average life expectancy. *(Japan)*

Discussion Topics

- The last two paragraphs leave the reader with the strange feeling that the author is accusing seniors of being wasteful of society's resources. "They take expensive ocean cruises . . . go on European vacations . . . and have unusual and costly hobbies." Wealthy seniors like other wealthy people can do what they like with their money. Nobody is going to Europe on their Social Security checks. How do you feel about seniors doing these things? Is it wasteful? Is it OK?
- If you were in the same position as the woman in "The Happy Golden Years," i.e., having a parent who is no longer able to maintain an independent existence, what would you do?

Grammar Presentation (pages 423–426)

Identify the Grammar

Examples of the target structures are not listed here since in this unit students will be finding

(continued)

Grammar Charts

- In the first chart ask students to compare the nonstandard conditions with the implied conditions. In general, which are easier to construct? *(nonstandard conditions)*
- Point out that most of the nonstandard condition structures are very commonly used in conversation except for one. Ask students if they can guess which it is. (But for, *which is, in fact, quite formal and very rarely used.*)
- Looking at the second chart, ask students to describe what is different in form between the inverted conditions and the standard conditions. *(word order, deletion of* if*)*
- Moving to the third and fourth charts, ask students what they notice about the form of the verbs in the subjunctive clauses. *(They're in the base form—they don't show agreement with the subject.)*

Grammar Notes

Note 1 *(Exercises 2–3)*

- Use the sentences in Chart 1 to practice forming implied conditions. Have students work in pairs. One partner covers the leftmost column and, looking at the implied condition column, re-creates the equivalent sentences using *with, without, but for, if so, if not,* and *otherwise,* while the other partner provides helpful feedback as needed. They then switch roles.
- Have students turn to page 427 in their books and do Part A of Discover the Grammar.
- Elicit other examples from the class. Start with a prompt such as this:
  I'd better balance my checkbook.
  Ask students to suggest some nonstandard conditions *(if not, otherwise)* and to complete the thought *(If not / Otherwise, I'm likely to bounce some checks.)*

Note 2 *(Exercises 3, 6)*

- Again, the charts provide good material for practice. This time, have students use Chart 2. Working in pairs, one partner covers the leftmost column, and looking at the standard condition column, re-creates the equivalent sentence as an inverted condition, while the

other partner provides helpful feedback as needed. They then switch roles.

- Have students turn to page 427 in their books and do Part B of Discover the Grammar.
- In small groups, have students create their own *if* clauses with *If I had . . . , If she should come . . . , If I were, . . . ,* etc. Each group presents their sentences to the other groups, who practice inverting them (*Should she come . . . ,* etc.).

Note 3 *(Exercise 6)*

Students will already be familiar with the structures in Note 3, having learned them in the last unit as present and past unreal conditionals. *If I were you* is a particularly useful structure in English. If you feel they need more practice with it, have them work in pairs posing problems, e.g., *My rent is too high,* and giving each other advice, e.g., *If I were you, I'd look for a new apartment.*

→ For additional practice, see the Supplementary Activities on page 108.

Notes 4–6 *(Exercises 4–6)*

- Have students turn to page 427 in their books and do Part C of Discover the Grammar.
- Ask students to underline the expressions that trigger the use of the subjunctive as you write the sentences on the board.
  1. *She <u>insists</u> I come over and help her at a moment's notice.*
  2. *. . . when I <u>suggest</u> she go out with me and take a walk, she gets angry.*
  3. *. . . I would have <u>recommended</u> she sell it a long time ago.*
  4. *. . . I'<u>d rather</u> she not go into a nursing home.*
  5. *. . . <u>it's important that</u> she have friends . . .*
  6. *I'd <u>propose</u> you find a retirement center . . .*
  7. *I'd <u>recommend</u> you look into them . . .*
  8. *. . . <u>it's essential that</u> we understand the value of the elderly in society . . .*
  Ask students what they notice about the use of *that* in these sentences. (That *is used after* it's + *adjective.*) Ask if *that* can be used after the underlined verbs. *(Yes, but it's not required.)* Ask students which sentence contains a negative subjunctive. *(4)* How is it formed? (Not *is added before the base form of the verb.*)
- Note 5 presents some useful alternatives to the subjunctive. Ask students to look at the above examples from the reading and consider in which cases the subjunctive might be replaced by a gerund phrase. *(2, 6, and 7; sentence 1 doesn't work because there is a change of subject which can't be expressed with the gerund.)*

- Point out that the last option presented in Note 5—verb + object + infinitive—is more conversational than the subjunctive and is likely to be preferred unless there is a good reason to use the subjunctive. Students should be familiar with this structure from their work in Unit 16. You may want to look at some sentences that can go both ways. Write some examples such as these on the board:

  He urged that we attend the meeting. He asked that I lend him some money.

  Have students express them differently:

  He urged us to attend the meeting. He asked me to lend him some money.

- Appendix 24 lists the verbs that can be followed by the subjunctive as well as those that take the form verb + object + infinitive. Have students look over the list and ask any questions they have. Some students may be surprised that the verbs *want* and *would like* are not listed in the Appendix, as in their language, the equivalents require the subjunctive. If *prefer* and *would rather* take the subjunctive in English, why shouldn't these verbs since they are so similar in meaning? The answer is that in languages not everything is strictly logical. In English the subjunctive these days is a relatively little-used form, and the verbs that still require its use simply need to be memorized.

- Have students work in small groups to generate two sentences each using the subjunctive after *demand, insist, propose, recommend,* and *suggest.* Let them then identify which of these could also be expressed using a gerund, for example:

  My teachers always demanded we be quiet in class.

  A friend of mine suggested I take this class. OR *suggested (my) taking . . .*

  My parents always insisted that I eat everything on my plate.

  My teacher recommended I read this book OR *recommended (my) reading*

- Review the examples in Note 6. The more informal option pointed out at the end of the note is more frequently used in conversation than the subjunctive version. Have students convert the first example in the note to the less formal version: *It's essential for elderly people to be treated with dignity.*

- Have students look once again at Appendix 24. Are there any adjectives listed there in addition to those in Note 6? *(obligatory, reasonable, unreasonable)*

- Have students practice the structure by completing these sentences:

  To be happy, it's important (essential, etc.) that a person have . . .

  To be a good parent (leader, etc.), it's important that a person be . . .

  To be a good parent, it's important that a person not . . .

  Then have students convert these sentence to the less formal, infinitive structure:

  To be happy, it's important to have/be, etc.

Focused Practice (pages 427–432)

Exercise 2
buddy: a friend

Exercise 3
in a rut: living or working in a situation that never changes, so that you feel bored

Communication Practice (pages 433–434)

Exercise 8
After students have answered the questions, play the audio program again and let them listen for examples of inverted conditions and the subjunctive. As they hear one of these, let them raise their hands. Pause the audio program, replaying it as necessary, and have students repeat the sentence.

1. *Had I known she was calling, I wouldn't have answered the phone.*
2. *I had to call and insist she come and get the kids.*
3. *It's important she pay more attention to those kids.*
4. *I suggest you call her back . . .*

Exercise 9
Invite students to rephrase the content of the statements in different ways using some of the structures they have learned in the unit. For example, *It's desirable for elderly parents to live with their children.*

Exercise 10
Ask students what they think about relationships between older and younger people. What do young people get from older people? What do older people get from younger ones?

Exercise 11

Questions to generate ideas and elicit vocabulary:

- Who are some of the older people you have spent time with?
- What did you learn from them?
- Which of them influenced you the most?
- What do you remember best about them?
- What memories / feelings would you like to share with them?

Further Practice

Discuss as a class: In many traditional societies, older people have typically been part of an extended family, living with their children, often taking care of young children while their parents go to work. Their home with the family is assured, and they are respected for the contribution they make to the household. In the United States, where independence and mobility are valued, grown children tend to live apart from their parents, often in distant parts of the country. For many older people, this means they will spend their last years alone, sometimes in the care of strangers. What do you think of this? Can anything be done to improve the situation for older people? In your home country where do older people generally live? What is it like for them?

GRAMMAR OUT OF THE BOX . . . . . .

Healthy living. Bring in a variety of magazine articles or Internet printouts about health-related issues—for example, achieving and maintaining a healthy weight, balancing work and family, working during retirement, eating a balanced diet, staying healthy during vacations, or managing stress in the workplace. Have students, working in small groups, read recommendations on one of the topics and discuss them. Then ask students to make notes about the main recommendations and get prepared to make a group report to the class. Encourage students to use the language they learned in this unit. Write the following opening lines on the board:

- *The article suggests (that) _____*
- *The experts recommend (that) _____*
- *You might _____; if so, _____*
- *Should you _____, _____*
- *Without perseverance, you won't be able to _____*
- *With a bit of patience, you'll soon be able to _____*
- *It's important (that) _____*
- *It's essential (that) _____*
- *It's advisable (that) _____*

Supplementary Activities

Unit 1   Notes 6–9

Have students look at Note 6, where an important contrast in usage between *will* (for unplanned action) and *be going to* (for a planned or already developing situation) is explained and exemplified. To provide practice applying this contrast, play "Let's Have a Party!"
• Start by volunteering, "I'll bring some fruit and cheese."
• Get students to offer to bring in different items, using the above structure. As they do, write each contribution on the board and the student's initials next to it.
• After this, go back and have the class remember who is bringing what. This time, since the action has been preplanned, the *be going to* future is needed. Give an example, e.g., "Tomiko is going to bring napkins." Then call on students.
• Point out that the present progressive can be substituted for *be going to* in these examples.
See Note 8. However, be sure students understand that the present progressive can be used for future meaning only in the case of preplanned activities.

Unit 2   Notes 1–3, 5–7

Draw the following timeline on the board:

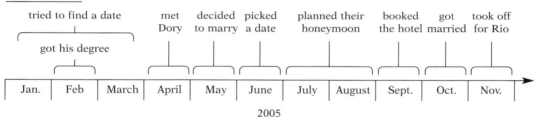

Mark's timeline

Write the following sentences on the board.

1. Mark and Dory _____ (know) each other since April, 2005.

2. In March, Mark _____ (not know) who he _____ (marry).

3. When Mark got his degree, he _____ (think) about finding a date.

4. When Mark _____ (meet) Dory, he _____ (try) to find a date for three months.

5. By the time Mark _____ (meet) Dory, he _____ (got) his degree.

6. When they _____ (decide) to marry, they _____ (pick) a date for the wedding.

7. When they _____ (book) the hotel, they _____ (plan) their honeymoon for two months.

8. By the end of September, they _____ (book) a hotel in Rio.

9. When they _____ (take off) for Rio, they already knew what hotel they _____ (stay) at.

Have students study the timeline and use appropriate forms of the verbs in brackets to complete the sentences about Mark and Dory.

Unit 3   Note 2

Draw the following box and chart on the board:

I see your point.	This printer is new.
He's tasting the sauce.	I feel bad about not telling the truth.
She's looking out the window.	He has a car.
I think it's ridiculous.	

Verb	Stative use	Active use
be		
have		
feel		
look		
see		
taste		
think		

Have students classify the examples in the box by writing them in the correct place in the chart. Then have students complete the chart with examples of their own illustrating the difference in meaning between the stative and active use of verbs. If necessary, allow students to use a dictionary for ideas, but encourage them to write their own examples, which can be adapted from the ones students find in their dictionaries.

Unit 4   Notes 3–6

• Enlarge, photocopy, and hand out the following conversations:

CONVERSATION 1
A: I don't like chocolate.
B: I do.

CONVERSATION 2
A: I like chocolate.
B: So do I. OR I do, too.

CONVERSATION 3
A: I don't like chocolate.
B: Neither do I. OR I don't either.

CONVERSATION 4
A: I don't like chocolate ice cream, but I do like chocolate cake. You don't like chocolate cake, do you?
B: No, I don't.

CONVERSATION 1
A: I've never been abroad.
B: I _____.

CONVERSATION 2
A: I've been abroad.
B: So _____. OR I _____.

CONVERSATION 3
A: I've never been abroad.
B: Neither _____. OR I _____.

CONVERSATION 4
A: I've never been abroad, but I have been to the north of our country. You haven't been to the north, _____?
B: No, I _____.

- Have students study the conversations in the first column, and then complete the conversations in the second column individually. Have students compare answers in pairs, and review as a class.
- Have pairs create their own four conversations based on the ones above. Encourage students to change the topic for each conversation. Have students submit their work to you for correction. Then have students practice the conversations without reading them.

Unit 5   Grammar Charts

To give students some practice listening to reduced forms, read these sentences and have students listen for the modals and the verb following them. Have students write the whole verb phrase.

You Say	Students Write
1. "Alice <u>couldn't a been thinking</u> very clearly."	couldn't have been thinking
2. "Tell Sara <u>she better come in</u> and talk to me."	she had better come in
3. "You <u>weren't sposta be</u> here until ten."	weren't supposed to be
4. "We <u>gotta leave</u> this place as soon as we can."	have got to leave
5. "Bill <u>might not a wanted</u> the marriage to work."	might not have wanted
6. "Sam's <u>gotta start paying</u> child support."	has got to start paying
7. "Bruce <u>hasta go</u> to court today."	has to go
8. "We <u>better get going</u> if we're <u>gonna make it</u>."	had better get going, going to make it
9. "<u>Arencha sposta be</u> at work now?"	Aren't you supposed to be
10. "You <u>don't hafta come</u> if you <u>don't wanna</u>."	don't have to come, don't want to

Unit 6   Notes 3–5

Have students individually write a true sentence about a classmate. It could be a fact they know or something they can see at the moment. Write these examples on the board:

- Bob is absent.
- Brenda is wearing smart clothes today.
- Sally looks tired.
- Sam passed his history exam.

Then have students sit in groups and share their sentences with their classmates, who should make speculations about them. Write this example on the board:

A: Bob is absent today.
B: He must be ill.
C: He can't be ill. He looked fine yesterday.
D: He must have overslept. He said his alarm clock was not working well.

Unit 7   Notes 3–5

Have students work in pairs and make up three simple stories (50–60 words) using non-count nouns. Point out that each story should contain at least five non-count nouns in uncountable or countable use. Have students look at Appendices 5 and 6 on pages A-4 and A-5 as they work and encourage them to be creative. Write this example on the board:

There was so much snow on the road that we had to stop at a gas station. There we ate some cake, drank a cup of hot coffee, and filled the tank with gasoline. We had our skiing equipment in the trunk, and we couldn't wait to get to the ski resort!

Invite students to share their best stories with the class.

Unit 8   Notes 2–6, 8

• On the board, write the following text based on the opening reading:

_____ (1) Easter Island lies in _____ (2) South Pacific Ocean. It is _____ (3) rather desolate place covered mostly by _____ (4) grassland, with _____ (5) trees that are no taller than 10 feet. _____ (6) island is famous for being one of _____ (7) richest sites of gigantic statues.

_____ (8) statues were made by _____ (9) people who inhabited _____ (10) island many years ago. _____ (11) Erich Von Daniken thinks that _____ (12) Easter Islanders did all _____ (13) work themselves. But how? Though _____ (14) wheel had been invented when the statues were built, they didn't have access to it. One convincing explanation is that they invented their own devices.

• Have students complete the story individually with *a, the,* or Ø.
• Have students compare answers with a partner, and then match each blank to the following uses, which you should write on the board:
—indefinite article + first mention:
—zero article + non-specific plural count noun:
—zero article + non-specific non-count noun:
—zero article + name of person or place:
—definite article + specific singular count noun:
—definite article + specific plural count noun:
—definite article + specific non-count noun:
—definite article +superlative adjective + noun:
—definite article + invention:
—definite article + name of a group of people:
—definite article + name of geographical place:

Review as a class. *(indefinite article + first mention: 3; zero article + non-specific plural count noun: 5; zero article + non-specific non-count noun: 4; zero article + name of person or place: 1, 11; definite article + specific singular count noun: 6, 10; definite article + specific plural count noun: 8, 9; definite article + specific non-count noun: 13; definite article +superlative adjective + noun: 7; definite article + invention: 14; definite article + name of a group of people: 12; definite article + name of geographical place: 2)*

Unit 9   Notes 2–5

- Write on the board a list of things people take or bring back from vacation:

cash	documentation	shaving cream	postcards
local currency	medications	toothpaste	souvenirs
traveler's checks	film	sunscreen	gifts
(other)	____	____	____

- Have pairs of students talk about the things they packed and brought back on an occasion when they went on vacation. Encourage students to ask follow-up questions. Point out they should use quantifiers. Write these examples on the board:

   A: When I went to France last year I took no cash, but I took a lot of traveler's checks.

   B: Didn't you take any local currency?

   A: No. When I got there I realized I didn't have any local money!

   A: Did you buy any souvenirs?

   B: I bought only one because I didn't have much money. But I bought lots of postcards!

Unit 10   Notes 4–5

- Draw the following chart on the board:

Object	Opinion	Size	Age	Shape	Color	Origin	Material
Favorite possession: ____							
Family heirloom: ____							
Other: ____							

- To provide practice with order of adjective and noun modifiers, have students write three objects they would like to describe in the first column, and then complete the relevant categories for each object. Point out that when necessary, students can write two modifiers for the same category. Then have students write a sentence describing each object.
- You may want to follow up by having students describe one of the objects to the class, withholding its name. The class tries to guess the object.

Unit 11   Note 7

- Tell students you'd like them to write five pairs of sentences about themselves, using time expressions to begin adjective clauses. The first item in each pair should begin with *when* or *that*. The second should omit these words.
  - —Elicit some opening lines. *(I [can/'t] remember . . . , I often think about . . . , I dream about . . .)*
  - —Elicit some words that refer to time. *(minute, moment, hour, day, month, summer, year, decade, century, period)*

- Have students exchange papers with a partner and:
  —ask each other questions.
  —tell each other which versions of the sentences they liked better.
- Have several students write their favorite sentences on the board. Which of these would be an interesting way to begin a short story? Have the class vote.

Note 8

To teach the distinction between identifying and nonidentifying clauses, ask students to construct two different types of sentences about other people in the class.
- Working individually, they create sentences with identifying adjective clauses containing no names. You may want to write these examples on the board:
  —The person (whom) I'm thinking of has dark brown hair, blue eyes, and . . .
  —One of the people who sits in the back row has . . .
  —A person in class (whom) I would like to know better has . . .
- Other students guess who each student has written about.
- Then, working in pairs, students create nonidentifying adjective clauses, using names. Write this example on the board:
  —Luis, who is originally from Venezuela, has lived in this city for eleven months.

Unit 12   Note 1

- Write the following sentences on the board:
  —He's the man with whom we had a meeting.
  —She's the woman to whom I brought the vase.
  —That's the company for which I used to work.
  —That's the film about which I wrote a review.
  —He's the painter whose exhibitions I usually go to.
- To give students practice of adjective clauses with prepositions, have students restate the sentences omitting the relative pronouns where possible and putting the preposition at the end. Write this example on the board:
  —He's the man we had a meeting with.

Note 2

- Write the following incomplete sentences on the board:
  I have two _____, both of whom _____.
  I have two _____, both of which _____.
  I have several _____, three of whom _____.
  I have many _____, none of whom _____.
  I have lots of _____, some of which _____.
- To give students practice of adjective clauses with quantifiers, have students complete the sentences on the board with true information about themselves. Write this example on the board:
  I have two brothers, both of whom are living abroad.

Unit 13   Note 6

Write the following prompts on the board:
- a mystery which might never be solved
- a crime that ought to be investigated further
- a criminal who may never be caught
- a public building that will be repaired
- a film that is going to be released soon

- a case that should have been made public
- a case that had to be kept secret
- my own idea: _____

To give students practice using the passive with modals, have students use five prompts from the board to write sentences expressing true facts / their own views about true facts. Follow up by having volunteers share their sentences with the class.

Unit 14   Grammar Charts

- Write the following categories on the board:

  1. *Stative Passive (Chart 1)*
  2. *Opinions or Ideas (Chart 2)*
  3. *Other Uses of the Passive.*

- Have students scan the reading for more examples of passive sentences and group these sentences into the categories above. *(1:* par. 2, . . . *the Asu may be related to . . . ; 2:* par. 5, *While in many cultures the excrement of animals is regarded as a valuable commodity, rac excrement is considered foul smelling and is thought to be quite dangerous to the environment;* last par., *It is especially hoped that anthropologists . . . will focus their research . . . ; 3:* par. 4, *The rac . . . is possessed by the vast majority of Asu;* par. 5, *Rac doctors must be given rather valuable charms in return for providing new foot apparel;* par. 6, *Racs are ridden a great deal and are often used as beasts of burden;* last par., *Much more research is needed.)*

Unit 15   Notes 2–5

- On the board, write the following incomplete sentences:

  My friend, _____, and I

  We became friends by _____.

  I remember _____ together when we were younger.

  When we get together we enjoy _____.

  We have a common interest in _____.

  His / Her passion is _____.

  He / She helped me when I had trouble _____.

  I don't mind his / her _____.

  He / She doesn't like being _____.

- Have students complete the sentences individually with true information about a good friend. Point out they should use gerunds or gerund phrases.
- Follow up by having students sit in groups and talk about their friends.

Unit 16   Note 2

Refer students to Appendix 14 for a list of verbs followed by the infinitive. Give them a few moments to read over the list and ask if they have any questions.
- Divide the class into small groups. Have each student choose a word from each column in the Appendix, write it down, and close their books.
- Write or elicit several verb phrases on the blackboard. These can be serious or amusing (e.g., *go on a trip, learn a new language, become president, write a novel*).
- Students look through the words selected in the first step to find any that combine well with these phrases and write out sentences using infinitive phrases to share with their group. For example, *Natasha expects to become president.*
- Ask each group to share a few sentences with the class.

Note 5

From their study of Appendix 12 in the last unit and Appendix 14 more recently, students are already familiar with the long lists of verbs followed by infinitives and gerunds, respectively. Now they need a chance to practice making the correct choices.
- Divide the class into two teams. Let each team spend a few minutes looking through Appendices 12 and 14 and making up sentences with them.
- Have a representative from each team select about fifteen words at random from the two appendices and write them on the board.
- Have another representative from each team come to the board. In turn, each one points to a word and calls on someone from the opposing team to make a sentence with it. Students score points for their team by using each verb, followed correctly by a gerund or infinitive, in a sentence.

Unit 17   Note 4

- To help students become aware of how placement of focus adverbs can affect meaning, write the following examples and explanations on the board:
  a. Even Joe enjoyed the party.
  b. Joe even enjoyed the party.

  1. Joe was reluctant to go to the party, but he finally decided to go, and, surprisingly, he enjoyed it.
  2. We didn't expect to enjoy the party, but we all did, including Joe.
  As a class, match the examples with the explanations. (a: 2; b: 1)
- Then write the following sentences on the board and have students work in pairs to write explanations for them.
  a. Only Sue can take part in the marathon.
  b. Sue can only take part in the marathon.
  c. Even Rod made a suggestion.
  d. Rod even made a suggestion.
  e. I didn't just phone.
  f. I just didn't phone.
To review, discuss the meaning of each sentence as a class.

Note 5

- To provide practice with negative adverbs, write the following sentences on the board:
  a. She rarely fights in combat.
  b. He had never considered joining the military.
  c. Women can serve in the military only in a few countries.
  d. They know little about the war.
  e. Wars can't be justified in any way.
  f. Neither Bruce nor Arnold agreed with me.
- Have students call out the verb or verb phrase in each sentence. Underline the verbs / verb phrases as students call them out. *(a. fights, b. had considered, c. can serve, d. know, e. can't be justified, f. agreed)*
- Have students restate the sentences starting as shown below. Remind students that if the verb is in the simple present or simple past, they will have to use *do / does* or *did*, respectively.
  a. Rarely . . .
  b. Never . . .
  c. Only in . . .
  d. Little . . .
  e. In no way . . .
  f. Bruce didn't agree with me. Neither . . .
Review as a class.

Unit 18   Note 6

Working in pairs, have students look through Appendix 20 to find conjunctions that have approximately the same meaning or can be used in some of the same situations as (1) *if (as long as, provided that, in case)* and (2) *even if (no matter if/whether, whether or not)*.

Note: *In case* has a very different meaning from *as long as* and *provided that* and is only sometimes roughly equivalent to *if*.

<u>If</u> it rains, we'll move inside. = <u>In case</u> it rains, we'll move inside. (NOT <u>Provided that</u> . . .)

<u>If</u> you help me, I'll help you. = <u>Provided</u> you help me, I'll help you. (NOT <u>In case</u> . . .)

Ask students to write a sentence for each of these conjunctions. Remind them to use commas where needed. Elicit some examples to go over with the class.

Unit 19   Note 3

• Draw the following event chain on the board:

What Sarah and Mike did on their first vacation day in London:

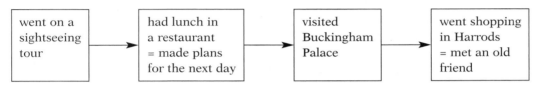

• Write the sentences below on the board. Have students use the information on the event chain to complete the sentences using adverbial phrases. Point out that the event that follows an equal sign (=) happened during the first event in the box.

After _____, they had lunch in a restaurant.

While _____, they made plans for the next day.

Before _____, they had lunch in a restaurant.

After _____, they went shopping in Harrods.

While _____, they met an old friend.

Unit 20   Note 4

• Write the following on the board:

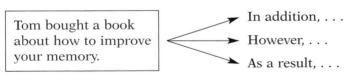

. . . his memory didn't improve.
. . . his memory improved.
. . . he bought some audiotapes.

Have students decide which statement could logically follow each transition.

- Follow the same procedure with the diagram below.

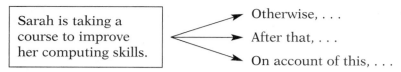

Sarah is taking a course to improve her computing skills.

Otherwise, . . .

After that, . . .

On account of this, . . .

. . . she's leaving work earlier.
. . . she'll try to get a new job.
. . . she might lose her job.
- Draw a new diagram on the board, and have students work in pairs to complete it with their own ideas.

?

Unit 21   Note 3

- To provide further practice with the type of clauses explained in Note 3, write the following sentences on the board:
  He's not here. That's worrying.
- Have students join the sentences to produce three new sentences with noun clauses starting with the opening lines below. Have students underline the noun clauses.
  The fact _____
  I'm worried by _____
  It's _____
- Review as a class. (*The fact that he's not here is worrying. I'm worried by the fact that he's not here. It's worrying that he's not here.*)
- Follow the same procedure with the following sentences:
  You don't like chocolate. I'm surprised.
  The fact _____
  I'm _____
  It's _____

Unit 22   Notes 2–4

- Write the following statements on the board, and have students find the mistake in each.
  Ann said Frances that she wanted to read the paper.
  Frances tell that she had already read it.
  Ann asked Frances that she could borrow the paper.
  Ann asked Frances if she always bought The New York Times?
  Frances asked Ann where had she left the paper.
- Have students compare answers with a partner. To review as a class, have students explain their corrections.

Note 6

• Draw the following chart on the board:

DIRECT SPEECH	INDIRECT SPEECH
"Weekly News comes out on Sundays."	Mark said that Weekly News comes out on Sundays.
"I arrived late this morning."	Mark has just told me he arrived late this morning.
"I'm going home."	Mark says he's going home.
"I'm tired."	Mark is saying that he's tired.

• Have students work in pairs to decide why it is not necessary to change the verbs in each reported statement.

Unit 23   Note 5

• Write the following statements on the board:

If I hadn't read that book, I wouldn't know the answer.	Past condition; past result
If I were rich, I would be in the Bahamas enjoying the sun.	Present condition; past result
If I hadn't been there, I wouldn't have gotten hurt.	Past condition; present result
If my car weren't at the garage, I would have lent it to you.	Present condition; present result

• Have students match the conditional sentences with the types of conditions and results they express they express.
• Then have students replace the underlined segments with their own ideas.

Note 6

• Write on the board:

Something I want now:

Something I regret about the past:

Something I'm not pleased with and I'd like to change in the future:

• Have students complete the items with their own ideas in note form. You may want to write examples on the board:

Something I want now: a car

Something I regret about the past: that I didn't pass the history test

Something I'm not happy with and I'd like to be different in the future: the fact that Maria smokes

• Then have students express their wishes with sentences starting with I wish. (I wish I had a car. I wish I had passed my history test. I wish Maria would stop smoking.)

- Write the following on the board:

  With a bit of luck, what will happen?

  But for your family's help, what would you do?

  Had you been born in the United States, what language would you be studying now?

  Were you a millionaire, where would you live?

  You might win the lottery one day; if so, what will you do?

- Have students answer the questions. Students should write complete sentences to practice implied and inverted conditions. Point out that the answers can be serious or amusing.
- Have volunteers share their answers with the class.

Scoring Rubric for Speaking

Tips for using the speaking rubric

• Give a copy of the rubric to the class before you use it.
• Tell students that you will evaluate their speaking using the rubric.
• The speaking rubric can also be found in a printable format on the Power Point® presentations CD-ROM found in the back of this Teacher's Manual.
• Give feedback for the different areas identified in the rubric: vocabulary, grammar, pronunciation, fluidity, topic organization, and communication. Point out some strong points and weak points. Use language that a student can understand and give examples of what the student did or didn't say when possible. Example comments: *You used a lot of vocabulary and expressions from the unit.* OR *You need to work on verb forms. Review the verb forms needed for the future conditional.* OR *Your sentences were usually complete and clear, but sometimes you hesitated a lot.*
• It's recommended that you discuss the assigned rating and your feedback with each student in a timely manner in order to be most effective and helpful.

SPEAKING RUBRIC

Rating	Vocabulary	Grammar	Pronunciation	Fluidity	Topic	Communication
4	Uses variety, with few errors	Uses a variety of structures, with few errors	Almost always clear and accurate	Speaks smoothly, little hesitation	Successfully organizes and develops topic	Communicates information and opinions effectively
3	Uses variety, makes some errors in word choice	Uses a variety of structures, makes some errors	Usually clear and accurate, some problem areas	Speaks with some hesitation, does not usually interfere with communication	Topic is organized, needs more development	Most information and opinions are communicated clearly
2	Uses limited vocabulary and expressions, some errors	Uses basic structures, makes frequent errors	Errors sometimes make it difficult to understand student	Speaks with hesitation, frequently interferes with communication	Topic not organized, needs development	Information and opinions are not clear
1	Uses basic vocabulary and expressions, makes many errors	Uses basic structures, makes many errors	Very weak; student cannot be understood	Hesitates frequently when speaking, interferes with communication	Does not stay on the topic	Is not able to communicate information and opinions

Scoring Rubric for Writing

Tips for using the writing rubric

- Give a copy of the rubric to the class before you use it.
- Tell students that you will evaluate their writing using the rubric.
- The writing rubric can also be found in a printable format on the Power Point® presentations CD-ROM found in the back of this Teacher's Manual.
- Give feedback by writing comments for the different areas identified in the rubric: topic, sentence structure, vocabulary, grammar.
- Use language that a student can understand and, when possible, give examples of what the student did or didn't do. Example comments: *You addressed the topic and gave very clear examples to support your ideas.* OR *You tried to use a lot of vocabulary and expressions from the unit, but review the meanings of the items I marked in red.* OR *You need to work on verb forms. Review regular and irregular verb forms in the simple past.*
- It's recommended that you discuss the assigned rating and your feedback with each student in a timely manner in order to be most effective and helpful.

Rating	WRITING RUBRIC
5	• Topic is addressed and well organized; includes clear explanations or details • Includes mostly complex sentence types, with few errors • Uses a variety of vocabulary and idiomatic expressions; makes few errors in word choice • Uses complex grammar structures, with few errors
4	• Topic is addressed and generally well organized; includes some explanations or details • Includes some variety of sentence types, but with occasional errors • Varies vocabulary and expressions, but makes occasional errors in word choice • Uses some complex grammar structures, but with errors
3	• Topic is not addressed completely, but writing is organized; explanations or details need more development • Uses little variety in sentence type, but does not have many errors • Attempts to vary vocabulary and expressions, but makes some errors in word choice • Does not use complex grammar structures, but does not make many grammar errors
2	• Topic is somewhat addressed, but writing is not organized and lacks explanations or details • Uses only basic sentence types and makes frequent errors • Uses limited vocabulary and with frequent errors • Uses simple grammar structures, but with some errors
1	• Topic is not addressed; there are no explanations or details • Most sentences have errors • Has many errors in vocabulary usage, even at the basic level • Uses only simple grammar structures, and makes many errors

Audioscript

Unit 1

Exercise 8 (page 14)

MOM: Tim? Come on! We're going to be late if you don't get up right now.

TIM: Why? Where are we going?

MOM: To the historical museum. Remember?

TIM: Do we have to? Amy and I want to go to the West Edmonton Mall.

AMY: That's right, Mom. Museums are boring.

DAD: But this is a really interesting museum. There'll be all kinds of things to learn.

TIM: Why do we have to learn things when we're on vacation?

AMY: Dad, can't you and Mom drop us off at the mall? Then you can go to the museum.

MOM: It's all arranged, kids. We're meeting the tour bus at 9:30. In fact, if we don't get down to the lobby, we're going to miss it.

TIM: Oh, no! Not a tour!

DAD: Yes. Sometimes a tour is the best way to see things.

AMY: I hate tours. If we have to go to the historical museum, can't we at least go by ourselves?

MOM: Come on, kids. We're going to be late.

AMY: Can we go to the mall later?

DAD: Sure. Tell you what. The tour will be over by 12:30. As soon as we get back from the tour, we'll go to the mall.

TIM: Can we go ice-skating at the mall?

MOM: Yes. As a matter of fact, we've got reservations for all of us to skate.

AMY: Right on, Mom!

Unit 2

Exercise 8 (page 28)

In other news, the first-ever wedding of a couple jumping from a plane in parachutes took places yesterday in the skies over Saskatoon, Saskatchewan, Canada. Samantha Yang and Darrell Hammer hired a minister, Reverend Robert Martinez, to jump with them out of a twin-engine Cessna and marry them in the air before they landed. Yang and Hammer met four years ago at a meeting of the Saskatoon Sky-Divers, of which they have been members for many years. To date, each of them has made over thirty jumps. Interviewed as to why they wanted to get married in such an unusual way, Yang said, "We're just adventurous souls, I guess. We like new and different things. We didn't want a conventional wedding." Hammer agreed, adding, "We were going to get married on a bungee jump, but when we got to thinking about it, we decided that would be just a little too dangerous. Plus, we couldn't find a minister who would bungee-jump with us."

Reverend Martinez had never made a parachute jump before yesterday. Asked if he had ever performed such an unusual wedding ceremony before, Martinez responded, "No, I think this one is the oddest. I used to be a pastor in Arizona. I would get some fairly unusual requests. I mean, for example, once I married two people on horseback. But nothing quite like this."

Would he do another parachute-jump wedding— or even another parachute jump? "I don't think so," Martinez said. "No, I think this is one for the scrapbook. At this point, I can just say, 'Been there, done that.'"

That's the news on the half hour. Stay tuned for our next broadcast on the hour.

Unit 3

Exercise 7 (page 43)

JIM: Hi, Mary. How are things going? You look like you lost your best friend.

MARY: Not well. I'm having some pretty serious money problems.

JIM: Why? What's wrong?

MARY: Well, someone got hold of my credit card number.

JIM: You mean somebody stole your credit card?

MARY: No. Somebody got the number. You've heard of identity theft? Well, this is a good example of it.

JIM: Oh, no! Really? I know that sort of thing happens, but I've never known anyone it happened to.

MARY: Yeah. The whole thing is really upsetting. Whoever got the number has charged $8,000 on my card.

JIM: How do you think it happened?

MARY: Well, I'm almost positive it was on the Internet. About two months ago I bought some CDs from a website and used my card. They said it was a secure site, but apparently it wasn't.

JIM: So what happens now? You won't have to pay the $8,000, will you?

MARY: Probably not, but I might have to pay something. You're supposed to report thefts like this immediately.

JIM: Didn't you?

MARY: No, not right away. I got a credit card bill with a big purchase on it that I couldn't remember making, but I thought it was probably my mistake, and I didn't do anything for a few days. By the time I reported it, there were a lot of other purchases.

JIM: I'm really sorry. This is terrible.

MARY: Thanks. You know, the Internet makes things easy. Maybe too easy.

JIM: Yeah. It's easy for us to get information, but it's also easy for criminals to get it. That's the downside of the Internet.

Unit 4

Exercise 7 (page 68)

MARY: Good evening. I'm Mary Mobley with tonight's edition of *Do the Right Thing*. The toll-free number is 1-800-555-9999. Call number 1, Sally from Toronto, you're on the air.

SALLY: Hi, Mary. First, let me tell you how much I enjoy your show. I don't care much for a lot of the stuff on radio, but I *do* listen to you.

MARY: Thanks, Sally. What's on your mind tonight?

SALLY: Well, I've been dating a man named Bob for a long time. We're engaged, but I just don't feel like I can marry him.

MARY: Why not? Don't you love him?

SALLY: I *did* love him at first—or at least I thought I did—and I *do* think a lot of him as a person. But the wedding is in three weeks. I've been thinking of just running away and never coming back.

MARY: Why haven't you done something before this?

SALLY: I *did* try to tell him a couple of weeks ago, but he just thought it was pre-wedding nerves.

MARY: Well, Sally, to me you don't sound at all sure of your feelings.

SALLY: No, I *am* sure. I don't want to marry him. I'm just worried about hurting him.

MARY: You don't have to hurt Bob, but you *do* have to tell him the truth. I wish you good luck. . . . Hello, Jerry from Tulsa.

JERRY: Evening, Mary. Thank you for taking my call. I wanted to ask you about a problem with my children.

MARY: OK, go ahead. What's the problem?

JERRY: They only call me when they want something, and all they really seem to care about is getting their inheritance. I'm not a rich man, but I **am** pretty well off, and I *have got* some money put away for them. The trouble is that they never come to see me. We *do* live in different parts of the country, so I guess that part is understandable. They've both e-mailed me recently, asking if they could have their inheritance early. My son wants to buy a house. He doesn't have the cash for a down payment, but he *does* earn enough to make the monthly payments. And my daughter and her husband want to buy a boat.

MARY: How old are they?

JERRY: They're both in their late twenties.

MARY: OK. What's your problem, then?

JERRY: I agreed to send the money. Can I withdraw my offer? I mean, would it be ethical?

MARY: Well, your children *do* sound a bit selfish. If you feel it'd be wrong to give them this money now, I'd suggest you just tell them that you've changed your mind. That *may* start them thinking a little and *might* even make them more concerned about you. Good luck. . . . Now, caller number 3, Helen from Kingston, New York, talk to me . . .

Unit 5

Exercise 6 (page 84)

BEV: Hello?

DAD: Hi, Bev. This is Dad.

BEV: Dad! Where are you? Mom's surprise party is supposed to start in fifteen minutes. Everybody's already shown up. We're just waiting for you and Ray and Mom.

DAD: Great. You don't think your mother has figured out what's going on, do you?

BEV: No, I'm sure she hasn't. She thinks we're all going to a concert this afternoon. She says she's really looking forward to it.

DAD: Good. Anyway, here's the problem, Bev. Ray and I are at the department store trying to find a gift for your mom, and we can't come up with anything. Do you think we could get away with not giving her a present today? If we took a little more time, we could find something really nice.

BEV: Dad! Of course not! Everybody who's here has brought something. You and Ray will be the only ones. And Dad, remember what you told me when I was a girl? Don't put things off till the last minute?

DAD: Yes, dear, I know. We should've gone shopping last week. But, honey, what do you suggest?

BEV: What about a camera?

DAD: She's got three cameras. In fact, she just got rid of one of her old cameras last week.

BEV: How about some article of clothing?

DAD: Great idea. A dress maybe?

BEV: Dad! You can't just buy her a dress. She'd never buy a dress without trying on several first.

DAD: Well, Bev, we're running out of time here. Can't you think of something?

BEV: Well, you might get her a blouse. She loves blouses.

DAD: No way, Bev. I tried that once, and your mother hated what I got her.

BEV: Well, . . . let's see. How about a couple of nice scarves?

DAD: Good! What material? What color?

BEV: Why don't you look for a couple of silk scarves in some conservative color?

DAD: Good idea. Will do. We'll get there as soon as we can.

BEV: OK, Dad. But hurry up. Mom could be home any minute.

Unit 6

Exercise 6 (pages 99–100)

PROFESSOR: OK, folks. Today we're going to talk about a question related to hearing. I want to begin by telling you about an experience I had the first time I heard my voice on tape. It was in a speech class when I was in college. The professor recorded our voices and then played them back. When I heard mine, I said, "That couldn't have been me. There's got to be some mistake. I don't sound like that." Now, I'd venture to say that all of you must have had this experience at one time or another. Am I right? Let me see a show of hands. . . . Uh-huh, just as I thought. Now, the question is why. Why do we hear our voices differently than others do? Based on what we've been studying, you should be able to figure this out. Allison, what do you think?

ALLISON: I think it must be because we're hearing the sound in a different way.

PROFESSOR: Very good. You've got the right idea. Now, anybody want to expand on that? Bart?

BART: It could be because the sound is traveling through different substances.

PROFESSOR: Right. Go on. Can you explain?

BART: Well, let's see. When somebody speaks, the sound of that person's voice comes to us through the air. We hear our own voice through our head.

PROFESSOR: Good, good. Uh, Kathy, can you add something?

KATHY: I agree with Bart when he says we hear our own voice through our own head. But don't we also hear it through the air? It might be a combination of the two things.

PROFESSOR: Yes. You're both right. You see, when we hear our own voice, we hear partly through our ears—externally. But we also hear through the bone in our head and through the fluid in our inner ear—internally. Most of the sound that we hear internally comes through liquid. . . . Now, here's one more question. Which sound is the "real" sound? The way other people hear our voices, or the way we hear them? Uh, Darren?

DARREN: I think the sound others hear has to be the real sound.

PROFESSOR: Anybody else?

KATHY: I'd say the opposite. The sound we hear must be the real sound.

PROFESSOR: Actually, Kathy is right. Internal hearing is of higher fidelity than external hearing.

Statements

1. That couldn't have been me.
2. There's got to be some mistake.
3. All of you must have had this experience at one time or another.
4. You should be able to figure this out.
5. It must be because we're hearing the sound in a different way.
6. It could be because the sound is traveling through different substances.
7. It might be a combination of the two things.
8. The sound others hear has to be the real sound.
9. The sound we hear must be the real sound.
10. Internal hearing is of higher fidelity than external hearing.

Unit 7

Exercise 7 (page 125)

Hello, everyone, and welcome to Global Gourmet. I'm Flo Nyberg, and today we're going to be making a wonderful dish called "pelmeni." Pelmeni is a traditional Russian dish that requires some time and work to prepare, but it is well worth the effort.

Pelmeni are delicious little meatballs wrapped in dough. Here are the ingredients you'll need for the meat mixture: 1½ pounds of hamburger (or other ground meat such as chicken or pork), 1½ chopped onions, 2 egg yolks, 3 tablespoons of water, a teaspoon of salt, and a half teaspoon of pepper. Now for the dough: To make it, you'll need 2 cups of flour, 1 teaspoon of salt, and a half cup of water. Now I'll give you a few minutes to get all those things together.

All right. Have you got your ingredients ready? I hope so. Here we go, then. First you need to make the dough. Mix the flour and salt together. Then mix it with the egg yolks and some of the water. Stir this mixture with a fork. Add the rest of the water. Work the mixture until it's smooth and not lumpy. Let the dough stand for one hour. Then roll it out with a rolling pin as thinly as possible.

The next step is to prepare the meat mixture. Simply mix the hamburger (or other meat), the chopped onions, the egg yolks, the salt, the pepper, and the water together.

Now here's the next step: Use a round cookie cutter to make circles from the dough. Each circle should be approximately two inches in diameter. Place a small amount of the meat mixture in the middle of each circle. Fold the edges of the circle over and pinch the edges together and you've got lots of little pelmeni. Drop a large number of these pelmeni into boiling water and let them cook. They'll be finished cooking when they rise to the surface. Spoon them out and serve them with sour cream and yellow mustard.

In Russia, hundreds of pelmeni are often made at one time—perhaps for banquets or perhaps to be frozen until needed. One person can easily eat 15 or 20 of them at a meal. Good luck and *bon appetit*. I'm Flo Nyberg. I'll be back tomorrow with another recipe on Global Gourmet.

Unit 8

Exercise 6 (page 138)

WIFE: Anything interesting in the paper?

HUSBAND: Not much. There's a story about the battle between the environmentalists and that Indian tribe that wants to hunt whales.

WIFE: Oh, yeah. What does it say?

HUSBAND: Oh, the usual nonsense. It's on the side of the environmentalists.

WIFE: Why do you think it's nonsense?

HUSBAND: Because it's too pro-environmentalist. It doesn't look at the Indians' point of view.

WIFE: You mean you support the Indians?

HUSBAND: Well, yes, basically.

WIFE: Why? Do you think they should be allowed to hunt whales?

HUSBAND: Well . . . yes, I think I do. I mean, after all, traditionally they supported themselves by whale hunting. They just want to get that situation back.

WIFE: Well, I don't support them. I believe in saving the whales.

HUSBAND: Why?

WIFE: Well, once years ago I saw a whaling ship bring in a whale and cut it up. It was a horrible experience. Whales should be left alone. Hunting them is cruel.

HUSBAND: Hmm. But do you feel that way about all animals? What about cattle? We had roast beef for dinner last night. Isn't it cruel to slaughter cattle for meat?

WIFE: That's different. Cattle are domestic animals. They're raised for food. Whales are intelligent animals. And some of them are endangered. If we allow whale hunting, they could become extinct.

HUSBAND: Yeah, you've got a point. But I still think we have to consider the Indians' point of view. They've hunted whales for centuries.

Unit 9

Exercise 7 (page 151)

MARY: Mmm. That was sure a great meal. Thanks for suggesting this restaurant, Mike.

MIKE: Glad you liked it. There aren't as many menu choices as at that restaurant we went to last month, but what they serve is really delicious.

BILL: Yeah. And the prices are lower here, too.

SALLY: Well, guys, Mary and I are going to the ladies' room. Back soon.

BILL: OK.

MIKE: All right, let me just get the check here. . . . Everything looks right. . . . Uh-oh!

BILL: What's wrong?

MIKE: I don't have my wallet! I must have left it somewhere, but I don't know where. Have you got any money?

BILL: I don't think so, but let me check. I didn't bring my wallet because you said you were paying. . . . Let me just look . . . oh yeah, I found a few dollars. How much is the bill?

MIKE: Fifty-five.

BILL: Oh, too bad. I've got less than 20.

MIKE: Have you got a credit card with you?

BILL: No, I don't. Actually, Sally and I don't have any credit cards at all. We don't use them.

MIKE: Hmm. Maybe Mary has her card or some money with her. I sure hope so. Otherwise we'll be washing dishes.

MARY: Hi, guys. We're back. Is the bill all taken care of?

MIKE: No, it's not. We've got a problem. I don't have my wallet. Do you have any money, Mary?

MARY: Gee, Mike, I don't know. Let me look. . . . Looks like I've got about $25.

MIKE: Hmm. Bill has about $15. It's still not enough to pay the bill. Do you have your credit card, Mary?

MARY: No, I don't think so. . . . Oh, wait a minute—I don't have my credit card, but here's my bank card. We can use it at an ATM.

MIKE: But there aren't any ATM machines here, are there?

MARY: Yes, there are. There's one in the hotel lobby.

MIKE: Whew! Saved. I just wonder what I could have done with my wallet . . .

Unit 10

Exercise 6 (pages 162–163)

DR. TANAKA: OK, Josh, let's get started. Our first meeting is only going to be a thirty-minute session. We don't want to make this a brain-breaker. Now, first I want you to tell me exactly how you feel when your teacher asks you to read.

JOSHUA: I feel like a total, complete idiot. And I feel like I have an ugly, high-pitched, squeaky voice.

DR. TANAKA: Your voice sounds fine, Josh. You're just going through a rapid adolescent growth period, so your voice is changing. It happens to a lot of twelve-year-old boys. All right. Now, the key to getting you over this fear-of-oral-reading problem is to distract you from thinking about how well you're doing. Let's think of a short, easy-to-remember phrase that you can keep in the back of your mind. When you're reading and you start to feel nervous or frustrated, you say it and distract yourself.

JOSHUA: How about "Roses are red, violets are blue"?

DR. TANAKA: That'll do fine. All right, let's put it to the test. I want you to read this passage. If you start feeling anxious, just start saying the phrase.

JOSHUA: "It was an icy, dark, stormy evening. It promised to be one of those famous three-dog nights." . . . What's a three-dog night?

DR. TANAKA: It's a night that's so cold that you need three, large, warm, furry dogs to sleep with to keep you warm. Anyway, you read that beautifully. Did you feel nervous?

JOSHUA: Just for a second, and I started saying the line from the poem. After that it was fine. I think I'm going to like this.

Unit 11

Exercise 7 (page 193)

JENNIFER: Hi, Bob. How's your new job?

BOB: Well, the pay is good, which is why I took the job in the first place. Other than that, it's pretty bad.

JENNIFER: Why?

BOB: Well, my boss works me like a slave. He's got me doing a lot of paperwork, which really makes me angry. I didn't take this job to be a paper pusher. The other thing is that I have a co-worker who's making things difficult for me. She's one of those people who can never say directly what's bothering her. They assigned me to be her partner without even consulting me, which is really irritating.

JENNIFER: Two months ago you told me you wanted this job more than anything. Now you're dissatisfied, which really surprises me. What happened?

BOB: Well, I guess I didn't research the company well enough, which makes me wonder whether I was too impulsive in the first place.

Exercise 9 (pages 193–194)

AL: Hi, Mom. Hi, Dad. Just thought I'd call and tell you about my week.

MOM: Hi, Al. How are things going now?

AL: Pretty well. I like the dormitory. The supervisor, who lives right down the hall from me, is really helpful. And he doesn't inspect our rooms.

DAD: How about your roommates, son?

AL: I really like the one who's from Minnesota. He's great to hang around with. I'm not so sure about the other one.

DAD: What about your courses? Are they hard?

AL: Well, my English course, which is really tough, is going to require a lot of writing. So is the history class that's held in the morning. The history class that I have in the afternoon looks like it's going to be the easiest.

MOM: One thing I'm curious about—is this an all-male dorm, or are there girls living there, too?

AL: Well, there are two parts to the building. The girls live on one side and the guys on the other. And there are three cafeterias. The girls who live on the second floor eat with us at the cafeteria on our floor.

DAD: What about your advisors? Advisors helped me a lot when I was in college.

AL: Well, my advisor, who is from Minneapolis, is wonderful. She's told me just what subjects I have to take.

MOM: OK, now I have another question . . .

Unit 12

Exercise 7 (page 205)

Good evening, all you movie buffs. I'm Penelope Truman with this week's Movie Mania. Run, don't walk, to the film festival being held this holiday weekend on the university campus. A series of all-time classics, some recent and some of which haven't been shown on the big screen in over a decade, will be shown in the film school auditorium. For the $20 admission price, you can see eight movies. Here are my special picks:

First: *A Beautiful Mind*, which was the creation of director Ron Howard, is a fascinating biography starring Russell Crowe and based on the life of M.I.T. professor and mathematical genius John Nash, who suffered from schizophrenia and had some very interesting delusions. You have to pay close attention to this one: which characters are real, and which aren't? Ultimately, it's a touching film for which Jennifer Connelly won an Oscar for her performance as Nash's wife.

Second: *Saving Private Ryan*, directed by Steven Spielberg, has a number of well-known stars, including Tom Hanks and Matt Damon. *Saving Private Ryan* is about an army captain assigned to take his men into a war zone in order to rescue a soldier whose brothers have all been killed in the war. It's the ultimate anti-war movie because it shows the horrors of war. This film, deserving of its Academy Awards, still makes me cry, and I've seen it five times.

Third: We don't see as many musicals as we used to, which is too bad, but they may be making a comeback. Even if you're not a fan of musicals, though, this one deserves your attention. *Chicago*, starring Renee Zellweger, Richard Gere, and Catherine Zeta-Jones, is a story of the almost lawless times in the city of Chicago after World War I. Zellweger plays a woman on trial for murdering her husband, and Gere plays the lawyer who defends her. Whoever would have thought Gere could sing and dance? Zeta-Jones won an Oscar for her role as a fellow prisoner.

Fourth: *Back to the Future*, the movie that was responsible for launching Michael J. Fox in his screen career, is about a teenager who has to travel back in time to arrange for his own parents to meet so that he won't cease to exist! *Back to the Future* is especially fun because it gives us a semi-objective comparison of our own era and an earlier one.

Finally: For all of you old-timers out there, a kiss may be just a kiss, but *Casablanca*, showcasing the talents of Humphrey Bogart and Ingrid Bergman, is more than just a movie. This picture is a must-see for all regarding themselves as serious movie-buffs. This movie, filmed in black and white, may not be a pretty picture, but it's certainly a profound one.

So, there they are. My spies tell me that tickets are likely to sell like hotcakes, in which case you'd better call right away or order your tickets online if you want to attend. I'm Penelope Truman for Movie Mania, and I'll see you at the movies.

SELECTED SENTENCES
1. Run, don't walk, to the film festival being held this holiday weekend on the university campus.
2. A series of all-time classics, some recent and some of which haven't been seen on the big screen in more than a decade, will be shown in the film school auditorium.
3. *A Beautiful Mind*, which was the creation of director Ron Howard, is a fascinating biography starring Russell Crowe and based on the life of M.I.T. professor and mathematical genius John Nash.
4. Ultimately, it's a touching film for which Jennifer Connelly won an Oscar for her performance as Nash's wife.

5. *Saving Private Ryan* is about an army captain assigned to take his men into a war zone in order to rescue a soldier whose brothers have all been killed in the war.
6. This film, deserving of its Academy Awards, still makes me cry.
7. *Chicago*, starring Renee Zellweger, Richard Gere, and Catherine Zeta-Jones, is a story of the almost lawless times in the city of Chicago after World War I.
8. *Back to the Future*, which is the movie that was responsible for launching Michael J. Fox in his screen career, is about a teenager who has to travel back in time to arrange for his own parents to meet so that he won't cease to exist!
9. *Casablanca*, showcasing the talents of Humphrey Bogart and Ingrid Bergman, is more than just a movie. This picture is a must-see for all regarding themselves as serious movie buffs.
10. This movie, filmed in black and white, may not be a pretty picture, but it's certainly a profound one.

Unit 13

Exercise 8 (page 232)

SADLER: OK, Mr. Akimura—just a few questions about the koala that was stolen. The koala's keeper was found by the janitor. Is that right?

AKIMURA: Yes. I had him examined by our resident physician. Apparently he'd been drugged. He's all right now.

SADLER: Had he been hit?

AKIMURA: No, there were no marks of any kind on his body.

SADLER: Have any other animals been stolen?

AKIMURA: Well . . . yes, as a matter of fact. Two sea turtles were taken two weeks ago.

SADLER: Why weren't we notified immediately?

AKIMURA: Well, you've heard that the zoo is currently being expanded, haven't you? The expansion depends on a 50 percent *yes* vote in the election. The expansion proposal isn't likely to get approved by the voters if they hear that animals are missing.

SADLER: What time was the keeper found?

AKIMURA: About 8 P.M. The laboratory and food preparation area gets cleaned every evening after the animals have been fed. The janitor was just starting his work when he noticed the keeper behind a table.

SADLER: Do you have any idea why these animals were taken? And by whom?

AKIMURA: Well, they're very valuable. They could be sold on the black market for a lot of money. We can only imagine that some underworld group is behind this.

Sadler: What about the janitor?

Akimura: What do you mean?

Sadler: Well, is he reliable? Has his background been checked?

Akimura: I'm not totally sure. He gave us good references when he was interviewed. I presume some checking was done, but I suppose we should look into it.

Sadler: That's all right. I'll get his references checked out when I go back to the office. We'll be in touch, Mr. Akimura.

Unit 14

Exercise 6 (page 245)

We interrupt our regularly scheduled program to bring you this news bulletin. A massive series of earthquakes has struck the nation, causing extreme damage to most major cities. The earthquakes are said to have registered a 9 on the Richter scale, although this information is considered preliminary. The minister of science has stated that the epicenter of the quakes was located in the Atlantic Ocean some 40 miles west of Gibraltar. According to unconfirmed reports, vast sections of the coastline are reported to be under water as a consequence of a gigantic tsunami that hit the coastal areas after the earthquakes. The exact number of casualties of the tsunami is not known, although it is estimated that more than 200,000 people have drowned. Serious flooding is believed to have occurred in cities farther inland. The president, who was vacationing at his mountain retreat, has returned to the capital. Looting is alleged to be taking place in most major cities, and it is assumed that the president will be speaking to the nation shortly, in an effort to reestablish law and order. As he was boarding his plane for the flight to the capital, the president said, "A grave tragedy has struck our nation. It is to be hoped that the citizens of Atlantis will conduct themselves in a calm, gentle, and law-abiding manner in our time of need." In the meantime, Atlanteans are advised to gather provisions and to head for the highest ground that they can find. Stay tuned for further bulletins.

Exercise 8 (page 246)

Quizmaster: All right, contestants, are you ready to begin? Here we go. For $500: A revolutionary leader from Venezuela, he was called the Liberator and is considered the father of South American democracy.

Contestant 1: Simón Bolívar?

Quizmaster: That's correct. Next question, for another $500: It is thought that he was the author of *The Iliad* and *The Odyssey*, both from Greek literature. However, it is not known for certain

whether he was one specific person or a composite of many people.

Contestant 3: Aristotle?

Quizmaster: I'm sorry. That is incorrect.

Contestant 2: Homer.

Quizmaster: Yes, that is correct. For $800: He was a philosopher who lived in Greece from approximately 427 to 347 B.C. His Dialogues are studied today all over the world. Some people say that the myth of Atlantis was created by him.

Contestant 2: Plato?

Quizmaster: Absolutely correct. For another $800: Born in India, he is known as the founder of Buddhism, a religion that is practiced by many people in Asia.

Contestant 1: Gandhi?

Quizmaster: No, I'm sorry. That's incorrect.

Contestant 2: Siddhartha Gautama?

Quizmaster: Yes, correct. Now, for $1,000: The second wife of King Henry VIII, she was eventually beheaded, but not before she became the mother of Queen Elizabeth I, regarded as one of the greatest of the English monarchs.

Contestant 1: Anne Boleyn?

Quizmaster: Yes, that's absolutely correct. Now for the last question. Contestant 2 is in the lead. For $1,500: One of the daughters of the ruling royal family in Russia, it was assumed that she was murdered in the 1917 revolution which brought the Bolsheviks to power. In the years since then, however, it has been persistently rumored that this one daughter somehow survived the assassination attempt and eventually made her way to America.

Contestant 2: Anastasia Romanova?

Quizmaster: Absolutely right! Congratulations, Contestant 2. You are the winner.

Unit 15

Exercise 8 (page 270)

Jane: Hello?

Brian: Hello. May I speak with Jane Travanti?

Jane: This is Jane.

Brian: Jane, my name is Brian Hansen. Dr. Ralph Stevens gave me your number. I understand that you belong to an orienteering club. I'm interested in joining a group like that and getting to know some people, and . . . he suggested calling you to find out some details. Would you mind giving me some information about your club and about becoming a member?

Jane: Sure, I'd be glad to. Are you new in town?

BRIAN: Yeah, I've been here about five months and haven't really met anyone. Dr. Stevens thinks I need to stop working so hard and try to enjoy myself more. He's probably right.

JANE: Have you ever done any orienteering before?

BRIAN: No, I haven't. Do you need to be experienced?

JANE: Not necessarily. You can learn. We've got several different levels of participants. You do need to be in good physical condition.

BRIAN: Well, I haven't been doing much exercising lately, but Dr. Stevens says I'm basically in good physical shape. So can you give me some details? How often do you go orienteering, and where do you go, and stuff like that?

JANE: Sure! We try to go at least twice a month, normally on Saturdays. Usually we go to the Sherwood Forest area. Sometimes we only manage to go once a month, but most months it's at least twice. In the summer we get around by running, but right now we navigate by cross-country skiing. Do you know how to ski?

BRIAN: I tried cross-country skiing a couple of years ago, but I haven't done it since then. I did pretty well at it, though. I still have my skis.

JANE: Great. Let's see . . . what else? Uhmm, oh the group is pretty diverse. There are some married people and their kids, some singles, all ages. But we're an actual club. We have dues of $40 a year. That's to pay for organizing the activities. Sounds like you'd like the club. It's a good way to make friends. The members really enjoy being together.

BRIAN: Sounds great to me. When's your next activity?

JANE: We're meeting on Saturday morning, the 15th, at 6 A.M. in front of Darcy's Coffee Shop in Stapleton. We'll get to the forest by carpooling. Do you know where Darcy's is?

BRIAN: I think so.

JANE: OK, good. Don't forget to bring your skis. And remember to bring a lunch—hopefully with a lot of high-protein stuff in it.

BRIAN: Super. I'll see you on the 15th at 6 A.M. Thanks a lot.

JANE: Sure. I'll look forward to meeting you in person. Bye.

Unit 16

Exercise 8 (page 284)

Good afternoon. Here is a bulletin from the Mason County Sheriff's Office. Charles Gallagher and two other inmates are reported to have escaped from the maximum security prison in Grandview. The three prisoners are thought to have escaped in a prison laundry truck. Authorities are not saying how the break could have taken place, but according to usually reliable sources, the three men are believed to have been helped in their escape by a prison employee. A new state-of-the-art security system was supposed to have been installed two months ago, but because of unexpected delays and postponements, it is not yet in place. Listeners should be aware that the three prisoners are thought to have weapons and are believed to be heading in the direction of Union City. Listeners are warned not to approach the prisoners but are asked to contact the Sheriff's Office or call the toll-free number, 1-800-555-9999, if they have any information.

Unit 17

Exercise 8 (page 308)

McGAFFEY: Our next caller is from Singapore. Here's Lu Adijojo. Lu, what's your view?

Lu ADIJOJO: Hello, Mike. Before I give my viewpoint, I just want to say how much I enjoy your show. I get a chance to listen only once a week or so, but I really like it.

McGAFFEY: Thanks. That's nice to hear. So how do you feel about what these two callers said? Do you agree with either of them?

Lu ADIJOJO: Well, I'm sort of in between. Basically, I guess I'm a little closer to the lady from Canada. I don't totally disagree with Jerry, but I do disagree with what he said about service needing to be voluntary. Like the second caller, I also think it should be required. But I do agree with Jerry about women in combat.

McGAFFEY: OK. Give me some specifics. Why shouldn't women be in combat?

Lu ADIJOJO: Well, one reason is that many women of military service age are mothers. I just don't think it's right for women to go off and fight when their children are at home. The motherly role is just too important.

McGAFFEEY: All right. What about his idea that fighting is not feminine?

Lu ADIJOJO: I agree with the lady on this part. There's no clear opposition between fighting in combat and being feminine. I just think it's not advisable for mothers. We don't allow women in Singapore to fight in combat, and not even pro-military people want to change that.

McGAFFEY: What do you think about Sarah's idea about national service in every country?

Lu ADIJOJO: I think it's basically a great idea. But I'm afraid this probably won't happen in most countries because there might not be enough money to carry it out.

McGAFFEY: All right, Lu. Thanks for your comments. Call me back sometime. . . . We'll be back after this commercial message.

Unit 18

Exercise 8 (page 323)

MARY: Thanks for tuning in to *Sports Talk*, all you listeners out there. I'm Mary Mobley, and today we're talking with Lillian Swanson, champion swimmer, whose Team Jamaica just won the world championship. Lillian will be participating in the upcoming Olympics as part of the Jamaican national team. Lillian, thanks so much for being here with us.

LILLIAN: Thanks for having me, Mary.

MARY: There are a million questions I could ask, Lillian, but I'll start with this one. From all appearances, you've had a charmed athletic career. To what do you attribute your success?

LILLIAN: Well, Mary, whenever I've been asked that question, I've always answered in the same way: It was because my parents loved and supported me.

MARY: OK. Tell us more. How did it all happen?

LILLIAN: It started when I was a girl in Jamaica. I learned to swim when I was four. I swam in the Caribbean, and swimming wasn't a big deal. It's the most natural thing in the world in Jamaica. I think I became a good swimmer because I had to swim in the Caribbean, which is a lot more difficult to swim in than a pool.

MARY: Who taught you to swim?

LILLIAN: My parents. My family and I spent a lot of time at the beach since we didn't have many toys or video games or things like that.

MARY: What did you mean when you said that your parents supported you?

LILLIAN: Well, when I was 12, I decided I wanted to become a champion swimmer and go to the Olympics someday. My parents said they'd pay for lessons and training if I would stick to my plan and practice regularly. So I did. They helped me become a disciplined person.

MARY: Twelve is pretty young to make a decision like that. Didn't you ever get tired of practicing all the time? And did you ever get discouraged?

LILLIAN: Sure I got tired of practicing, lots of times. And yes, I got discouraged whenever I had a hard time learning a new stroke.

MARY: Any regrets?

LILLIAN: None at all. Because swimming is a total passion for me, I can't imagine myself doing anything else. But I owe it all to my parents. Once I started my lessons, they wouldn't let me quit.

MARY: Well, Lillian, thanks very much for talking with us. And good luck in the Olympics.

LILLIAN: Thanks. My pleasure.

Unit 19

Exercise 6 (page 338)

Good afternoon. This is the latest news from the World Broadcasting Network. The cease-fire has been broken in Franconia. Asked whether he would attend next week's peace conference in Geneva, rebel leader Amalde declined to commit himself, saying that the success of the conference depends on the good-faith actions of Mr. Tintor, the country's president. Mr. Amalde went on to say that Mr. Tintor could demonstrate good faith by agreeing to free elections. Interviewed about Mr. Amalde's comments, an aide to President Tintor, speaking off the record, said he did not expect the conference to take place as scheduled. One of the key issues to be discussed is amnesty for the rebels.

Meanwhile, researchers from the Global Health Foundation announced plans to test a new vaccine for AIDS. Acknowledging that the current vaccine is ineffective, the researchers claim that their new vaccine is a marked improvement over the existing one and believe that it holds great promise.

A new nation comes into existence at midnight tonight. To be known as the Central Asian Republic, the new nation has been carved out of the eastern portion of Spartania. According to its new president, the new country will need billions of dollars of foreign aid in order to be a viable state.

Finally, here is today's human interest story: In St. Louis, Missouri, 16-year-old Sam Michaels was saved from drowning in a swimming pool by 12-year-old Carrie Hutchinson. Being unable to swim, Michaels had almost given up hope of being rescued. Having heard his cries for help, Hutchinson located him, jumped into the water, and pulled him to safety by using the lifesaving techniques she had learned in swimming class. Michaels, grateful for the rescue, said he planned to start swimming lessons immediately.

That's the news from the World Broadcasting Network. Stay tuned for further developments.

Unit 20

Exercise 6 (page 351)

LEADER: All right, folks, we're ready to start Part 2 of the workshop. Let's just review the points we made before. First, it's important to get people's names in your short-term memory. When you're meeting clients, it's crucial to be able to remember and use their names. Clients like to be called by their names, and it's good for business. Therefore, it's absolutely essential that you say the people's names when you meet them. Second, you need to notice one particular thing about each person and link that thing with the person's name. For example, suppose the person has strong, prominent eyebrows.

And suppose the person's name is Ed. You can link the "e" in *eyebrows* with the "e" in *Ed*, and then you have an easier . . . Yes, may I help you?

VISITOR: Yes. My name is Keoki Kendall.

LEADER: Excuse me, Mr. Kendall, but we're in the middle of a workshop here. I'd . . .

VISITOR: I won't keep you long. I want everyone to put your hands up. Hands up!

SARAH: He's got a gun.

VISITOR: Hands up! Quick! Everyone! . . . Thank you. You have all been very cooperative. You may put your hands down now. Thank you. Aloha.

BOB: What in the world was that about?

MIKE: Come on, you guys. He wasn't for real.

SARAH: What? Are you kidding?

MIKE: Didn't you notice? That was a toy gun he had. Besides that, Marsha, you didn't really act like this was an interruption. So this must have all been planned.

LEADER: Yes, Mike, you're right. It was all planned. But I'll bet he had you going for a minute. Right, Bob?

BOB: I'll have to admit it.

LEADER: All right. The question is what you got out of the experience. Let's see what you remember. How was he dressed?

SARAH: He had on a suit, a tuxedo actually, but he wasn't wearing a white shirt.

LEADER: OK, good. What color was his shirt? . . . No one remembers? All right. What about his shoes? What color were they?

MIKE: Brown?

LEADER: Sorry. As a matter of fact, they were black. What was his name?

SARAH: Uh . . . I think his first name was . . . Keoki?

LEADER: That's right. Very good. Now why do you think you were able to remember that name?

SARAH: Well, it's an unusual first name—except in Hawaii.

LEADER: Good. Now what was his last name?

MIKE: I think it was Kendall. I don't think I would have remembered it, except for the fact that you repeated it when you said, "Excuse me, Mr. Kendall."

LEADER: Right. Excellent. Now what was the last word he said?

BOB: Aloha.

LEADER: Very good. Why were you able to remember it?

BOB: Well, it's not the usual way we say good-bye. Everyone knows the word, of course. But people don't say it much.

LEADER: Right. OK. Now let's just sum up the point here. You were able to remember some of the particulars about our visitor but not all of them. It's true that you were distracted. That was deliberate. But . . . most importantly, if you're going to improve your memory and use your memory well, you're going to have to learn to focus your attention consistently. You were able to remember the flashy things, and that's a good start. But it's the ordinary things you have to work on. You have to pay attention to those things, too.

Unit 21

Exercise 6 (page 375)

JEAN: Hi, Greg.

GREG: Hi, yourself. How's it going?

JEAN: Great. Hey, do you want to hear a joke?

GREG: A joke? Why do you think I'd want to hear a joke?

JEAN: Don't you like jokes?

GREG: Not usually.

JEAN: Why not?

GREG: Well . . . what bothers me about jokes is that they're too . . . programmed.

JEAN: I don't know what you mean.

GREG: Somebody tells a joke, and you're expected to laugh, whether you think it's funny or not. The other problem is that you're forced to be dishonest.

JEAN: You're too sensitive. Don't laugh if you don't think it's funny.

GREG: But everybody thinks you're no fun if you don't laugh.

JEAN: What?

GREG: Well, a lot of times I don't get what the point of the joke is. I feel like I'm stupid when that happens.

JEAN: I know what: I'll tell you a funny story—not exactly a joke—and let's see if you understand.

GREG: Oh, all right. Go ahead.

JEAN: OK, here we go. According to a report on the radio, there was a middle school in Oregon that was faced with a unique problem. A lot of girls were beginning to use lipstick, and they would put it on in the girls' bathroom. There was nothing wrong with that, but after they'd put it on, they'd press their lips against the mirror just to make sure the lipstick was on right, and that would leave dozens of lip prints all over the mirror. So finally the principal of the school decided that something had to be done about the problem.

GREG: So what did he do?

JEAN: It wasn't a he; it was a she. Anyway, here's what she did: She told all the girls to report to the bathroom, and she met them there with the school custodian. She explained to the girls that all the lip prints were causing a major problem for the custodian because he had to clean the mirrors every day. To show the girls how difficult it was to clean the mirrors, she asked the custodian to clean one of them. He took out a mop with a long handle, dipped it into the toilet, and then cleaned the mirror with it. Ever since then there haven't been any lip prints on the mirror.

GREG: Gross. Pretty funny, though.

JEAN: Are you sure you're not just saying that just so you don't feel stupid?

GREG: Nope. It wasn't exactly a joke, but it was funny.

Unit 22

Exercise 7 (page 392)

Good evening. I'm Allison Kramer, and here are the news headlines. Mt. St. Andrea erupted at 5:45 A.M. A cloud of ash is covering the local area, and visibility has been strongly affected. Amazingly, there have been no deaths reported so far. In political news, Senator Diana McLeod is leading her challenger, Marcine Miller, by eight points in the latest GGG poll. The election, as you are probably aware, is only a week away. Ms. Miller says that despite being behind in the polls, she is confident that she will win. In sports news, the Seattle Mariners defeated the Atlanta Braves in Game 7 of the World Series by a score of 1–0. This is the Mariners' first championship. That's news on the hour. We'll be back in thirty minutes. I'm Allison Kramer.

Unit 23

Exercise 7 (page 418)

SALLY: Hi, April. What's wrong? You look upset about something.

APRIL: I am. I wish Bob and I weren't going together.

SALLY: Why?

APRIL: He asked me if he could borrow my workbook for French class—to copy it. We have to turn our workbooks in on Friday. I've finished mine, but Bob's done almost nothing.

SALLY: I hope you're going to tell me you said no.

APRIL: I said yes.

SALLY: April! I wish you hadn't done that.

APRIL: Well, I knew it wasn't a good idea to lend it to him, but I thought he'd break up with me if I refused.

SALLY: This is trouble, girl.

APRIL: What would you have done?

SALLY: I would have told him no, plain and simple.

APRIL: Easier said than done. He's very persuasive, and he is my boyfriend.

SALLY: It's the wrong thing to do.

APRIL: Yeah, I know. If the teacher finds out, she'll fail both of us.

SALLY: Probably. But the main problem is that it's just wrong. You worked for your grade. He's done nothing. It's not fair to you, and it's not fair to anyone who's done the work.

APRIL: Well, it's too late now, isn't it?

SALLY: Have you given it to him?

APRIL: No, not yet.

SALLY: Then it's not too late. If I were you, I'd call him up and tell him I'd changed my mind.

APRIL: How can I do that? What can I say?

SALLY: Just tell him you won't be able to do it because your conscience is bothering you.

APRIL: What should I do if he gets mad and says he wants to break up?

SALLY: Say good-bye. He's not worth having as a boyfriend if that's his reaction.

APRIL: I guess you're right. Have you got any courage pills?

Unit 24

Exercise 8 (page 433)

MARGE: Hello?

NANCY: Hi, Marge. It's Nancy. Got a moment? I need some advice.

MARGE: Sure. What's the problem?

NANCY: My daughter Amanda called an hour or so ago and asked me to babysit. When I said no, she almost demanded I do it. I gave in and said yes, but I wish I hadn't. Had I known she was calling, I wouldn't have answered the phone. What would you suggest?

MARGE: Has this been happening a lot?

NANCY: Yes, it has. It's the fifth time in three weeks. The last time it happened, it was 10 o'clock at night, and I was feeling sick. I had to call and insist she come and get the kids.

MARGE: Did she?

NANCY: Yes, but she was mad. I love her and my grandchildren, but enough is enough.

MARGE: What's her problem, anyway? Why is she asking you to babysit all the time?

NANCY: Well, both she and Stan have strange work schedules. She's been working overtime.

MARGE: They seem pretty well off to me. Why is Amanda working so much?

NANCY: She and Stan want to buy another house. Personally, I think she's been neglecting the children. It's important she pay more attention to those kids.

MARGE: Well, this isn't a matter of survival. They have a nice enough home already. I suggest you call her back and tell her you've changed your mind. You're not her slave.

NANCY: Thanks, Marge. That was my thought, too. I just wanted some support.

MARGE: Absolutely! You raised one family; you shouldn't have to raise another.

Student Book Answer Key

UNIT 1 Present and Future Time
(pages 2–15)

After You Read 1. b   **2.** b   **3.** b

1

A. 1. Used to narrate events in sequence: finds, asks, says, counters, throws up, walks, goes, agree.
Used to show actions in progress: is admiring, are smiling.

2. present perfect. The author uses that form here to connect the past and present: to show a state that began in the past and continues to the present moment.

3. you're visiting (present progressive as future); you leave (simple present as future); you'll be relaxing (future progressive); you'll have been traveling (future perfect progressive); it'll be (unplanned future with *will*); if you do (two actions in the future, simple present in the dependent clause); you'll be able to get (two actions in the future, *will* in the independent clause); I'm going to give (planned future with *be going to*); once you learn (two actions in the future, simple present in the dependent clause); you'll like (two actions in the future, *will* in the independent clause).

B. 2. present   **5.** future   **7.** future
3. present   **6.** future   **8.** future
4. future

2

2. has been shining (OR has shone)
3. 've visited (OR 've been visiting)
4. 'm going (OR 'm going to go)
5. get
6. 've been staying (OR 'm staying)
7. 'm going (OR 'm going to go)
8. are (OR have been)
9. love
10. are going (OR are)

3

2. 'll find   **8.** says
3. holds   **9.** travels
4. has continued   **10.** goes
5. is focusing   **11.** keeps
6. 've been trying   **12.** concludes
7. has kept   **13.** pleases

4

Possible answers:
2. 've also stayed   **8.** tour
3. have toured   **9.** arrive
4. spend (OR are spending)   **10.** spend (OR are spending)
5. start   **11.** leaves
6. finish   **12.** will be
7. travel

5

2/B Take it easy. We'll be there in a few minutes—as soon as we cross the big bridge coming up. See it?

4/B I'll have a splitting headache by the time we get there if you don't stop complaining. There'll still be some bargains!

8/B Next time you go to the flea market, I'm staying home!

6/B Yes, you are. You're making me nervous. Just stop making all that noise!

1/A Can't you drive a little faster? By the time we get to the flea market, they'll have sold all the best items. Those antique vases I love will be all gone.

5/A Well, excuse me for living! But I'm not complaining!

3/A Yes. But we're *already* an hour late. We'll have missed all the best bargains.

7/A Next time, we're going to leave home two hours earlier. That way, even if we get lost, we'll still have time to get some good bargains. You know how I love to bargain.

6

Answers will vary.

7

I am writing these words in English because I need the practice. At this moment I am on an airplane over the Pacific Ocean, on my way to a year of study at Columbia University in the United States. I am looking forward to being there, but I am also a little afraid. What ~~do~~ *will* I find when I ~~will get~~ *get* to America? Will the Americans be arrogant and violent? Will I make any friends? ~~Am I~~ *Will I be* happy?

These were the words I wrote in my diary on the airplane last month. But ~~I'm here~~ *I've been here* for a month now, and I've found that things are a lot different from what I expected. I've found that the majority of people here are friendly. They ~~are going~~ *go* out of their way to help you if you need it.

On television, the news programs ~~are speaking~~ *speak* a lot about bad events like accidents, murders, diseases, and fights. But I don't see as much violence in my life as I do on television. I have not been mugged and I don't worry all the time about my safety.

Two of the ideas I had about the United States, however, ~~will seem~~ *seem* to be true. One is that Americans ~~aren't paying~~ *don't pay* much attention to rules. One of my best American friends says, in fact, "Rules are made to be broken." The other idea I had is about the American family. In Asia the family is very important, but some Asian people ~~are thinking~~ *think* that the family ~~is meaning~~ *means* nothing in the United States. ~~I'm not knowing~~ *I don't know* if this is true or not. But I think it might be true, since my American friends almost never ~~are mentioning~~ *mention* their parents or their brothers and sisters. Anyway, I am going to have a chance to see a real American family. ~~I go~~ *I'm going* with my roommate Susan to spend Thanksgiving break with her family in Pennsylvania. When I ~~will see~~ *see* her family, I will understand more.

8

2. F	6. T	9. T
3. F	7. F	10. F
4. T	8. F	11. F
5. F		

9–11

Answers will vary.

UNIT 2 Past Time   (pages 16–32)

After You Read   1. b   **2.** a   **3.** b

1

A. 1. did, do; knew, know; got, get; came, come; took, take; was, be; said, say; thought, think; won, win

  2. Sentence: *Runze hadn't met Weinlick before she picked up a candidate survey on the Monday before the wedding.* Forms: past perfect *(hadn't met)*, simple past *(picked up)*. Past perfect to show which action happened first, simple past to show which action happened second.

B. 2. earlier: *He just didn't know* / later: *whom he would be marrying*
  3. earlier: *Friends would repeatedly ask Weinlick* / later: *when he was going to tie the knot*
  4. earlier: *Runze hadn't met Weinlick* / later: *before she picked up a candidate survey*
  5. earlier: *Weinlick had prepared everything* / later: *By the time the wedding day rolled around*

C. 2. F   **5.** F
  3. H   **6.** F
  4. H

2

2. didn't happen	8. wanted
3. met	9. made
4. had	10. led
5. thought	11. 've never met
6. called up	12. has always loved
7. asked	13. 've never been able

3

2. 'd sleep	5. used to be	8. 'd spend
3. 'd go	6. used to live	9. used to think
4. 'd go	7. used to be	

4

Possible answers:

2. By the time they both returned to their hometown about a year ago, Jim had completed four years of military service and Jennifer had graduated from college.
3. Before they saw each other again, Jennifer had started teaching and Jim had taken a job as a computer programmer.
4. When they ran into each other in a drugstore one morning, neither had gone out on any dates.
5. Because he had woken up with a splitting headache, Jim drove to Olson's Drugstore.
6. Because Jennifer's younger sister had fallen and hurt herself and needed medicine, Jennifer also went to Olson's.
7. Before a week had passed, Jim asked Jennifer out on a date.
8. When Jim and Jennifer had dated for three months, they got married.

5

2. I thought I'd probably feel just a little bit trapped . . .
3. I thought we were going to live in an apartment . . .
4. I expected that there wouldn't be as much money to spend . . .
5. I hoped that we would be happy . . .
6. I was sure that we were going to have a lot of fun together . . .
7. I didn't think I'd see as much of my buddies . . .
8. I figured that we were going to be taking a lot of trips . . .

6

Possible answers:

1. David was finishing a student teacher program, and Elizabeth was attending nursing school.
2. She used to be a pharmacy student.
3. She felt she would have more of a chance to help people.
4. Both marriages were arranged by others.
5. David's great-grandfather was going to do missionary work in Alaska.
6. The committee thought the woman in New York would make him a good wife.
7. The due date for their first child was the third anniversary of their marriage.

7

I just had to write today. It's our six-month anniversary. Jim and I ~~are~~ (have been) married six months as of today. So maybe this is the time for me to take stock of my situation. The obvious question is whether I'm happy I ~~get~~ (got) married. The answer is "Absolutely." When I remember what my life ~~has been~~ (was) like before ~~we're getting~~ (we got) married, I realize now how lonely ~~I've been~~ (I was) before. Jim is a wonderful guy. Since we both work, we ~~took~~ (take) turns doing the housework. He's really good about that. When we ~~have been~~ (were) dating, I wasn't sure whether or not ~~I'll~~ (I'd) have to do all the housework. But I ~~wasn't having~~ (didn't have) any reason to worry. Today we split everything 50 / 50. The only complaint I ~~was having~~ (have) is that Jim snores at night. When I tell him that, he only says, "Well, sweetie, you snore too." I don't believe it. But if this is our only problem, I guess we're pretty lucky.

Well, ~~I would have~~ (I've had) a long and tiring day, but it's almost over. It's time to go to sleep.

8

Possible answers:

2. Each of them has made over 30 jumps.
3. They've been members of the group for many years.
4. They were going to get married on a bungee jump.
5. They thought it would be too dangerous.
6. They couldn't find a minister who would bungee jump with them.
7. No, Reverend Martinez had never done this kind of wedding before.
8. No, Reverend Martinez wouldn't do another wedding like this one.

9–12

Answers will vary.

UNIT 3 Simple and Progressive: Action and Non-Action Verbs (pages 33–45)

After You Read 1. a **2.** a **3.** b

1

A. Non-action verbs: is / are; has / have; want; looks; love; sounds

B.
2. A	**7.** S	**12.** A
3. A	**8.** S	**13.** S
4. S	**9.** A	**14.** S
5. A	**10.** A	**15.** S
6. S	**11.** S	

C. Sentences with *there:*
There's no doubt that . . .
Are there ways to gain . . . ?
. . . if there's an emergency . . .
. . . there are countless benefits of cars . . .
There are other negatives . . .
If a technological product is there . . .

2

2. seeing	**6.** hears	**9.** is
3. smells	**7.** is thinking	**10.** is being
4. sees	**8.** tastes	**11.** are having
5. has		

3

2. freely	**5.** good	**8.** quickly
3. simply	**6.** clearly	**9.** easily
4. rapidly	**7.** well	**10.** angry

4

Possible answers:

2. There has never been complete peace in the world. (OR There will never be complete peace in the world.)
3. There were between 200 and 300 million people on the Earth in 1 A.D.
4. There were automobiles after 1910.
5. There was no television before 1920.
6. There are no humans on others planets now.
7. There were deaths from smallpox before the 20th century.
8. There were no personal computers before 1950.
9. There have been DVD players since the 1990s.
10. There will be just under 8 billion people on the Earth by 2025.

5

Possible answers:

2. Volleyball is a sport I play well.
3. Spaghetti is a food that tastes good to me.
4. I feel bad when I lose my temper.
5. Algebra is a school subject I do well in.
6. I feel strongly about helping the poor.
7. Blue is a color I look good in.
8. A cruise around the Caribbean is a vacation that sounds interesting to me.
9. Garlic is something that smells awful.
10. Rio is a place that looks beautiful.

6

It seems
~~It's seeming~~ that I constantly hear the same
We need
thing: "Cell phones are dangerous. ~~We're needing~~ to restrict them. People are dying because of
I think
cell phones." Well, ~~I'm thinking~~ cell phones themselves aren't the problem. I'm completely opposed to restrictions on them.

First, people say cell phones are dangerous to health, so they should be limited. Supporters
are
of this idea say there ~~are being~~ studies showing that cell phones produce radiation that is harmful to users. I think this is nonsense.
sounds
There hasn't been any real proof. It'~~s sounding~~
doesn't
like just another study that ultimately ~~isn't~~
mean
~~meaning~~ anything.

Second, a lot of teachers are proposing that we not allow cell phones in classes because
angry
they're a distraction. I feel pretty ~~angrily~~ about this. Here's a good example. Two weeks ago in
had
my history class, one of the students ~~was having~~ her cell phone on because her mother was really sick and might need a ride to the hospital. The student's mother couldn't contact anyone else. In fact, the mother did call, and the student found someone to help her. What if her cell phone hadn't been on? The teacher
bad
would have felt pretty ~~badly~~.

Third, people argue that using a cell phone while driving is dangerous. I disagree. It's no
dangerous
more ~~dangerously~~ than turning on the car

radio or eating a sandwich. People do those things when they drive. The law says you must always have one hand on the steering wheel. It's possible to use a cell phone ~~correct~~ *correctly* with one hand. I use my cell phone ~~careful~~ *carefully*; I always keep one hand on the wheel. Maybe there should be training in ways to use a cell phone ~~good~~ *well*, but we shouldn't prohibit using cell phones in cars.

This has always been a free country. I hope it stays that way.

2. She is having serious money problems.
3. Someone got hold of her credit card number.
4. This is a good example of identity theft.
5. $8,000 is involved.
6. Mary gave her credit card number on a website that probably wasn't secure.
7. People are supposed to report problems like this immediately.
8. Mary reported the problem a few days later.
9. She thought it was her mistake.
10. The downside is that it's easy for criminals to get information.

Answers will vary.

PART I From Grammar to Writing
(pages 46–48)

1

2. fragment—no subject and no verb
3. sentence
4. fragment—no subject
5. fragment—no subject and no verb
6. sentence
7. fragment—no verb
8. sentence

2

SENTENCES

1. Sherry, Akiko, and Lisa took a one-day trip to Barcelona.
2. They stayed in a youth hostel for a very reasonable price.

3. They visited the Sagrada Familia, Gaudí's famous church.
4. All three girls were impressed by the church's beauty.
5. Nearing the top, Akiko began to feel dizzy and had to start down again.
6. Sherry and Lisa continued climbing.
7. Both she and Lisa agreed that the view was magnificent.
8. The three decided to return to Barcelona.

REWRITTEN PARAGRAPH

In late December, Sherry, Akiko, and Lisa took a one-day trip to Barcelona. Not knowing anyone there, they stayed in a youth hostel for a very reasonable price. On their one day in the city, they visited the Sagrada Familia, Gaudí's famous church. All three girls were impressed by the church's beauty and decided to climb to the top instead of taking the elevator. Nearing the top, Akiko began to feel dizzy and had to start down again. Sherry and Lisa continued climbing. However, even Sherry, who had done a great deal of mountain climbing in Canada, felt nervous and unprotected at the summit. Both she and Lisa agreed that the view was magnificent and the climb well worth it. The three decided to return to Barcelona as soon as they could.

3

Last ~~last~~ summer when my wife and I were traveling in Morocco, we had one of the most interesting bargaining experiences ~~ever we~~ *ever. We* were in an open-air market in Rabat, and I really wanted to buy a Moroccan *jellaba*, a long, heavy, ankle-length ~~garment there~~ *garment. There* were several different shops where jellabas were sold, but Heather and I were drawn to one shop in ~~particular I~~ *particular. I* tried one jellaba ~~on it~~ *on. It* fit perfectly, and I knew it was the one I wanted, so I asked the merchant how much it ~~was he~~ *was. He* said it was ~~$200 now~~ *$200. Now* I've always been uncomfortable about bargaining, so I was ready to pay his ~~price Heather~~ *price. Heather* took me aside, however, and said that was too much and that he expected me to ~~bargain when~~ *bargain. When* I said I couldn't bargain, she told me that bargaining was part of the game and that I should offer

less. I
him ~~less I~~ sighed, tried to swallow the lump in
$100. He
my throat, and suggested ~~$100 he~~ smiled and
$110. He
asked for $150, whereupon I offered ~~$110 he~~
head. Heather
looked offended and shook his ~~head Heather~~
away. I
grabbed my hand and we started walking ~~away I~~
thought that was going to be the end of the
experience, but then the merchant came
$125. I
running after me, saying he'd accept ~~$125 I~~
ended up buying the jellaba for that amount,
it. Since
and I still have ~~it since~~ then I've never been
bargain.
afraid to ~~bargain~~

Answers will vary.

UNIT 4 *Be* and Auxiliaries in Additions, Tags, and Short Answers (pages 56–71)

After You Read **1.** a   **2.** b   **3.** a

1

A. **2.** Sam is <u>a perfectionist</u>; so (is) Jerry.

3. Jerry, always a high achiever, was <u>president of his high school class</u>. So (was) Sam.

4. Jerry has <u>been a leader in most of his enterprises</u>. So (has) Sam.

5. Sam always <u>tries to obey rules</u>. Jerry (does) too.

6. Jerry has <u>never liked liberal ideas</u>. Neither (has) Sam.

7. Does this sound like <u>some crazy new theory</u>? It (isn't)

8. They were <u>there</u> before any other children (were).

9. They sense that they have <u>to become different from the oldest child</u>, so they (do).

10. Based on this idea, we might expect powerful political figures, such as U.S. presidents, <u>to be firstborns</u>. They usually (are), says Sulloway.

11. But this is perhaps <u>too much of a generalization</u>. Yes, maybe it (is).

B. **2.** But they <u>are</u> both firstborns.
3. Like firstborns, they <u>do</u> identify with their parents.
4. Shy children . . . may not become leaders even if they <u>are</u> firstborns.
5. . . . the theory of birth order <u>does</u> appear to be generally valid.
6. . . . but they <u>will</u> maximize the quality of those relationships.

2

2. h	**5.** g	**8.** c
3. e	**6.** j	**9.** b
4. i	**7.** d	**10.** a

3

2. do	**6.** did	**10.** will
3. will	**7.** have	**11.** we can't
4. it won't	**8.** have I	**12.** will
5. did do	**9.** it is	

4

Possible answers (Note: In the contrast sentences, but, however, *and* though *are appropriate in each case.)*
2. I'm not, though.
3. My brother and sister do, however.
4. Neither had anyone else in my family.
5. They shouldn't, though.
6. But my brother's family hasn't.
7. She does speak it, though.
8. Neither has our daughter. (OR Our daughter hasn't either.)
9. So has Katie. (OR Katie has, too.)
10. Theresa does, though.

5

BRENT: Jeremy, come on into the living room. There are some things we need to talk about.

JEREMY: Dad, if it's about the broken window in the bathroom, I can explain. I guess I (did) break it, but I didn't mean to. It was an accident, really.

BRENT: It wasn't the window I wanted to talk about. I (was) wondering how it got broken, though.

JEREMY: It's not the window? What (do) you want to talk about, then?

BRENT: Well, for one thing, I got a letter in the mail from your teacher, Ms. Hammond. She says you haven't been studying and you might fail. You (do) want to pass the seventh grade, don't you?

JEREMY: Of course, Dad. And I (have) been studying. I just keep forgetting to turn in my homework.

BRENT: She says you don't pay attention in class, either, and you're always staring out the window.

JEREMY: Dad, she just doesn't like me. I (do) pay attention. Just because I'm not looking at Ms. Hammond doesn't mean I'm not paying attention to what she's saying. . . . She's boring, too.

BRENT: Jeremy, I've known Ms. Hammond for a long time. Her classes may not always be fun, but she (does) know how to teach. From now on, I want you to study every evening from 7:00 until 9:00, and I'm going to call Ms. Hammond every week to see if you're turning in your homework. And I (will) call every week. Don't think I won't.

JEREMY: Do I still get to watch TV and play video games?

BRENT: Not during the week until your grades improve. You can't have any of your friends over during the week either. Of course, you (can) read a book if you've got your homework done. OK. Now, let's talk about the window. What (did) happen to the window?

6

Dear Mr. and Mrs. Washburn,

I'm writing to give you a progress report on Jeremy. In general, I'd say he's doing better than
before, though he ~~is~~ *isn't* doing as well as he could. He still has a tendency to daydream a little too
much, but he ~~doesn't~~ *does* seem to be paying better attention in class. One of his weak subjects is
science; ~~neither~~ *so* is math. He scored high in math on the national achievement tests a month ago,
though, so he ~~is~~ *does* have a chance of passing his

math class. However, he ~~is~~ *is not* passing at the
moment. ~~Either~~ *Neither* is he passing science. He is doing very well in English, though, and he's
doing reasonably well in history and art ~~either~~ *too*. The main problem I'm having is getting Jeremy
to turn in his work; still, he ~~didn't~~ *did* submit three assignments last week. I appreciate your efforts to monitor his study time in the evenings.
Children today have so many distractions, ~~do~~ *don't* they? Your son is lucky to have parents who
care about education; many ~~don't~~ *do not*. Jeremy is
doing better; he ~~isn't~~ *is not* out of trouble yet. Please keep up the supervised work at home, and call me if you have any concerns.

7

2. T	**6.** F	**10.** T
3. T	**7.** F	**11.** F
4. F	**8.** T	**12.** T
5. F	**9.** F	

8–11

Answers will vary.

UNIT 5 Modals to Express Degrees of Necessity (pages 72–88)

After You Read 1. b **2.** b **3.** a **4.** a

1

1. a	**4.** a	**7.** b
2. b	**5.** a	**8.** b
3. b	**6.** a	**9.** b

2

2. had to worry
3. supposed to do
4. were supposed to leave
5. Should we have left
6. don't have to leave
7. should you tip
8. you're supposed to do
9. should you leave
10. ought to have given
11. could have left

3

Possible answers:

1. should have
2. is not supposed to
3. should
4. must
5. should have
6. don't have to

4

Possible answers:

2. They should have arranged their shoes so that they were pointing toward the door.
3. They shouldn't have said anything about the gift.
4. They shouldn't have taken a rock and roll CD as a gift.
5. Helen shouldn't have taken the sushi.
6. They should have refused the first offer of a drink.
7. They could (OR might) have taken a box of chocolates.
8. They could (OR might) have taken flowers.
9. They could (OR might) have declined the sushi.
10. They could (OR might) have left earlier.

5

Dear Masako,

Sorry it's taken me so long to write. I should ~~of~~ *have* gotten to this weeks ago, but I've been so busy. I'm really looking forward to the holidays and seeing all you guys again.

School is going well. It's tough but really interesting, and I'm sure I ~~should~~ *ought* to be studying even more than I have been. Part of the problem is that I'm taking too many classes. You're only ~~suppose~~ *supposed* to take five a term, but I'm taking six.

Anyway, I've gotten to know a lot of new people, including several Australians. I have this one really good friend, a girl named Jane. She invited me to her house last week for a party. Actually, it was my birthday, but I didn't know she knew that. I thought it was a party like any other. I figured ~~I better~~ *I'd better* take some kind of gift, but I couldn't decide what it ~~must~~ *should* be. Finally I came up with the idea of a bouquet of flowers. As soon as I got to the party, I gave it to Jane, and she was really happy to get them. But then the funniest thing happened. I guess I ~~should expect~~ *should have expected* something was up from the mysterious way Jane was acting, but I didn't. This was a surprise party—for me! As soon as I took off my coat and sat down, a lot of people jumped up from behind sofas and other places where they'd been hiding and shouted "Surprise! Happy birthday!" I was embarrassed, but I ~~might not have been~~ *shouldn't have been*, because everyone was really friendly, and pretty soon I forgot about my embarrassment. Then they gave me presents. I was about to put them away, but Jane said, "Aren't you going to open them?" I didn't know what to do. In China you ~~shouldn't have opened~~ *shouldn't open* gifts right when you get them, but apparently you are supposed to in Australia. So I opened them. The nicest gift was a new blouse from Jane. She told me I must ~~have gone~~ *go* and try it on immediately, so I did. It's beautiful. Anyway, what a party! I thought I knew all about Australian culture, but I guess I'm not as familiar with it as I thought. The custom of opening up presents in front of the gift giver is a strange one to me.

The weather is kind of chilly. How is it back in Singapore? Nice and warm? ~~Must~~ *Shall* I bring you something special from Australia when I come?

Well, Masako, I'm running out of space, so ~~I~~ *I've* got to sign off. Write soon.

Best,
Tong-Li

6

Possible answers:

2. Bev says they shouldn't delay the gift because everyone else has brought something.
3. He says they should have gone shopping last week.
4. He thinks they shouldn't get Mom a camera.
5. She thinks they shouldn't get Mom a dress.
6. She thinks they might get her a blouse.
7. She thinks they ought to get Mom a couple of nice scarves.
8. She says they'd better hurry up because Mom could be there any minute.

7–10

Answers will vary.

UNIT 6 Modals to Express Degrees of Certainty (pages 89–102)

After You Read **1.** a   **2.** b   **3.** c

1

A. . . . Columbus <u>may not have been</u> the first . . .
. . . Vinland <u>must have been</u> . . .
. . . Vinland <u>couldn't have been</u> . . .
<u>Could</u> the climate <u>have been</u> . . .
. . . Vinland <u>may have been</u> what is now . . .
. . . individuals <u>may have sailed</u> from Japan . . .
. . . the Japanese <u>may have introduced</u> . . .
. . . how <u>could</u> the voyage <u>have happened</u> . . .
. . . Japanese fishermen <u>might have been swept</u> . . .
. . . theory <u>may sound</u> unlikely. . .
. . . <u>may be disproved</u> eventually. . .
. . . pottery evidence <u>must mean</u> . . .

B. 2. a   **6.** a
3. a   **7.** a
4. b   **8.** b
5. a

2

2. may have had to
3. might be
4. could be working
5. must have
6. might be meeting
7. should be
8. must have been visiting

3

2. could have caused
3. must be
4. might have brought
5. could . . . have disappeared
6. could . . . have existed
7. had to have existed
8. must have become
9. Could there really have been
10. might be
11. may have influenced
12. might be

5

One <s>must</s> *might* think that with all the scientific progress that has been made in the last century, researchers would be able by now to answer this very simple question: Why do we itch? Unfortunately, scientists can't answer this question with any certainty. They simply don't know.

There are some clear cases involving itching. If a patient goes to her doctor and complains of terrible itching and the doctor finds hives or some other kind of rash, the doctor will probably say that she <s>must eat</s> *must have eaten* something she was allergic to—or that she <s>must not have been</s> *must have been* stung or bitten by some insect. This kind of case can be easily explained. Most itching, however, does not have an obvious cause.

Here's what scientists do know: Right under the surface of the skin there are sensory receptors that register physical stimuli and carry messages to the brain. These receptors detect pain and let the brain know about it. If there is a high level of physical stimulation to the body, the sensory receptors <s>might carried</s> *might carry* a message of pain to the brain. If the level of physical stimulation is low, the sensors <s>might be report</s> *might report* it as itchiness.

There has been a lot of speculation about the function of itching. Some researchers think it's possible that the function of itching <s>has to be</s> *may/might/could be* to warn the body that it is about to have a painful experience. Others theorize that early humans <s>might developed</s> *might have developed* itching as a way of knowing that they needed to take insects out of their hair. Still others believe that itching <s>could have been</s> *could be* a symptom of serious diseases such as diabetes and Hodgkin's disease.

One of the most interesting aspects of itching is that it <s>may have be</s> *may be* less tolerable than pain. Research has shown, in fact, that most people tolerate pain better than itching. Many people will allow their skin to be painfully broken just so they can get rid of an itch.

6

2. a   **5.** a   **8.** a
3. b   **6.** a   **9.** b
4. b   **7.** b   **10.** a

Possible answers:

1. The woman might have given police a description of the thief. (OR Someone could have seen the thief break into the woman's house.)
   The police must have put the man in jail. (OR The man could have appeared before a judge.)
2. The girl must not have tied the other end of the rope to something. (OR The dog might have broken the rope. OR Someone else could have untied the rope.)
3. The girl must have correctly pointed the signpost in the direction she had come from. (OR Someone else might have come along and told the girl which way to go. OR The girl could have remembered going there before.)
4. The man must have been struck by lightning. (OR The man's car could have caught fire.)

8–11

Answers will vary.

PART II From Grammar to Writing
(pages 103–105)

1

Correct choice: c

2

POSSIBLE CORRECTIONS

1. Casablanca is a city where exciting and mysterious things happen.
2. There are a number of reasons why college isn't for everybody.
3. Wild animals don't make good pets.
4. Regular exercise has many benefits.

3

Correct choice: b

PROBLEMS WITH THE OTHER CHOICES

a. There is no independent clause.
c. This is a possible title, but there is no independent clause and no verb.
d. This sentence is about just one detail in the paragraph.

4

POSSIBLE TOPIC SENTENCES

1. There are several reasons why public transportation is better for me than driving my own car to work.
2. I have three main reasons for preferring to watch movies on the big screen rather than on video.
3. I like to plan my own vacations instead of going on tours.
4. In my view, cats make better pets than dogs.

5

Answers will vary.

UNIT 7 Count and Non-Count Nouns
(pages 114–127)

After You Read 1. a   **2.** b   **3.** a

1

2. Underline *things*, *people*, and *days*; circle *food* and *diet*.
3. Underline *issue*; circle *food*.
4. Underline *lives*; circle *time* and *convenience*.
5. Underline *machines* and *snacks*; circle *soda* and *candy*.
6. Underline *kind*; circle *nutrition* and *stuff*.
7. Underline *family*; circle *weight* and *food*.
8. Underline *diet*; circle *evidence* and *gain*.

2

2. a piece of	**5.** pieces of	**8.** a cup of
3. a speck of	**6.** a drop of	**9.** a matter of
4. a pound of	**7.** piece of	**10.** period of

3

2. cuisines	**6.** flavoring	**10.** spices
3. rules	**7.** ways	**11.** menu
4. foods	**8.** century	**12.** fusion
5. rolls	**9.** chefs	

4

2. a work	**7.** a time	**12.** Soda
3. progress	**8.** criteria	**13.** milk
4. a history	**9.** time	**14.** a people
5. a talk	**10.** Work	**15.** a film
6. space	**11.** fish	**16.** peoples

5

Answers will vary.

6

Dear Kids,

    Your mom and I are having a wonderful time in Brazil. We landed in Rio de Janeiro on Tuesday as scheduled and made it to our hotel without any problems. On Wednesday we walked and sunbathed on Copacabana and Ipanema beaches. The only problem was that I dropped my camera and got ~~sands~~ *sand* in it, and now it's not working. Actually, there's one other problem: We don't have enough ~~furnitures~~ *furniture* in our hotel room. There's no ~~places~~ *place* to put anything. But everything else has been great. We went to a samba show, and even though it was intended for ~~tourist~~ *tourists*, it was a lot of fun.

    The Brazilian people ~~is~~ *are* very friendly and helpful. On Friday we had a flight to Sao Paulo scheduled for 9:00 A.M., and we missed the bus and couldn't get a taxi. But we were saved by one of the hotel ~~employee~~ *employees*, who gave us a ride to the airport. We got there just in time. Now we're in Sao Paulo. It's an exciting place, but I can't get over the ~~traffies~~ *traffic*. It took two ~~hour~~ *hours* to get from our hotel to the downtown area. Yesterday we had lunch at a famous restaurant where they serve *feijoada*, which is ~~typical Brazilian foods~~ *a typical Brazilian food*. It had so much spice in it that our mouths were on fire, but it was delicious. Tonight we're going to have dinner at another restaurant where they serve all kinds of meat. They raise a lot of cattle in Brazil, and ~~meats are~~ *meat is* very popular. This restaurant is one of the most famous ones.

    The other thing about Brazil that's really interesting is the amount of coffee the Brazilians drink. They have little cups of ~~coffees~~ *coffee* several times a day—called *caffezinho*. We tried it; it's very strong and sweet.

    That's all for now. Your mom hasn't had ~~a time~~ *time* to go shopping yet, which is good. You know how much I hate shopping.

Love,
Dad

7

2. hamburger	**7.** a teaspoon of
3. chicken and pork	**8.** 2 cups of
4. 1½ pounds of	**9.** 2 inches
5. 2 . . . yolks	**10.** 15 or 20
6. 3 tablespoons of	

8

STUDENT B'S COMPLETIONS
1. a grain of rice
2. a speck of dust
3. a game of soccer
4. a branch of astronomy
5. a clap of thunder

STUDENT A'S COMPLETIONS
6. a piece of advice
7. a grain of sand
8. a bolt of lightning
9. a piece / an article of furniture
10. an article of clothing

9–10

Answers will vary.

UNIT 8 Definite and Indefinite Articles (pages 128–140)

After You Read 1. b **2.** b **3.** a

1

A.		
2. D	**5.** I	**8.** G
3. I	**6.** G	**9.** I
4. G	**7.** G	**10.** D

B.	
1. b	**4.** a
2. a	**5.** b
3. b	

2

EXCERPT 1

2. an	**7.** the
3. the	**8.** the
4. the	**9.** —
5. the	**10.** —
6. —	

EXCERPT 2

1. The	**7.** the	**13.** the
2. the	**8.** the	**14.** the
3. —	**9.** the	**15.** the
4. —	**10.** the	**16.** —
5. —	**11.** the	**17.** the
6. a	**12.** the	**18.** the

3

EXCERPT 1

2. the	**5.** the	**8.** the
3. A	**6.** the	**9.** —
4. the	**7.** the	**10.** the

EXCERPT 2

1. The	**6.** the	**11.** the
2. a	**7.** The	**12.** —
3. —	**8.** the	**13.** the
4. an	**9.** —	**14.** the
5. the	**10.** the	

4

1. A television set is an electronic device that receives electromagnetic waves, converts the waves into images, and displays them on a screen. / The television set was invented in the 1920s by Farnsworth and Zorinsky.
2. A wheel is a circular device that turns around a central point. / The wheel was invented 5000 to 6000 years ago.
3. A clarinet is a woodwind instrument that uses a reed. / The clarinet was invented around 1700.
4. Guitars are stringed instruments that typically have six strings. / The guitar was invented in the 1400s in Spain.
5. Automobiles are self-powered traveling vehicles. / The automobile was invented in 1874 by Siegfried Marcus in Vienna.
6. Telephones are communication devices that convert sound signals into waves and reconvert them into sounds. / The telephone was invented in 1878 by Alexander Graham Bell.

5

People say we are now able to perform ~~a~~ genetic engineering. I am against this for several reasons. First, it is dangerous to tamper with ~~the~~ nature because we don't know what will happen. We could upset *the* balance of nature. For example, people are against ~~a~~ mosquito because it carries malaria. Suppose we change the DNA of the mosquito so that it will die off. That will stop ~~a~~ malaria, but it will upset *the* ecological balance because certain other species depend on *the* mosquito. If we destroy it, these other species won't be able to survive. This will have *a* serious effect on *the* environment.

Second, genetic engineering will take away people's control over their own lives. Suppose scientists develop the capability to isolate *a* gene for violent behavior and they eliminate this gene from future generations. This may eliminate a violence, but I believe that behavior is *a* matter of choice, and this type of genetic engineering will eliminate choice. It will make people behave as others have determined, not as they have determined, and it will take away an individual responsibility.

Third, genetic engineering will remove chance from our lives. Part of what makes ~~the~~ life interesting is unpredictability. We never know exactly how someone, or something, is going to turn out. It's interesting to see what happens. As far as I am concerned, we should leave genetic engineering to *the* Creator.

6

2. a	**5.** a	**8.** b
3. a	**6.** b	**9.** b
4. b	**7.** b	**10.** b

7–10

Answers will vary.

UNIT 9 Quantifiers (pages 141–152)

After You Read 1. b **2.** a **3.** b

1

2. yes	**6.** no	**10.** no
3. no	**7.** yes	**11.** no
4. no	**8.** no	**12.** no
5. no	**9.** yes	

2

2. any	5. number of	8. few
3. less	6. a lot of	9. little
4. some	7. many	10. a little

3

2. less	7. both of	12. most of
3. enough	8. $40	13. a couple of
4. more	9. fewer	14. some
5. a few	10. much	15. every
6. one of	11. few	

4

2. fewer	6. a great deal of
3. more	7. many
4. less	8. much
5. few	

5

Answers will vary.

6

My fellow citizens. We are at a time in our history when we need to make some real sacrifices. Recent presidents have made *a great many* ~~a great deal of~~ pledges they didn't keep. You may not like everything I tell you tonight, but you deserve to hear the truth. On the economy, we've made *a little* ~~little~~ progress, but we still have a *deal of* great ~~many~~ work to do, so there are several measures I'm proposing. First, I want to raise taxes on the very wealthy because *few* ~~a few~~ of them are really paying their share. Second, *many of the* ~~many of~~ members of the middle class are carrying an unfair tax burden, so I'm asking for a tax cut for the middle class. If I'm successful, most of you in the middle class will be paying 10 percent less in taxes next year, though *a few* ~~few~~ of you in the higher income group may see your taxes rise *a little* ~~little~~. How do I intend to make up the lost revenue? The problem with the national income tax is that there are *many* ~~much~~ loopholes in

the current law which allow *some* ~~any~~ people to avoid paying any taxes at all. My additional plan is to replace the lost revenue with a national sales tax, which is fairer because it applies to *all* ~~every~~ people equally. Third, we have no money to finance health care reform, and we've made *little* ~~a little~~ progress in reducing pollution and meeting clean air standards. Therefore, I am asking for a 50-cent-a-gallon tax on gasoline, which will result in many more people using public transportation, and will create additional revenue. Thus, we will have enough of money to finance our new health care program and will help the environment at the same time.

7

2. a	6. b
3. b	7. b
4. b	8. a
5. a	

8

ANSWERS TO TEAM A'S QUESTIONS
1. Canada has fewer people.
2. Canada has more land area.
3. Venezuela produces less oil.
4. Somalia has no snowfall.
5. Libya has few rivers.
6. Monaco has a small number of people.
7. South Africa produces a large amount of gold.
8. Aswan, Egypt, has little rainfall.

ANSWERS TO TEAM B'S QUESTIONS
1. Spain has fewer people.
2. Brazil has more land area.
3. The United States produces less oil.
4. Costa Rica has no military.
5. Yemen has few rivers.
6. San Marino has a small number of people.
7. France uses a large amount of nuclear energy
8. Antofagasta, Chile, has little rainfall.

9–10

Answers will vary.

UNIT 10 Modification of Nouns

(pages 153–166)

After You Read **1.** b **2.** a **3.** a

1

2. Circle *team*, *team*, *match*; underline *Soviet*, *men's*, and *semifinal* once; *U.S.*, *ice*, *hockey* twice.

3. Circle *squad*, *medals*, *all-stars*; underline *unbeatable*, *Soviet*, *last*, *four*, *National* once; *gold*, *Hockey*, *League* twice.

4. Circle *friends*, *The Lord of the Rings*; underline *film-buff* and *Academy-Award-winning* three times.

5. Circle *creatures*, *effects*; underline *awesome*, *special* once; *strange-looking* three times.

6. Circle *treatment*, *conflict*; underline *serious*, *profound*, *heartwarming* once; *age-old* three times.

7. Circle *expectations*; underline *parents'* once; *career* twice.

8. Circle *basis*; underline *actual*, *scientific* once.

9. Circle *condition*, *dystonia*, *function*, *concentration*; underline *medical*, *focal*, *abnormal*, *extreme* once; *muscle* twice.

10. Circle *slope*, *move*; underline *steep*, *icy*, *every* once.

2

2. new silk
3. ugly purple denim
4. suitable dress-up
5. important, interesting (OR interesting, important)
6. good memorable
7. sloppy, unstylish
8. round blue sapphire
9. oval green emerald
10. excellent tomato and cheese
11. fancy dress-up
12. beautiful purple denim

3

2. one-paragraph
3. 300-page
4. six-year
5. stress-related
6. eyesight-related
7. 10-gallon
8. performance-induced
9. two-month

4

Possible answers:

2. A long-haired cat came to our house and never left.
3. My dad loves his comfortable old jacket.
4. A surprise birthday party is an amusing and interesting experience.
5. An eleven-year-old child won the national spelling contest.
6. *Titanic* is an award-winning movie.
7. My husband built a three-legged table.
8. I'm fascinated by unusual-looking people.
9. She was wearing a short blue cotton skirt.
10. The Chinese jade bowl we bought is worth a lot of money.
11. My grandmother works in a sixty-story building.
12. My daughter can easily lift a 40-kilo bag.

5

It's midnight, the end of a long day. My first
                    medical school
week of ~~school medical~~ is over, and I'm exhausted but happy! I'm so glad I decided to go to university. It was definitely a good decision. I'm not completely sure yet, but I think I want to go into child psychology because I love working with children—especially nine- and
10-year-
~~10 years~~-old kids.

Yesterday our psychology class visited a
large new   *troubled middle-class*
~~new large~~ hospital where many ~~middle-class troubled~~ children go for treatment. I expected to see a lot of boys and girls behaving badly, but most of them were pretty quiet and relaxed. They just looked like they needed
            warm personal
some ~~personal warm~~ attention.

Today in our surgery class we had a bright
                        young Brazilian
hardworking teacher, a ~~Brazilian young~~ doctor who was substituting for our usual professor.
            helpful foreign
We got a ~~foreign helpful~~ viewpoint on things.

The only thing I don't like about medical
                disgusting cafeteria
school is the ~~cafeteria disgusting~~ food. I'm
                            tasty hot
going to have to start getting some ~~hot tasty~~
                        favorite local
Chinese food from my ~~local favorite~~ place.

Well, it's time for me to get some sleep. I hope
this ~~computer new~~ *new computer* program works correctly. I'll
write again soon.

Jennifer

6

A. 2. F   **5.** T   **7.** F
     3. T   **6.** T   **8.** T
     4. F

B. 2. We don't want to make this a <u>brain-breaker</u>.
    3. I feel like a <u>total, complete</u> idiot.
    4. And I feel like I have an <u>ugly, high-pitched, squeaky voice</u>.
    5. You're just going through a <u>rapid adolescent growth period</u>.
    6. It happens to a lot of <u>12-year-old boys</u>.
    7. Now, the key to getting you over this <u>fear-of-oral-reading problem</u> is to distract you from thinking about how well you're doing.
    8. Let's think of a <u>short, easy-to-remember phrase</u> that you can keep in the back of your mind.
    9. "It was an <u>icy, dark, stormy evening</u>."
    10. "It promised to be one of those <u>famous three-dog nights</u>."
    11. What's a <u>three-dog night</u>?
    12. It's a night that's so cold that you need <u>three large, warm, furry dogs</u> to sleep with to keep you warm.

7

Answers will vary.

8

1. b   **2.** b   **3.** a   **4.** b

9–11

Answers will vary.

PART III From Grammar to Writing
(pages 167–172)

1

2. <u>The Siberian tiger and the blue whale</u> are endangered species.
3. <u>That man who is sitting at the mahogany desk</u> is our loan officer.

4. <u>Relatively few adults or teenagers</u> are able to handle credit cards wisely.
5. <u>The expectation that we will like well-known works of art, literature, or music</u> can detract from our appreciation of them.

2

2. Much of what you were told was inaccurate.
3. Neither of those two politicians is in favor of cutting taxes.
4. None of the work has been completed successfully.
5. Very 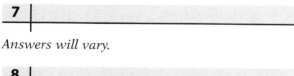little of this work can be done by one person working alone.
6. The singing of that famous Australian opera star is uplifting.

3

2. are   **5.** were
3. isn't   **6.** weren't
4. have

4

2. are   **4.** is
3. was   **5.** are

5

2. their   **5.** him or her   **7.** his or her
3. his or her   **6.** them   **8.** their
4. their

6

2. are   **5.** have
3. has   **6.** his
4. is

7

Many parts of our once-beautiful city ~~is~~ *are* starting to look like mini garbage dumps. You will recall that legislation requiring recycling within the city limits ~~were~~ *was* passed last year, and the mayor and other local politicians ~~encourages~~ *encourage* us to recycle, but in my apartment complex

there are
~~there's~~ no bins for recycling. The result is that
their
people take no responsibility for ~~his~~ own
his or her
actions, and everyone tosses ~~their~~ trash and
recyclables (glass, plastic bottles, cans, etc.)
right in with the food that is being thrown
away. Neither the manager of the complex nor
have
the owners of the building ~~has~~ bought any new
containers for items that are supposed to be
recycled. So what else can everybody do but
his or her
mix ~~his~~ trash together? Either the manager or
are
the owners ~~is~~ responsible for breaking the law
here. Not us! Meanwhile, trash cans in the
are
downtown area ~~is~~ overflowing with garbage,
are
and vacant lots all around the city ~~is~~ littered
with soda cans, broken glass, and paper. The
owner and publisher of your newspaper,
has
Stanford Black, ~~have~~ always been a supporter
of a clean environment. I urge your paper to
take leadership in solving this problem.

8

Answers will vary.

UNIT 11 Adjective Clauses:
Review and Expansion (pages 180–194)

After You Read 1. a   2. b   3. a

1

A. 2. yes   **6.** no
  3. no   **7.** no
  4. yes   **8.** no
  5. yes

B. 1. Try to place people you know into one or
    more of the categories. (OR who(m) you
    know OR that you know)
  2. This category has to do with the kind of
    information we notice and remember
    easily. (OR which we notice OR that we
    notice)
  3. Barbara is less interested in the sofa and
    more interested in the tense way the hosts
    are talking with each other. (OR that the
    hosts)

C. 2. Are you the kind of person <u>who</u>
    <u>resembles a sunflower</u>? I
  3. They developed a test, <u>which has been</u>
    <u>refined many times over the decades</u>. NI
  4. An introvert is a person <u>whose energies</u>
    <u>are activated by being alone</u>. I
  5. Mary starts to open up once she meets
    some people <u>who make her feel</u>
    <u>comfortable</u>. I
  6. He is imagining a time <u>when he was</u>
    <u>hiking alone in the mountains</u>. I
  7. Good examples are Jack and Barbara,
    <u>who have been married for years</u>. NI
  8. Jack, <u>whose parents own a sofa company</u>,
    notices that their hosts have bought a
    new sofa. NI
  9. The loan officer, <u>who makes Gary feels</u>
    <u>criticized</u>, is only trying to do his job. NI
  10. However, Gary takes his comments
    personally, <u>which classifies him as a</u>
    <u>feeler</u>. NI

2

2. which   **5.** who   **8.** whose
3. which   **6.** whom   **9.** no pronoun
4. who   **7.** who   **10.** who

3

2. where she worked
3. that he worked for
4. he worked
5. which bothers me
6. when her performance was
7. everyone likes
8. that has
9. when he was hired

4

Possible answers:
  2. The company, which is named Excelsior
    Computer, has existed for 15 years.
  3. The building where we do most of our work
    is located downtown.
  4. The office that I work in has been
    remodeled.
  5. Darren Corgatelli, whose wife is my aunt, is
    the boss.
  6. Darren, whom I've known since I was a
    child, is an excellent boss.
  7. Sarah Corgatelli, who is Darren's wife,
    keeps the company running smoothly.
  8. I joined the company in 1995, when I
    graduated from college.

9. I really appreciate my colleagues, whose advice has been invaluable.

10. Part of my job is telemarketing, which I like least.

5

2. which is why
3. the other prisoners looked up to
4. where he's been working
5. the psychiatrists considered
6. which is the reason
7. who has been in trouble
8. an opinion which / that makes me
9. whom the other prisoners respected
10. where he has been working
11. whom the psychiatrists considered
12. evidence which (OR that) makes me

6

Dear Mom and Dad   September 28

   Well, the first week of college has been tough, but it's turned out OK. My advisor is a lady who ~~she~~ is also from Winnipeg, so we had something

that (OR *which* OR *no pronoun*)

~~when~~ we could talk about. Since I haven't decided on a major, she had me take one of

   that (OR *which*)

those tests ˅show you what you're most

interested in. She also had me do one of those personality inventories that ~~they~~ tell you what kind of person you are. According to these

        who

tests, I'm a person ~~whom~~ is classified as an extrovert. I also found out that I'm most

          that (OR *which*)

interested in things ˅involve being on the stage

                which

and performing in some way, ~~that~~ doesn't surprise me a bit. I always liked being in school plays. Remember? I signed up for two drama courses. Classes start on Wednesday, and I'm getting to know the other guys in the

          where

dormitory ~~which~~ I live. It's pretty exciting being here.

   Not much else right now. I'll call in a week or so.

                     Love,
                     Al

7

1. a   **2.** b   **3.** b   **4.** a   **5.** b

8

Answers will vary.

9

1. a   **2.** b   **3.** a   **4.** b   **5.** b   **6.** a

10–11

Answers will vary.

UNIT 12 Adjective Clauses with Prepositions; Adjective Phrases   (pages 195–209)

After You Read 1. b   **2.** a   **3.** c

1

A.

reasons → all of which she dismissed quickly . . .

book → on which it is based

forces → representatives of which are hobbits, men, a good wizard, an elf, and a dwarf

actors → all of whom distinguish themselves

characters → most of whom are interesting and believable

B. 2. anyone who (OR that) continues to wear it
   3. which (OR that) is called the Shire
   4. which are represented by
   5. who is inclined to ask
   6. who (OR that) is interested in cinema
   7. who include
   8. which (OR that) is based on

2

2. both of which were directed by Steven Spielberg
3. all of whom are highly regarded European directors
4. all of which have earned a great deal of money
5. both of whom have played the role of James Bond
6. none of whom are known as singers

3

2. *Spider-Man*, based on the popular comic book, is the fifth-highest-earning movie of all time.
3. *The Matrix* and *The Matrix: Reloaded*, starring Keanu Reeves, are both very popular.
4. James Cameron has directed many big movies, including *Titanic, True Lies*, and the *Terminator* films.
5. The Harry Potter novels, written by J. K. Rowling, have translated well to the screen.
6. *Star Wars, The Empire Strikes Back,* and *Return of the Jedi*, featuring Harrison Ford, Carrie Fisher, and Mark Hamill, were conceived, written, and directed by George Lucas.

4

Possible answers:

2. Many recent science fiction films have been financially successful. They include *The Phantom Menace, Independence Day*, and *Spider-Man I* and *II*.
3. The top-earning animated films are *The Lion King* and *Shrek*. I've seen both of them.
4. *Chicago* was the best picture of 2002. It features three well-known actors.
5. Sequels to big movie hits may lose their appeal. This will cause filmmakers to become more creative.

5

Answers will vary.

6

Dear Brent,

Sarah and I are having a great time in Los Angeles. We spent the first day at the beach in Venice and saw where *The Sting* was filmed—

you know, that famous movie ~~starred~~ *starring* Paul Newman and Robert Redford? Yesterday we went to Universal Studios and learned about all

the cinematic tricks, most of ~~that~~ *which* I wasn't aware of. Amazing! The funny thing is that even

though you know the illusion ~~presenting~~ *presented* on the screen is just an illusion, you still believe it's real when you see the movie. Then we took the tram tour around the premises and saw several

actors working, some ~~which~~ *of whom* I recognized. I

felt like jumping off the tram and shouting, "Would everyone ~~is~~ famous please give me your autograph?" In the evening we went to a party at the home of one of Diana's friends, many of

~~them~~ *whom* are connected with the movie business. I had a really interesting conversation with a

fellow ~~works~~ *working* in the industry who claims that a

lot of movies ~~making~~ *made* these days are modeled conceptually after amusement park rides. Just like the rides, the movies start slowly and easily, then they have a lot of twists and turns ~~are~~ calculated to scare you to death, and they end happily. Maybe *Pirates of the Caribbean* is an example. Pretty fascinating, huh? What next?

Sorry to spend so much time talking about movies, but you know what an addict I am.

Anyway, I'll let you know my arrival time, ~~that~~ *which* I'm not sure of yet, so that you can pick me up at the airport.

Love you lots,
Amanda

7

2. F	5. F	8. F
3. F	6. T	9. T
4. T	7. F	10. F

8–11

Answers will vary.

PART IV From Grammar to Writing (pages 210–213)

1

2. Tom, who is clearly an extrovert, loves meeting new people.
3. Sandra, who is very quick to make friends, loves to have friends over for dinner.
4. Tom and Sandra have two married sons, both of whom live abroad.
5. The son who is older lives with his family in Britain.
6. The son who is younger lives with his family in southern Italy.
7. Tom and Sandra own a house in the city and one in the country. The one where they spend most of their time is in the city.
8. The house that they spend summers in is located in New Hampshire.

1. a. College students who live close to campuses spend less money on gas.

b. College students, who are expected to study hard, have to become responsible for themselves.

2. a. People, who are the only animals with a capacity for creative language, have highly developed brains.

b. People who live in glass houses shouldn't throw stones.

3. a. The car, which was invented in the late 19th century, has revolutionized modern life.

b. The car which I would really like to buy is the one in the far corner of the lot.

4. a. Science fiction movies, which have become extremely popular in the last two decades, often earn hundreds of millions of dollars for their studios.

b. The science fiction movies which have earned the most money collectively are the *Star Wars* films.

5. a. The panda that was given to the National Zoo died recently.

b. The panda, which is native only to China, is on the Endangered Species List.

1. A film produced by George Lucas is almost a guaranteed success.

2. A film directed by Steven Spielberg is likely to be a blockbuster.

3. *A Beautiful Mind,* directed by Ron Howard, won the Academy Award for best picture.

4. Many Canadians, including Donald Sutherland and Michael J. Fox, are major international film stars.

5. The Universal Studios facility located in California was established decades ago.

6. The Cineplex theater complex near our neighborhood has 12 separate theaters.

Dear Mom and Dad,

Thanks again for bringing me down here to the university last weekend. Classes didn't start until Wednesday, so I had a few days to get adjusted. I'm signed up for five classes: zoology, calculus, English, and two history sections. It's a heavy load, but they're all courses that will count for my degree. The zoology class, which meets at 8:00 every morning, is going to be my hardest subject. The history class that I have in the morning is on Western Civilization; the one that I have in the afternoon is on early U.S. history. Calculus, which I have at noon every day, looks like it's going to be relatively easy. Besides zoology, the other class that's going to be hard is English, which we have to write a composition a week for.

I like all of my roommates but one. There are four of us in our suite, including two girls from Texas and a girl from Manitoba. Sally, who is from San Antonio, is great; I feel like I've known her all my life. I also really like Anne, the girl from Manitoba. But Heather, the other girl from Texas, is kind of a pain. She's one of those types of people who never tell you what's bothering them and then get hostile. All in all, though, it looks like it's going to be a great year. I'll write again in a week or so.

Love,
Vicky

Answers will vary.

UNIT 13 The Passive: Review and Expansion (pages 220–234)

After You Read **1.** a **2.** a **3.** b

1

A. and B.

has been discovered *a*

were found *a*

must have been deposited *a*

has been searched *a*

has been found *a*

had to have been killed *c*

have . . . been discovered *a*

Is . . . known *b*

has been released *a*

have . . . buried *c*

a
has been told

a
will . . . be found

2. T; are caught   6. T; are rewarded
3. I; disappear   7. I; don't realize
4. I; go   8. T; are watched
5. T; is helped

3

2. are being questioned
3. was being opened
4. was being helped
5. are being withheld
6. are currently being interviewed

4

2. haven't been cracked
3. was sighted
4. was found
5. was determined
6. had been abandoned
7. had been set
8. might have been threatened
9. was caused
10. hasn't been proved (OR proven)
11. was considered
12. was accompanied
13. were received
14. have been discovered
15. Could she and Noonan have been killed
16. shouldn't be solved

5

A. 1. b   2. b   3. a   4. a   5. b   6. b

B. 2. have them enlarged
   3. getting his car tuned up
   4. have the windshield replaced
   5. got lunch delivered
   6. gotten analyzed
   7. had completed the work
   8. had finished the report
   9. had it typed
   10. having their kitchen remodeled

6

Possible answers:
2. An eight-year-old boy was crossing the intersection of 4th and Madison.

3. He was hit by a blue late-model Toyota Corolla.
4. The Toyota disappeared from the scene immediately.
5. The boy sustained massive injuries.
6. He was taken to Downtown Medical Center.
7. At present he is being cared for in the Intensive Care Unit.
8. His condition is described as critical.
9. Anyone with information is asked to call 444-6968.
10. A reward is being offered.

7

believe
In our day we ~~are believed~~ in science and have the feeling that every question can be
explained
~~explain~~ and every problem can be solved. But some of us want the opposite. We don't want everything to be explained. We like puzzles. We
needed
feel that mystery is ~~needing~~ in our lives.

The mysterious crop circles that have ~~been~~ appeared around the world in the last 25 years or so are an example of this. These formations
been
have ˄ reported in more than 20 countries, including the United States, Canada, and
found
Australia. But most of them have been ~~finding~~ in grain fields in southern England. These circles, which are large and flat, are ~~being~~ caused by a force that flattens the grain but
being
does not destroy it. They are still ~~been~~ made.
been
How have these circles ˄ produced? By whom have they been made? Since the first discovery of the circles, many explanations have been proposed. According to some people, the circles
have
~~has~~ been made by spirit creatures like fairies.
caused
Others say they have been ~~causing~~ by "Star
have
Wars" experiments or are messages that ˄ been left by extraterrestrials visiting our planet. Two British painters, David Chorley and Douglas Bower, say they ~~were~~ made the crop circles over a period of years as a joke. If this is true, however, how can we explain the crop circles in Australia and Canada and other places?

They couldn't all have ~~being~~ *been* made by Chorley and Bower, could they?

In 2002, movie director M. Night Shyamalan released his movie *Signs,* which is about the crop circle question. The movie shows clearly that the crop circles *were* made by invading aliens from beyond our solar system. This is one interesting and enjoyable theory. More explanations like it ~~get~~ *are* needed. What's fun is speculation. The mystery doesn't need to be solved.

2. b	**5.** b	**8.** a
3. a	**6.** b	**9.** b
4. b	**7.** a	

9

PROMPTS//COMPLETIONS

1. A.1//B.2	**6.** B.6//A.9
2. A.2//B.3	**7.** B.7//A.8
3. A.3//B.4	**8.** B.8//A.5
4. A.4//B.1	**9.** B.9//A.7
5. B.5//A.6	

ORDER OF PROMPTS: 1, 3, 2, 7, 5, 8, 4, 9, 6

MYSTERY OBJECT: a sandwich

10–12

Answers will vary.

UNIT 14 The Passive to Describe Situations and to Report Opinions (pages 235–256)

After You Read **1.** b **2.** a **3.** b

1

A. 2. S	**5.** O	**8.** O
3. O	**6.** O	**9.** S
4. S	**7.** O	**10.** O

B. 1. no, no	**3.** yes, yes
2. no, no	**4.** yes, yes

2

2. are surrounded by
3. is composed of (OR is divided into OR is made up of)
4. is found (OR is located)
5. is composed of (OR is made up of)
6. is bordered by
7. is composed of (OR is divided into OR is made up of)
8. is divided into
9. are located
10. are found in (OR are located in)

3

A. 2. was thought to be
   3. is claimed to be
   4. are regarded as
   5. were believed to be
   6. have been considered
   7. is said to live
   8. was regarded as
   9. is assumed to be
   10. are alleged to be

B. 3. It is claimed that Lee Harvey Oswald was the assassin of President John Kennedy.
   5. In the Middle Ages, it was believed that fairies and other spirit creatures were real.
   7. It is said that Bigfoot, a large, mysterious forest creature, lives in the Pacific Northwest.
   9. Today, it is assumed that William Shakespeare was the author of the plays credited to him . . .
   10. From time to time, it is alleged that certain people are criminals . . .

4

Answers will vary.

5

Every area of the world has its own legends, and Asia is no different. One of the most famous Asian legends is about the Abominable Snowman, also called the yeti, of the Himalayas. Is the yeti just a legend that is ~~believe~~ *believed* because people want things to be real, or does he really exist?

The yeti *is* thought to be a huge creature— perhaps as tall as eight feet. His body is

supposed to be covered with long, brown hair.
He ~~says~~ *is said* to have a pointed head and a hairless face that looks something like a man's. It is ~~claiming~~ *claimed* that he lives near Mount Everest, the highest mountain in the world, which ~~locates~~ *is located* on the border of Nepal and Tibet.

Sightings of the yeti have been reported for centuries, but the yeti was ~~make~~ *made* known to the rest of the world only in 1921. In that year, members of an expedition to climb Mt. Everest saw very large tracks in the snow that looked like prints of human feet. No conclusive evidence of the yeti's existence was found during that expedition, but interest was stimulated. Other expeditions were made. In 1951, explorer Eric Shipton led a search in which some gigantic, human-appearing tracks were found. Once again, the yeti himself was not seen. In 1969, Sir Edmund Hillary, who is regarded *as* one of the greatest climbers ever, arranged another expedition, this time with the intention of not only seeing the yeti but of capturing him. Once again, tracks were discovered, but that was all. Hillary eventually decided the footprints might simply *be* considered normal animal tracks enlarged by the daytime melting of the snow. In 1964, Boris F. Porshev, a Russian scientist, said that he believed that the yeti actually existed. He theorized that the yeti is a surviving descendant of Neanderthal man, a creature who is believed to ~~live~~ *have lived* from 200,000 to 25,000 years ago and is thought by some to be an ancestor of modern humans. Porshev has never actually been able to spot the yeti, however.

The mystery continues. Does the yeti really exist, or do people just want to believe he exists? It seems to me that there must be more to this mystery than just melted tracks. Centuries of reports by Himalayan trail guides must mean something. Besides, other yeti-type creatures have been reported—most notably, Bigfoot in North America. Time will tell, but maybe we shouldn't be so quick to dismiss the Abominable Snowman as nothing more than an entertaining story.

6

2. F	**6.** F
3. F	**7.** T
4. T	**8.** F
5. F	

7

Suggested answers:
1. Americans. "USA" spelled backwards.
2. funny
3. the car ("rac" spelled backwards)
4. tires
5. It is engine exhaust.
6. gas stations / oil companies
7. It isn't just exotic cultures that have strange customs and rituals.

8

1. e	**4.** a
2. f	**5.** b
3. d	**6.** c

9–11

Answers will vary.

PART V From Grammar to Writing (pages 248–250)

1

Rolleen Laing poured herself a second cup of coffee as she ate her breakfast, which consisted of a fried egg, *an* orange, and a piece of dry toast. She was 62 years old and had been successful as a university professor, *a* writer of detective fiction, and an amateur detective. Just then, the telephone rang. It was Harry Sadler, a local police detective. Ever since Rolleen had helped Harry crack a murder case several years previously, she had been called in as an unofficial consultant on several cases. She had helped Harry solve cases involving a hit-and-run victim, a murdered television executive, and, most recently, *a* koala stolen from the city zoo.

"Hi, Rolleen. This is Harry. You're needed on another case. It's a robbery this time. Some thieves broke into the art museum and stole a

Van Gogh, a Picasso, *a* Gauguin, and a Matisse. Meet me at the museum at 10:00, OK?"

2

2. According to historical records, the American outlaw Billy the Kid was known as a fearless gunfighter, was hunted by the law, and *was* killed in a gunfight.

3. Anthropologists speculate that the Anasazi might have been attacked by unfriendly tribes, decimated by crop failures, or *driven away by drought* ~~drought might have driven them away~~.

4. After Amelia Earhart's airplane was lost, naval investigators searched for debris, interviewed residents of South Pacific islands, but *found no trace of Earhart and her navigator* ~~no trace of Earhart and her navigator was found~~.

5. According to legend, the continent was struck by devastating earthquakes, inundated by floods, and *swallowed up by the ocean* ~~the ocean swallowed it up~~.

3

On the evening of August 6, 1930, Judge Force Crater, a wealthy, successful, and good-looking New York lawyer, disappeared without a trace. Earlier in the evening he had been seen with friends at a Manhattan restaurant and *observed* ~~they observed him~~ departing. At 9:10 P.M. he walked out the door of the restaurant and hailed a taxi. He was soon driven away. No one ever saw or heard from him again. It was 10 days before he was even reported missing. On August 16, his wife called his courthouse, *asked the secretary* ~~the secretary was asked~~ of his whereabouts, and learned that he was probably off on political business. This news reassured Mrs. Crater somewhat, but when he still hadn't turned up by August 26, a group of his fellow judges started an investigation. A grand jury was convened, but its members could not come to any conclusion as to what had happened to Judge Crater. They theorized that the judge might have developed amnesia, ~~might have~~ run away voluntarily, or been a crime victim. His wife disagreed with the first two possibilities, holding that he had been murdered by someone in the Tammany Hall organization, the political machine that controlled New York City at the time. The mystery remains unsolved to this day. Crater could have been killed by a Tammany Hall agent, *murdered by a girlfriend* ~~a girlfriend could have murdered him~~, or kidnapped by an organized crime group. He might in fact have suffered from amnesia, or *he might have planned his own disappearance.* ~~his own disappearance might have been planned by him~~. Reports of Judge Crater sightings have continued to surface over the last 70 years.

4

Answers will vary.

UNIT 15 Gerunds (pages 258–271)

After You Read **1.** T **2.** F **3.** T **4.** F

1

A. 2. O   **5.** C   **8.** O
   3. S   **6.** OP   **9.** C
   4. OP   **7.** C

B. 2. Y   **6.** N
   3. N   **7.** Y
   4. Y   **8.** Y
   5. Y

2

2. vegetating   **10.** working
3. worrying   **11.** playing
4. not having   **12.** collecting
5. not working   **13.** singing
6. making   **14.** not singing
7. socializing   **15.** singing
8. having   **16.** orienteering
9. meeting

3

2. Bob's helping   **6.** my becoming
3. My boss's criticizing   **7.** their being
4. Her living   **8.** Our getting
5. Mary's advising

2. seeing
3. having enrolled
4. assigning
5. arguing
6. having said

7. studying
8. helping
9. passing
10. having told

5

A. *Possible questions:*
1. Do you prefer being asked out on a date or asking someone yourself?
2. Are you more interested in entertaining yourself or in being entertained by others?
3. Do you prefer preparing dinner yourself or being invited to dinner by friends?
4. Do you like being told what to do or giving orders?
5. Do you like figuring things out yourself or being shown how to do things?
6. Do you prefer being given advice by friends or giving your friends advice?

B. *Possible answers:*
1. I prefer asking someone myself. I don't like being asked out on a date.
2. I'm more interested in being entertained by others. I don't like entertaining myself.
3. I prefer being invited to dinner by friends. I don't like preparing dinner myself.
4. I prefer giving orders. I hate being told what to do.
5. I like figuring things out myself. I don't like being shown how to do things.
6. I like being given advice by my friends. I don't like giving my friends advice.

6

Answers will vary.

7

Dear Adam,
    I've been here for three days and am having a great time, but I can't help ~~wish~~ *wishing* you were here too. Tell your boss I'm really angry at him. Not ~~let~~ *letting* you take any vacation time qualifies him for the Jerk-of-the-Year Award. (Just kidding. Don't say that!)
    Believe it or not, the first night I missed ~~to hear~~ *hearing* all the city noises, but I haven't really

had any trouble ~~to get~~ *getting* used to the peace and quiet since then. Everything's all so relaxed here—there's no ~~rush~~ *rushing* around or ~~write~~ *writing* things down in your Daily Planner. ~~Get~~ *Getting* out of New York City was definitely what I needed, even if it's only for two weeks. The ranch has lots of activities—horseback ~~ride~~ *riding*, river ~~raft~~ *rafting* on the Rio Grande, ~~to hike~~ *hiking* in the wilderness—you name it. The ranch employees do everything for you—being taken care of is nice, for a change, and I love ~~be~~ *being* chauffeured around Santa Fe in the ranch limousine. Tonight a group of us are going out to a country western dancing place called Rodeo Nites in Santa Fe, so having taken those two-step dance lessons last summer will come in handy. It's just too bad you couldn't come along so we could both have a good time. Tomorrow we're all going to Taos Pueblo to watch some ~~weave~~ *weaving* being done and to see some Native American dancing, which is great because I'm really interested in ~~learn~~ *learning* more about Native American culture. And I'm looking forward to ~~see~~ *seeing* Carmen at the Santa Fe Opera on Saturday.
    I'll write again in a day or two. Miss you lots.
              Love,
              Louise

8

2. F
3. F
4. T

5. F
6. T
7. T

8. F
9. T
10. T

9–11

Answers will vary.

UNIT 16 Infinitives (pages 272–294)

After You Read 1. b   **2.** b   **3.** a

1

A. 2. O
   3. S
   4. SC

5. O
6. O
7. SC

8. S
9. O

B. 2. F **5.** T
   3. F **6.** F
   4. T

2

2. warned me not to put off
3. were willing to allow me to make
4. was important to experience
5. forced me to study
6. was fortunate to graduate
7. expected to pass
8. required us to write
9. refused to accept
10. caused me to fail
11. advised me to retake
12. encouraged me to start

3

2. not to have heard
3. not to have understood
4. to have gotten
5. to have finished
6. to have been hit
7. to have fed
8. not to have done

4

2. to be helped by a passing motorist
3. your phone service to be disconnected
4. to be notified by the police
5. to get stopped by a police officer
6. to be questioned by your teacher

5

Possible answers:
2. Jack types too slowly to finish the report on time.
3. Marcy will have enough money to buy her friend's car.
4. Eve waited too long to start preparing the meal.
5. Sally didn't eat enough to stay healthy.
6. Carlos is intelligent enough to pass the course.

6

Answers will vary.

7

I just had to write tonight. Until now I've
                          to
never had the courage ^ do this, but now I do.

                                    confront
I've decided to ~~have confronted~~ Sarah about
her irresponsibility. This is something that has
been bothering me for some time now, but
                                    to
somehow I've always been reluctant ^ force the
issue. So here's the situation: Sarah invites
people ~~for~~ to do things, but she doesn't follow
through. Last week she asked my fiancé, Al,
        to
and me ^ have dinner, and she also invited our
friends Mark and Debbie. The four of us made
        to
plans ~~for~~ go to her house on Friday evening.
                                    to ask
Something told me I should call Sarah ~~asking~~
what we should bring, and it's a good thing I
did. Sarah said, "Dinner? I'm not having dinner
tonight. I know I mentioned it as a possibility,
but I never settled it with you guys. You
misunderstood me." Well that's just silly. She
        to plan
said ~~planning~~ on it for Friday evening at 7 P.M.
When I told the others, they were furious. Al
                    to be
said, "I don't expect ~~being~~ treated like royalty.
                be
I do expect to ~~have been~~ treated with
consideration." So tomorrow I'm going to call
Sarah up and make my point. I'm not going to
            to
allow Sarah ^ make my life miserable.

   Enough for now. Time for bed.

8

2. They are believed to have escaped in a prison laundry truck.
3. They are believed to have been helped by a prison employee.
4. The security system was supposed to have been installed two months ago.
5. The prisoners are thought to have weapons.
6. They are believed to be heading in the direction of Union City.
7. Listeners are warned not to approach the prisoners.
8. They are asked to contact the Sheriff's Office.

9–12

Answers will vary.

PART VI From Grammar to Writing
(pages 287–289)

1

2. Lately I've been trying to stop speeding in
traffic, ~~to schedule~~ *scheduling* too many activities, and rushing through each day like a crazy person.

3. To have a happier family life, we should all focus on eating meals together, on airing our problems and concerns, and on ~~take~~ *taking* time to talk to one another.

4. Mr. Mason's planning the agenda, Ms. ~~Bono~~ *Bono's* renting the hall, and Mrs. Tanaka's arranging for the guest speakers made the conference a success.

5. Ken's life is vastly changed because of his having stopped working all the time, ∧*having* joined a singles group, and having met some interesting new friends.

2

2. I'm advising you not to sell your property, take out a loan, and ~~not to~~ buy a new house right now.

3. Most presidents want to be reelected to a second term, ∧*to be* taken seriously by other world leaders, and to be remembered fondly after they leave office.

4. To be hired in this firm, you are expected to have earned a bachelor's degree and ~~having~~ *to have* worked in a bank for at least two years.

3

What are you most afraid of? Are you worried about being cheated, ~~to lose~~ *losing* your job, or contracting a deadly disease? Well, if you're like the vast majority of Americans, you fear standing up, ~~to face~~ *facing* an audience, and ~~to deliver~~ *delivering* a speech more than anything else. Surveys have found that anxiety about public speaking terrifies Americans more than dying does. Somehow, people expect to be laughed at, ridiculed, or to be scorned by an audience.

Many college students fear public speaking so much that they put off taking a speech class or even ~~to think~~ *thinking* about it until their last term before graduation. Speech instructors and others familiar with the principles of public speaking stress that the technique of desensitization works best for overcoming speech anxiety. This idea holds that people can get over their fear of speaking in public by enrolling in a course, ~~to attend~~ *attending* the class faithfully, and ~~to force~~ *forcing* themselves to perform the speech activities. Once they have discovered that it is rare for people to die, ~~making~~ *to make* fools of themselves, or to be laughed at while making a speech, they're on their way to success. Consequently, their anxiety becomes a little less each time they get up and talk in public. It may take a while, but eventually they find themselves able to stand up willingly, ~~speaking~~ *speak* comfortably, and ~~expressing~~ *express* themselves clearly.

4

Answers will vary.

UNIT 17 Adverbs: Functions, Types, Placement, and Meaning
(pages 296–309)

After You Read 1. T   **2.** F   **3.** F

1

A. 2. S   **5.** S   **8.** M
   3. S   **6.** M   **9.** N
   4. F   **7.** F   **10.** T

B. 2. N   **6.** Y
   3. Y   **7.** N
   4. N   **8.** N
   5. N

C. 1. There goes the difference between the sexes.
   2. At the top of the list are service jobs like working in daycare centers or hospitals.
   3. Not only should it be allowed, but it should also be promoted.

4. No way is combat non-feminine!
5. Neither do I.
6. Here's Lu Adijojo.

2

Each sentence can have the sentence adverb in two other positions.

2. Unfortunately, military service can be dangerous.
3. I'm against the death penalty essentially because I consider it cruel and unusual punishment.
4. There's certainly a lot more violence in movies than in the past.
5. Nuclear weapons can be eliminated, hopefully.
6. A vaccine against AIDS can be found, possibly.
7. The prime minister's position is clearly wrong.
8. Actually, there's increasing opposition to people's owning SUVs.

3

2. b   **3.** a   **4.** b   **5.** a   **6.** b   **7.** b   **8.** a

4

2. Rarely do women fight alongside men in combat.
3. In no way is military service useless.
4. Neither will poverty.
5. Not only do we need to stop global warming, we also need to find new energy sources.
6. Never had it occurred to me that SUVs could harm the environment, but I learned they could.

5

Possible answers:

2. Seldom are homeless people treated kindly.
3. Hopefully, national service will be established soon.
4. Here are my arguments against the cloning of humans.
5. I can't think of even one reason to support him.
6. I'm basically not in favor of cloning. (OR I'm not in favor of cloning, basically.)
7. I don't just like her policies; I strongly support them.
8. In no way do I support hunting.

6

2. even . . . has
3. Only in . . . is military service required
4. Not only . . . but they also allow
5. just aren't required
6. Only in . . . are women required

7

Dear Dad,

I'm sitting in the train station, waiting for the 5:25 to get here, so ~~just I~~ *I just* thought I'd drop you a quick note. I've been attending the conference on reducing global warming. Actually, I almost didn't get to go to the conference because ~~almost we~~ *we almost* didn't get our taxes done on time. Vicky and I stayed up until midnight last night, though, and I mailed the forms this morning.

I hate income taxes! Only once in the last ten years ~~we have~~ *have we* gotten a refund, and this time the tax return was so complicated that ~~Vicky got even~~ *even Vicky got* upset, and you know how calm she is. Maybe we should move to Antarctica or something. No taxes there.

Besides that, we've been having a few problems with Donna. It's probably nothing more serious than teenage rebellion, but whenever we try to lay down the law, she gets defensive. Rarely if ever ~~she takes~~ *does she take* criticism well. The other night she and her friend stayed out until 1 A.M.—this was the second time in two weeks—and when we asked her what they'd been doing she said, "~~Just we were~~ *We were just* talking and listening to dance music at the Teen Club. Why can't you leave me alone?" Then she stomped out of the room. Fortunately, Sam and Toby have been behaving like angels—but they're not teenagers!

Meanwhile, Donna's school has started a new open-campus policy. Students can leave the campus whenever they don't have a class. ~~Even they don't have~~ *They don't even have* to tell the school office where they're going and when they'll be back. No way ^ *do* Vicky and I ~~do~~ approve of that policy. School time, in our view, is for studying and learning, not for socializing. Little *do* those school officials realize how much trouble teenagers can get into whenever they're roaming around unsupervised.

Well, Dad, here *comes the train* ~~the train comes~~. I'll sign off now. Write soon.

Love,
Ken

8

2. a	**6.** b
3. b	**7.** b
4. a	**8.** a
5. b	

9–10

Answers will vary.

UNIT 18 Adverb Clauses
(pages 310–325)

After You Read **1.** Y   **2.** N   **3.** Y

1

A. *Paragraph 1, four adverb clauses to be underlined:*
1. As I was watching the Olympics the other night,
2. when he said that bowling, roller skating, tug-of-war, ballroom dancing, and chess have been proposed for future Olympic games
3. by the time the 2008 Beijing Olympics start?
4. after I get up in the morning

B. *Paragraph 3, three adverb clauses to be underlined:*
1. Although athletes still try to achieve their personal best,
2. while that rival is an also-ran
3. Since there are ever-increasing possibilities for product endorsement,

C. **2.** *when* When the Olympic games started about 2,700 years ago in Greece, the contests held were basically those related to war.

3. *contrast* Although athletes still try to achieve their personal best, the emphasis has shifted away from the individual pursuit of excellence.
4. *under what conditions* If you add to that the cost of parking and eating, the cost was up to at least $75.
5. *where* We see it wherever we look.

2

2. If the score is forty–love, one player's score is zero. (tennis)
3. You can't play this game unless you have ice skates and a puck. (ice hockey)
4. You go to the free throw line after you've been fouled. (basketball)
5. Though you can't use your hands, you may use your head. (soccer)
6. You've finished the course when you've run 42.2 kilometers. (the marathon)
7. Your team can't bat until the other team makes three outs. (baseball)
8. If your team scores a touchdown, it earns six points. (American football)

3

Possible answers:
2. Although (OR Though OR Even though OR While) Greek city-states were often at war with one another, Olympic contestants stopped fighting during the games.
3. The ancient Olympic games were outlawed by the Roman emperor Theodosius I after they had been held for over 1,000 years.
4. He outlawed them in 393 A.D. because (OR since) Romans thought Greeks wore too few clothes.
5. French educator Pierre de Coubertin revived the Olympics since (OR because) he thought they would promote international peace.
6. Tug-of-war was dropped from the Olympics in 1920 when (OR after OR because OR since) American and British athletes disagreed about how it should be played.
7. New Olympic sports often first appear as demonstration events before they are adopted as medal sports.
8. Any sport can potentially become a medal event if (OR provided that) it can be scored and fulfills certain criteria.

2. The Quiksilver Invitation surfing competition had to be canceled because the waves were just too big (OR since the waves were just too big).

3. the waves were too dangerous (OR he might endanger his own life OR someone might have been hurt trying to rescue him).

4. you can ride the biggest wave of the year and get it on film.

5. they want the ultimate thrill.

6. Although exact figures on how many extreme athletes exist are hard to come by,
(Other possible subordinating conjunctions: *though, even though, while*)

7. when I started doing rescues 20 years ago
(No, the sentence will not make sense with *whenever.*)

8. because nobody goes there.
(Other possible subordinating conjunctions: *since, as*)

9. an educational program was started

Possible answers:
1. if the player makes the basket.
2. unless the player misses the basket.
3. Although the Blues are losing,
4. even though very few people are watching.
5. Because the slope was icy,
6. until the ice melts. (OR until it snows again.)

Answers will vary.

A lot of people are criticizing school sports these days. Some say there's too much

while
empahsis on football and basketball, ~~if~~ there's not enough emphasis on education. Others say the idea of the scholar-athlete is a joke. Still others say sports provide a way of encouraging violence. I think they're all wrong. If anything, school sports help prevent violence, not encourage it. Why do I think sports are a positive force?

because (OR *since* OR *as*)
For one thing, sports are positive ~~even though~~ they give students opportunities to be involved in something. Every day on TV we hear that violence is increasing. I think a lot of people

don't
get involved in crime when they ~~won't~~ have enough to do to keep themselves busy. After

you
~~you'll~~ play two or three hours of basketball, baseball, or any other kind of sport, it's hard to commit a violent act even if you want to.

Second, sports teach people a lot of worthwhile things, especially at the high school level. When they play on a team, students learn

Whenever
to get along and work with others. ~~Wherever~~ their team wins, they learn how to be good

loses
winners; when their team ~~will lose~~, they find out they have to struggle to improve. They discover that winning a few and losing a few are part of the normal ups and downs of life. Also, there's no doubt that students improve their physical condition by participating in sports.

because (OR *since* OR *as*)
Finally, sports are positive ~~although~~ they allow students who do not have enough money to go to college to get sports scholarships and improve their chances for a successful life.

If
~~Whereas~~ a young basketball player from a small village in Nigeria can get a scholarship to play for say, UCLA, he will have a chance to get an education and probably make his life better.

If
~~Wherever~~ a young woman with little money is accepted on the University of Toronto swim team and gets a scholarship, she'll have the chance to earn a college degree and go on to a

Although (OR *Though* OR *Even though*)
high-paying job. ~~Because~~ school sports programs have some deficiencies that need to be corrected, their benefits outweigh their disadvantages. I should know because I'm one of those students. School sports must stay.

8

Suggested answers:
2. She learned to swim when she was four.
3. Lillian thinks she became a good swimmer because she had to swim in the Caribbean.
4. They spent a lot of time at the beach because they didn't have many toys or video games.
5. When she was 12, Lillian decided she wanted to become a champion swimmer and go to the Olympics someday.
6. Lillian's parents agreed to pay for lessons if Lillian would stick to her plan and practice regularly.

7. She got discouraged whenever she had a hard time learning a new stroke.
8. Lillian can't imagine herself doing anything else because swimming is a total passion for her.
9. Once Lillian started her lessons, her parents wouldn't let her quit.

9–12

Answers will vary.

UNIT 19 Adverb and Adverbial Phrases (pages 326–339)

After You Read 1. T 2. T 3. F

1

A. Upon opening the door . . .
  After being rushed to a hospital . . .
  . . . after being turned over to the police
  After returning to the United States . . .
B. Having spent a wonderful day . . .
  Having heard Reg and Maggie speak on French television . . .
C. 2. Y **6.** Y
  3. Y **7.** Y
  4. N **8.** Y
  5. N

2

2. Reg carefully considered the options before he sped away.
  Reg carefully considered the options before speeding away.
3. Because the criminals were a deadly threat, Reg floored the gas pedal.
  (cannot be shortened)
4. When Reg saw a police car parked on the shoulder, he pulled over to alert the authorities.
  Seeing a police car parked on the shoulder, Reg pulled over to alert the authorities.
5. As Nicholas lay on his deathbed, Reg and Maggie decided that something good ought to come out of the situation.
  (cannot be shortened)

6. Because the criminals thought the Greens had precious stones, they fired shots that killed Nicholas.
  Thinking the Greens had precious stones, the criminals fired shots that killed Nicholas.

3

B. 2. no
  3. She came to the zoo last year after being taken from owners.
  4. no
  5. yes
  6. On April 11, while (OR after) giving birth to a stillborn calf, Champakali died.
  7. Damini stood still in her enclosure. She barely nibbled at the two tons of food in front of her.

4

Possible answers:
2. Noticing their interest in him, the boy offered them a guidebook.
3. They told the boy they couldn't buy anything, not having any local money.
4. Impressed by the boy's responsibility, they decided to go back and buy a guidebook.
5. Finding an exchange kiosk, they changed some money.
6. Having gotten some local money, they looked for the boy but couldn't find him.
7. After being told where the boy might be, they located him.
8. Having found the boy, they bought a map from him.

5

If you're at all like me, you tire of requests
to help others. ~~Hitting~~ *Hit* by seemingly constant appeals for money to support homeless shelters, the Special Olympics, or the like, I tend to tune out, my brain numbed. I don't think I'm selfish. But ~~subjecting~~ *subjected* to so many requests, I only remember the flashy ones. By ~~being argued~~ *arguing* that I don't have enough money to help others, I am able to ignore the requests. Or at least that was the way I saw the situation before *being* sent by my magazine to South America to do a human-interest story on homeless children.

heard
Having ~~hearing~~ many TV requests asking viewers to sponsor a child overseas, I always said to myself, "I'll bet the money is pocketed by some local politician." My opinion changed when I saw the reality of the life of a poor child.

Having landed (OR Landing)
~~While landing~~ in Santa Simona, I took a taxi to my hotel in the center of town,

Sitting
where I met Elena, a girl of 10 or 11. ~~Sat~~ on a dirty blanket on the sidewalk in front of the hotel, she caught my eye. Elena was trying to earn a living by selling mangoes. Smiling at me, she asked, "Mangos, señor?—Mangoes, sir?" I bought some mangoes and some other fruit, and we talked together. Elena's life had been difficult. Her parents were both dead, and

had
she lived with an elderly aunt. Having ʌpolio at the age of five, she now walked with a limp. She and her aunt often went hungry.

Investigating
~~Investigated~~ the question the next day, I talked to several different authorities.

Convinced
~~Having convinced~~ that money from sponsors does in fact get to those who need it, I knew my attitude had to change. Learning that I could sponsor Elena for less than a dollar a day, I began to feel ashamed; after all, I spend more than that on my dogs. But what remains most vivid in my mind is my vision of Elena. She didn't beg or feel sorry for herself. Selling her mangoes, she earned a living, and her spirit shone through in the process. So I say to all of you reading this: The next time you hear an ad about sponsoring a child, pay attention.

6

Possible answers:
2. Mr. Tintor could demonstrate good faith by agreeing to free elections.
3. The president's aide spoke off the record.
4. They acknowledged that the current AIDS vaccine is ineffective.
5. The new nation is to be known as the Central Asian Republic.
6. It will need billions of dollars of foreign aid in order to become a viable state.
7. He had almost given up hope because he was unable to swim.
8. Hutchinson rescued him by using the lifesaving techniques she had learned in swimming class.

7–9

Answers will vary.

UNIT 20 Connectors (pages 340–362)

After You Read 1. a   **2.** a   **3.** b

1

A. 1. There is evidence, <u>moreover</u>, . . .
  2. <u>Furthermore</u>, the first syllable . . .

B. 1. <u>However</u>, just as you say . . .
  2. I wouldn't be too concerned, <u>though</u>, . . .
  3. It, <u>in contrast</u>, . . .
  4. <u>However</u>, there are things
  5. Or were you, <u>instead</u>,

C. 1. <u>therefore</u>, I decided to do
  2. <u>Thus</u>, we are able to
  3. <u>Because of this</u>, we may
  4. <u>Consequently</u>, elderly people

D. 1. <u>First</u>, let's distinguish
  2. <u>Second</u>, let's look
  3. Suppose, <u>for example</u>,
  4. Let's say, <u>for instance</u>,

2

Possible answers:
2. He was having problems remembering his appointments, so he bought a daily planner.
   He was having problems remembering his appointments; consequently, he bought a daily planner.
3. It's important for Nancy to take her medications, but she forgot today.
   Although it's important for Nancy to take her medications, she forgot today.
   It's important for Nancy to take her medications; however, she forgot today.
4. Jack remembers everyone's name, and he never forgets a face.
   Jack remembers everyone's name; in addition, he never forgets a face.

3

2. first	**5.** therefore	**8.** otherwise
3. second	**6.** In addition	**9.** And
4. however	**7.** Meanwhile	**10.** As a result

Possible answers:

1. Hank didn't have time to take a shower, and he didn't have time to eat breakfast.

   Hank didn't have time to take a shower. In addition, he didn't have time to eat breakfast.

2. He ran out of the house, but he left his wallet on the table.

   He ran out of the house. However, he left his wallet on the table.

3. He was driving too fast, so a police officer stopped him.

   He was driving too fast. Consequently, a police officer stopped him.

4. Hank didn't have his driver's license, and he didn't have his car insurance.

   Hank didn't have his driver's license. Besides that, he didn't have his car insurance.

5. While this was happening, Hank's co-workers were waiting for him at work.

   Meanwhile, Hank's co-workers were waiting for him at work.

6. Hank's boss told him he had to improve his memory, or there could be serious consequences.

   Hank's boss told him he had to improve his memory. Otherwise, there could be serious consequences.

October 12th

Yesterday I drove my car to the downtown campus of the college. I usually have trouble finding a parking place, ~~however~~ *but* this time it was almost impossible. There were simply no parking places anywhere near the campus, ~~therefore~~ *so* I had to park in the downtown mall, which is about a mile away. When I finished class, I walked back to the mall. ~~Therefore~~ *However*, I couldn't remember where I'd parked my car! Believe it or not, it took me 45 minutes to find it, and I was about ready to panic when I finally did. That was the last straw. I've decided that I'm going to send my car to a new home in the suburbs.

I used to think that a car was the most wonderful thing in the world. I loved the freedom of being able to come and go to my part-time job or to the college whenever I wanted. A year ago I was in a carpool with four other people, ~~nevertheless~~ *but* I hated having to wait around even though my carpool members weren't ready to leave, so I started driving alone. ~~Although~~ *However*, I've changed my mind since then. Now it's clear to me that there are just too many disadvantages to having a car in town. ~~Accordingly~~ *For instance*, sitting stalled in your car in a traffic jam is stressful, ~~besides~~ *and* it's a phenomenal waste of time. In addition, it would cost me $200 a month to park my car in the city (which is why I don't do that), ~~moreover~~ *and* there's always the chance it will be vandalized. ~~Nonetheless~~ *Therefore*, I've decided to leave it at my cousin Brent's house in the suburbs. Otherwise, I'll end up going broke paying for parking or memory improvement. My car will have a good home, and I'll use it just for longer trips. When I'm in the city, ~~although~~ *though*, I'll take the bus or the tram, ~~otherwise~~ *or* I'll walk. Who knows? They say you can meet some interesting people on the bus. Maybe I'll find the love of my life. My only problem will be remembering which bus to take.

Possible answers:

2. People like to be called by their names, and it's good for business.

3. You need to notice one particular thing about a person and link that thing with the person's name.

4. The visitor told them to put their hands up.

5. a. The man had a toy gun.

   b. The leader didn't act like this was an interruption.

6. It's not the usual way to say good-bye.

7. They have to learn to focus their attention consistently.

Answers will vary.

PART VII From Grammar to Writing
(pages 354–357)

1

2. F As soon as I've saved enough money.
3. S Although China is overpopulated, <u>it is trying to correct the problem</u>.
4. S <u>We won't solve the problem of illiteracy</u> until we provide enough teachers.
5. F If a young basketball player from Nigeria can get a scholarship.
6. F Because I was one of those students.
7. S <u>The economy is perhaps too dependent on high-tech industries</u>.
8. S Carried out right, <u>this procedure would cause the economy to expand</u>.
9. F By the time the train finally arrived in Boston.
10. S <u>We need to make some personal sacrifices if we want to help the poor</u>.

2

The life of Stella and Hank Wong has improved immeasurably‚ₓ S̶ince they both got new jobs. Stella got a position as a proofreader and editor at a publishing companyₓ t̶hat is pioneering new workplace methods. Hank was hired as a full-time consultant for an engineering firm. The difference between their new jobs and their old ones can be summed up in one word: flextime. Until they secured these new position‚ₓ Stella and Hank had a very difficult time raising their two small children.

Their life was extremely stressful‚ₓ B̶ecause they were at the mercy of a nine-to-five schedule and had to pay a lot for day care. In order to get to work on time‚ₓ t̶hey had to have the children at the day care center by 7:30 every morning. Both of their new companies, however, offer a flextime schedule. As long as Stella and Hank put in their 40 hours a week‚ₓ t̶hey are free to work‚ₓ w̶hen it is convenient for them. Now they can take turns staying home with the children, and day care is just a memory. Best of all, the children are much happier‚ₓ B̶ecause they are getting the attention they need.

3

_C_ 1. Violence exists nearly everywhere in the world, and it is spreading.
_X_ 2. Since we usually watch TV at home in our living room, a TV show doesn't seem like a special event.
_C_ 3. The population will continue to increase, but natural resources won't.
_X_ 4. We must make trains fast and comfortable if we expect people to use them.
_S_ 5. I listened politely for a while and then excused myself.
_C_ 6. The governor isn't in favor of higher taxes, nor does he encourage the development of mass transit.
_C_ 7. We don't have to buy a lot of groceries all at once, for we can always stop at the supermarket on the way home from work.
_X_ 8. Tim passed his driving exam with flying colors, though he could use some practice in parallel parking.
_X_ 9. As I was entering the dining car, a violent lurch of the train threw me to the left.

4

Possible answers:
1. Drake tried to think of a justification for his actions, but he was unable to come up with a single thing.
2. Although Drake tried to think of a justification for his actions, he was unable to come up with a single thing.
3. Because dams provide a great many economic benefits, I don't think they should be removed.
4. Dams provide a great many economic benefits. Therefore, I don't think they should be removed.
5. Bruce is an excellent athlete, and he is a top student.
6. Bruce is an excellent athlete. In addition, he is a top student.

5

Answers will vary.

UNIT 21 Noun Clauses: Subjects, Objects, and Complements (pages 364–377)

After You Read 1. F   2. T   3. F

1

A. <u>What wasn't so admirable</u> was the rivalry among the three. **S**

<u>What the sons wanted</u> was a secure place in their mother's affections. **S**

<u>That the boys were intensely competitive</u> had always bothered the lady. **S**

They didn't understand <u>that their mother loved each boy for his own uniqueness</u>. **O**

The boys realized <u>that their mother's final days were approaching</u>. **O**

Each searched for a way to prove <u>he was the best son</u>. **O**

Each boy promised to buy her <u>whatever she wanted</u>. **O**

He was sure <u>that the mansion would be the very best thing any of them could give her</u>. **C**

B. Each brother was constantly trying to figure out <u>how he could outdo the other two</u>.
Direct question: How could he outdo the other two?

. . . but she didn't know <u>what to do about it</u>.
Direct question: What should / could she do about it?

Curly, son number three, was in a dilemma, wondering <u>what he could do to top the gifts of the other two brothers</u>.
Direct question: What could he do to top the gifts of the other two brothers?

One could ask the parrot <u>whatever one wanted to know</u>.
Direct question: What did one want to know?

I don't know <u>if you believed me</u>, though, when I said that I didn't need anything.
Direct question: Did you believe me . . . ?

I don't know <u>what you mean</u>, son.
Direct question: What do you mean?

2

2. what the name of the nearest town was
3. if there was a telephone booth nearby
4. if there were any towing companies
5. if he knew
6. how long he had lived
7. what his name was
8. if he knew anything at all

3

A. *Possible answers:*
1. What is a pun?
I don't know what a pun is.
2. What does hyperbole mean?
I have no idea what hyperbole means.
3. What is the humor of the unexpected happening?
I'm not sure what the humor of the unexpected happening is.
4. How does repetition work in humor?
I'm not entirely sure how repetition works in humor.
5. What is the humor of the incongruous situation?
I don't have a clue what the humor of the incongruous situation is.
6. How does sarcasm differ from other humor?
I don't know how sarcasm differs from other humor.
7. Why is it impossible to tickle yourself?
I'm not sure why it is impossible to tickle yourself.
8. What are endorphins?
I have no clue what endorphins are.

B. *Possible answers:*
1. What is a pun?
A pun is a kind of humor that depends on similarities in sound or meaning between two words.
2. What does hyperbole mean?
Hyperbole means exaggeration.
3. What is the humor of the unexpected happening?
An example of the unexpected happening is when a woman opens her purse, and a bird flies out of it.
4. How does repetition work in humor?
Repetition works by repeating an element in a humorous story.
5. What is the humor of the incongruous situation?
The humor of the incongruous situation depends on normal things happening in unusual places.
6. How does sarcasm differ from other humor?
Sarcasm is often more biting and hurtful than other humor.
7. Why is it impossible to tickle yourself?
It is thought that we must perceive tickling as a pretended attack by someone.
However, our brain is aware of itself.
8. What are endorphins?
Endorphins are hormones that are created in the brain when we laugh or exercise.

4

Possible answers:

1. *Honk if you're illiterate*: What's funny about this is that anyone who is illiterate couldn't read the bumper sticker.
2. *If you don't like the way I drive, stay off the sidewalk*: What this is referring to is some people's tendency to drive wildly—even going onto the sidewalk.
3. *Missing: Husband and Dog. Attention: $100 reward for dog*: What's funny about this is the fact that some wives like to joke about their animals being more valuable than their husbands.
4. *Change is inevitable—except for vending machines*: What the humor depends on is the pun on the meaning of *change. Change* means "alteration in circumstances" or "excess money returned when one makes a purchase." Vending machines sometimes do not return change correctly or at all.
5. *I'm in no hurry. I'm on my way to work*: What this is about is the feeling on the part of some employees that work is not satisfying or fulfilling.
6. *Everyone is entitled to my opinion*: What the humor depends on is the similar saying, "Everyone is entitled to his or her opinion."
7. *Forget about world peace. Visualize using your turn signal*: What the humor depends on is a commonly seen bumper sticker that says "Visualize World Peace." This bumper sticker asks people to think of less grand things than world peace (while driving) and concentrate on driving properly.
8. *Eschew obfuscation*: What the humor depends on is knowing the meanings of *eschew* and *obfuscation. Eschew* is a fancy word for "avoid." *Obfuscation* is a fancy way to say "making things confusing."

5

1. Make sure ~~is~~ the joke you're telling *is* funny.
2. The best jokes are broad enough so that everyone can enjoy them. Be certain that no one will be embarrassed by ~~that~~ *what* you tell.
3. Also make certain that ~~whichever~~ *whatever* you're saying won't embarrass anyone.
4. Ask yourself ~~is~~ *if* the joke you want to tell *is* vulgar. If it is, don't tell it.

5. Before you begin, be certain you remember what ~~are the key details~~ *the key details are*. Run through them in your mind before you start speaking.
6. Make sure ~~what~~ *that* you have everybody's attention when you're ready to start.
7. Be certain ~~whether~~ *that* you remember what the punch line of the joke is. Nothing is worse than listening to a joke when the teller can't remember the punch line.
8. The fact ~~can you~~ *(that) you can* remember a joke doesn't guarantee success. You have to make the experience a performance. Be animated and dramatic.
9. ~~If~~ *Whether (or not)* to laugh at your own jokes is always a question. Many comedians are criticized because they laugh at their own jokes. Don't laugh at what you're saying. Let others do the laughing.

6

Suggested answers:

2. The expectation is that you'll laugh, whether you think the joke is funny or not.
3. If you don't laugh, everyone thinks you're no fun.
4. The other problem is that you're forced to be dishonest.
5. He feels like he's stupid.
6. The problem was that they were leaving lip prints all over the mirror.
7. The principal of the school decided that something had to be done about the problem.
8. The principal wanted to show the girls how difficult it was to clean the mirror.

7–9

Answers will vary.

UNIT 22 Direct and Indirect Speech
(pages 378–404)

After You Read 1. b   **2.** a   **3.** b

1

A. 2. "Candidate Q is gaining momentum and that Candidate R is losing ground." → The reporter's claim that Q was gaining and that R was losing ground is unsupported.

3. "Candidate A leads Candidate B by five points." → The reporter said Candidate A led Candidate B by five points.
"This represents an increase of one point since a week ago." → The reporter said this represented an increase of one point since the previous week . . .
OR
". . . the Blues have to win 7 seats . . ." → . . . he stated that the Blues had to win 7 seats . . .
OR
". . . more than 100 million Americans breathe polluted air." → The reporter said more than 100 million Americans breathed polluted air.

4. ". . . the profits of XYZ Corporation have dropped from 15 percent to 10 percent . . ." → the reporter said the profits of XYZ Corporation had dropped . . .

5. ". . . there is a greater chance that Candidate A will win the election . . ." → . . . the reporter said there was a greater chance that Candidate A would win the election . . .

6. "This represents an increase of one point since a week ago . . ." → The reporter said this represented an increase of one point since the previous week . . .

B. 2. I   **3.** I   **4.** C   **5.** I   **6.** C

2

2. The headline said scientist Linda Buck unlocked the secret to the sense of smell.
3. The headline said Mt. St. Helens could erupt again.
4. The headline said a new tax cut would be passed soon.
5. The headline said Senator Mason was running behind his opponent.
6. The headline said mercury-contaminated fish are / were dangerous to eat.
7. The headline said a new miracle drug had been perfected.

3

2. Sam asked, "Where was the Rosetta Stone found?"
3. Bob asked, "How long did the Revolutionary War last?"
4. Minnie asked, "What were the last two states to join the Union?"

5. William asked, "Can a person born outside the country become president?"
6. Grant asked, "What was the Boston Tea Party?"
7. Amanda asked, "How many electoral votes does it take to become president of the United States?"
8. Zelda asked, "Is population growth increasing worldwide?"

4

Possible answers:
2. (that) I could
3. her what she needed
4. (that) she had
5. (me) how they worked
    (OR [me] how they work)
6. call (OR called)
7. ask (OR asked)
8. if there had been
9. hadn't predicted
10. (that) there had
11. had been
12. had happened
13. had been saying
14. would lose
15. looked like he was losing
16. they would see what happened
17. was going

5

Possible answers:
2. A member of the City Council said (that) construction on the new subway system had been started a year previously.
3. A reporter remarked that it probably wouldn't be finished on schedule.
4. Another member of the City Council observed (that) the assistant mayor had resigned the day before.
5. A townsperson said (that) the voters didn't want taxes raised now.
6. Another townsperson added (that) they wanted tax relief this year.
7. The mayor claimed (that) the citizens of that town were better off than they had been four years before.
8. The former mayor pointed out that serious crime had increased since then.
9. The mayor added (that) life was better here than in most places.
10. Another townsperson commented (that) he had made that claim in the previous election campaign.

January 20

Dear Emily,

I just wanted to fill you in on Tim's school adventures. About two months ago Melanie said she ~~feels~~ *felt* we should switch Tim to the public school. He'd been in a private school for several months, as you know. I asked her why ~~you~~ *she* thought that, and she said, "He's miserable where he is, and the quality of education is poor." I couldn't help but agree. She said she thought we ~~can~~ *could* move him to the local high school, which has a good academic reputation. I ~~told~~ *said (OR told her)* that ˣI agreed but that we should ask Tim.ˣ The next morning we asked Tim if he ~~wants~~ *wanted* to stay at the private school. I was surprised at how strong his response was. He ~~said~~ *told* me that he hated this school and didn't want to go ~~here~~ *there* any longer. So we changed him. He's been at the new school for a month now, and he's doing well. Whenever I ask him ~~does he have~~ *if he has* his homework done, he says, "Dad, I've already finished it." He's made several new friends. Every now and then he asks us why ~~didn't we~~ *we didn't* let him change sooner. I'm just glad we moved him when we did.

Not much else is new. Oh, yes—I do need to ask ~~are you~~ *if you are* coming for the holidays. Write soon and let us know. Or call.

Love,
Charles

2. The reporter said (that) a cloud of ash was covering the local area.
3. The reporter said (that) there had been no deaths so far.
4. The reporter said (that) Senator McLeod was leading her challenger by eight points.
5. The reporter said (that) the election was only a week away.
6. The reporter said (that) Marcine Miller was confident that she would win.

7. The reporter said (that) the Mariners had won Game 7 of the World Series by a score of 1–0.
8. The reporter said (that) this is / was the Mariners' first championship.

Answers will vary.

PART VIII From Grammar to Writing (pages 395–398)

1

2. "Sally, how would you evaluate your education?" the reporter queried.
3. "I absolutely love going to school!" Sally responded.
4. "Jim," Frank said, "you're crazy if you think it's going to be easy to get a job."
5. Frank said, "Jim, don't be a fool!"
6. The union spokesperson asked the management team, "When are you going to start taking our concerns seriously?"

2. Company President Bates responded that there was simply no money for salary raises.
3. TV reporter Joan Matthews asked Fumiko if she agreed with Janice that cloning should be banned.
4. Frank asked Jim what he would do if he couldn't find a job after he quit school.
5. Professor Martin asked Russell if he intended to go to graduate school after earning his bachelor's degree.

Suggested answers:
2. commented   5. maintained
3. noted   6. added
4. claimed

Suggested answers:
2. Keith asked, "Valerie, what made you come to that conclusion?"
3. Valerie responded, "Ben doesn't have any real friends on the team."
4. She added, "His coach said he's seemed miserable for quite a long time."
5. Keith said, "I think you're probably right."

6. Keith asked, "Should we allow him to quit the team or encourage him to take up another sport?"

Answers will vary.

UNIT 23 Conditionals; Other Ways to Express Unreality (pages 406–420)

After You Read **1.** a **2.** b **3.** b **4.** b

1

1. If I don't take my medicine regularly, I go into shock.
2. He's going to faint if he doesn't get out of the sun.
   . . . he'll kill us and steal the car if we pick him up.
   There won't be anything worth buying if we don't get there soon.
   . . . if you can just take me to the bus station, I'll be on my way.
   I'll be surprised if we ever hear from him, though.
3. If only that chest of drawers would still be there!
   If only I weren't so forgetful.
4. I'd sure get out of this heat if I were him.
   If I had a nickel for all the times we've done things because of your male intuition, I'd be a rich woman.
5. If you hadn't come along when you did and taken me to the pharmacy, I might have died.
   At the very least, I would have become very ill if you hadn't been there to help.
   If I had been fortunate enough to have any children of my own, I couldn't have had any nicer ones than you two.
6. We'd probably have that chest of drawers if we'd gotten here earlier.

2

2. If diabetics don't take their insulin, they sometimes go into shock.
3. We will run out of energy if we don't develop alternate fuel sources.
4. If global warming continues, the polar icecaps could melt.

5. A Venus flytrap dies if it doesn't get enough water.
6. If present trends continue, the world population will reach nine billion by 2060.

3

2. will you give
3. I will
4. what would you do
5. you found
6. I'd take
7. it weren't
8. I wouldn't be
9. I'd keep
10. how would you feel
11. you were
12. I'd want
13. if I were
14. I'd call
15. I'll do it
16. if you really think

4

Possible answers:
A. 2. They wish it weren't raining.
   3. He wishes she would say yes.
   4. He wishes she would change her mind.
   5. She wishes she hadn't broken her leg.
   6. She wishes she were playing.

B. 2. If only it weren't raining.
   3. If only she would say yes.
   4. If only she would change her mind.
   5. If only I hadn't broken my leg.
   6. If only I were playing.

5

2. were coming
3. wouldn't have done
4. had been
5. would have turned out
6. they hadn't
7. wouldn't have picked
8. I'd been betting
9. you would have won
10. you'd bet
11. You'd be
12. wouldn't be
13. you'd made it

6

June 4
   This has been one of those days when I wish
I ~~would have~~ *had* stayed in bed. It started at 7:30 this morning when Trudy called me up and asked me for "a little favor." She's always asking me to do things for her and never wants

to take any responsibility for herself. She acts
as if the world owes her a living. I wish she
didn't
~~doesn't~~ think like that. Today she wanted me
to take her to the mall because she had to get
her mother a birthday present. At first I said
I couldn't because I had to be downtown at
11 A.M. for a job interview. Trudy said she'd do
asked
the same for me if I ~~would ask~~ her. Then she
said it wouldn't take long to drive to the mall
and I'd have plenty of time to get downtown
from there. I gave in and agreed to take her,
but something told me I shouldn't. If I had
listened to my inner voice, I might have ~~had~~ a
job right now. When we were on the freeway,
there was a major accident, and traffic was tied
up for over an hour. By the time we got to the
mall, it was 11:30, so I missed the appointment.
would have gotten *had*
I think I probably ~~would get~~ the job if I ~~would~~
~~have~~ managed to make it to the interview,
because my qualifications are strong. If only
hadn't
I ~~wouldn't have~~ listened to Trudy! I just wish
didn't (OR *wouldn't*)
she ~~doesn't~~ ask me to do things like this. If she
hope
asks me again, I ~~wish~~ I don't agree.

7

Possible answers:
2. Sally wishes April hadn't let him copy her
   workbook.
3. April thought Bob would break up with her
   if she refused.
4. Sally would have told him no.
5. The teacher will probably fail both of them if
   she finds out.
6. Sally would call Bob up and tell him she had
   changed her mind.
7. April should tell him she won't be able to do
   it because her conscience is bothering her.
8. If Bob gets mad and says he wants to break
   up, April should say good-bye.

8

ANSWERS TO TEAM A'S QUESTIONS
1. You would be in Tegucigalpa if you were in
   the capital of Honduras.
2. You would have to be at least 35 years old if
   you were president of the United States.
3. You would be traveling in North or South
   Korea if the monetary unit were the won.

4. You would be in Cambodia if you were
   visiting Angkor Wat.
5. You would have been Napoleon if you had
   been the emperor of France in 1802.
6. You would have been Jawaharlal Nehru if you
   had been the first prime minister of India.
7. You would have been from Italy if you had
   been Marco Polo.
8. You would have climbed Mt. Everest if you
   had been with Edmund Hillary and Tenzing
   Norgay.

ANSWERS TO TEAM B'S QUESTIONS
1. You would be between 80 and 89 if you were
   an octogenarian.
2. You would be traveling in Peru if you were
   in Machu Picchu.
3. You would be a whale if you were the largest
   mammal.
4. You would be in Venezuela if you were
   standing and looking at Angel Falls.
5. You would have been Alexander Graham
   Bell if you had been the inventor of the
   telephone.
6. You would have been a dinosaur if you had
   been a stegosaurus.
7. You would have been an emperor if you had
   been Genghis Khan.
8. You would have been the founder of
   Buddhism if you had been Siddartha
   Gautama.

9–11

Answers will vary.

UNIT 24 More Conditions;
The Subjunctive   (pages 421–444)

After You Read 1. Y   2. N   3. Y   4. N

1

A. 1. If so, I'd say she needs a situation . . .
   2. Otherwise, the problem will just get worse.
   3. Without it, they would have been in
      trouble.

B. 1. Had I known how things were going to
      turn out, . . .
   2. Should that happen, . . .

C. insists I come
   suggest she go
   recommended she sell
   I'd rather she not go

important that she have
propose you find
recommend you look into
essential that we understand

D. 1. Y   **2.** Y   **3.** N   **4.** N   **5.** Y

2

2. If so, that would solve your problem.
3. And if not, what can I do?
4. Without cigarettes, I can't make it through they day.
5. You can do it with a buddy who has the same problem.
6. I'd be lonely but for my friends. (OR I'd be lonely without my friends.)

3

A. 2. Had she known
3. otherwise
4. with
5. If so
6. If not

B. 2. If she had known
3. If she didn't find a job
4. If she had a bit of luck
5. If they were hiring
6. if they weren't hiring

4

1. e (that) she spend
2. c (that) she go
3. d (that) she stay
4. f (that) Dad (OR he) stay
5. b (that) I do
6. a (that) he do

5

Possible answers:
A. 2. advisable that they make
3. crucial that an elderly person see
4. necessary that their children visit
5. important that a senior stay
6. essential that every elderly person be treated

B. 2. advisable for them to make
3. crucial for an elderly person to see
4. necessary for their children to visit
5. important for a senior to stay
6. essential for every elderly person to be treated

6

Answers will vary.

7

December 10
Dear Henrietta,

It's time I wrote and filled you in on what's been happening since I left Russellville. I finally got a job! Remember when you suggested I just
go
~~went~~ walking around, getting a sense of what St. Louis was like? A few weeks ago I was getting rather worried since I had spent most of the money I had saved to get me through the job-hunting period. It's not easy for a 60-year-old woman to find a job, you know. I had gotten to the point where it was absolutely
find   *come*
essential that I ~~found~~ something or ~~came~~ back to Russellville. So I decided to follow your
Had I known (OR *If I had known*)
advice. ~~I had known~~ how easy this would be, I would have tried it the first week I was here. I started walking around in the downtown area, and before I knew it, I saw a beautiful little florist's shop. I walked right in, unafraid, and asked if they needed anyone. Can you believe that they did?

I was really happy in my job until my boss hired a new assistant manager who has been making my life miserable. Among other things,
that I make
he demands ~~me to make~~ coffee for him. He
I do
also insists that ~~I'm doing~~ other things that aren't in my job description. I took this job to work with plants, not to serve him coffee. I think I need to tell him where I stand. It's
stop
important that he ~~stops~~ treating me as his personal slave.

I have a few days off for the holidays. Do you have some time off? If so, how about coming down here for a visit? Wouldn't that be fun? I have a spare bedroom in my apartment. If you can come, I suggest you ~~to~~ drive, as it isn't far. Please write and let me know.

Love,
Doris

8

Possible answers:
2. The daughter almost demanded that she do it.

3. Had she known who was calling, she would not have answered the phone.

4. She had to call and insist that her daughter come and pick up the kids.

5. It is important that the daughter pay more attention to the kids.

6. She suggests the mother call her daughter back and tell her she has changed her mind.

 9–12

Answers will vary.

PART IX From Grammar to Writing
(pages 435–438)

 1

2. Thain asked Donna to pull over; his intuition told him the old man needed their help.

3. Kate knew she had to change her relationship with her boss, **but** she didn't know how to do it.

4. **Although** (OR **Though**) Donna wished they had gotten to the yard sale on time, she was glad they had stopped to help the old man.

2

2. Thain and Donna drove to a pharmacy. **They** got the old man his insulin.

3. Donna wanted to get to the yard sale; there was a chest of drawers for sale.

4. Donna didn't want to stop for the old man, **but** Thain persuaded her it was necessary.

5. **Although** (OR **Though**) Harold says he will seek professional help to overcome his anger, there is no assurance that he will carry out his promise.

6. **Feeling** dominated by her mother-in-law, **Nancy** needed to take assertive action.

 3

2. Nancy says she wants to do something worthwhile. **If** so, she should consider volunteer work.

3. I need to get a bank loan; otherwise, I'll have to file for bankruptcy.

4. Ben and Carolyn would like to send Jim to a private school. **However**, the school is expensive, and Jim doesn't want to go.

5. Fred and Claudia love their new neighborhood; in fact, they're going to buy a house there.

 4

Suggested answers:

Call it either intuition or good vibrations. **W**hatever you want to call it, it works. **L**ast summer, I was one of four members of a committee to hire a new head nurse at the nursing home where I work. **W**e interviewed two candidates as finalists, a man named Bob and a woman named Sarah. **O**n paper, Bob was better qualified; he had a master's degree while Sarah had only a bachelor's degree. **H**owever, Sarah was the one who really impressed us; she answered all of the questions straightforwardly and simply. **B**ob, on the other hand, evaded some of our questions while simultaneously trying to make us think he knew everything and could do everything. **A**ll of us on the committee just liked Sarah better. **I**n fact, she got the job because she was the person we all felt we wanted to work with. Our intuition wasn't wrong; she's turned out to be a wonderful nurse.

 5

Answers will vary.

Using the PowerPoint® presentations

The PowerPoint presentations are saved as .PPS files, which means that they open in Slide Show view and cannot be edited. The instructions in this section explain the basic steps of opening and using the PowerPoint presentations.

2.1. Start a Presentation

2.1.1. Windows

• Insert the PowerPoint® presentations CD-ROM into the CD-ROM drive. On most computers, a Contents page will open automatically.
• If the Contents page does not open automatically, open **My Computer**, double-click on the CD-ROM drive, and then double-click on the "**Start.html**" file.
• On the Contents page, click the link for "**PowerPoint presentations.**"
• Click the link for the presentation you wish to view.

2.1.2. Macintosh

• Insert the PowerPoint® presentations CD-ROM into the CD-ROM drive.
• Double-click on the CD-ROM drive icon, the symbol that looks like a CD.
• Double-click on the "**Start.html**" file.
• On the Contents page, click the link for "**PowerPoint presentations.**"
• Click the link for the presentation you wish to view.

2.2. Advance Through Slides

To advance from one slide to the next or from one animation to the next, click the left mouse button, the **Down Arrow** button (↓) or the **Right Arrow** button (→) on the keyboard.

2.3. Go Back Through Slides

To go back to previous slides, or to go back through the animations on a slide, click the **Up Arrow** button (↑) or the **Left Arrow** button (←) on the keyboard.

2.4. Exit a Presentation

Press the "**Esc**" (escape) button on the keyboard.

Technical Support

For Technical Support, email
EPSupport@pearsoned.com

License Agreement

READ THIS LICENSE CAREFULLY BEFORE OPENING THIS PACKAGE. BY OPENING THIS PACKAGE, YOU ARE AGREEING TO THE TERMS AND CONDITIONS OF THIS LICENSE. IF YOU DO NOT AGREE, DO NOT OPEN THE PACKAGE. PROMPTLY RETURN THE UNOPENED PACKAGE AND ALL ACCOMPANYING ITEMS TO THE PLACE YOU OBTAINED THEM. *THESE TERMS APPLY TO ALL LICENSED SOFTWARE ON THE DISK EXCEPT THAT THE TERMS FOR USE OF ANY SHAREWARE OR FREEWARE ON THE DISKETTES ARE AS SET FORTH IN THE ELECTRONIC LICENSE LOCATED ON THE DISK:*

1. **GRANT OF LICENSE and OWNERSHIP:** The enclosed data disk ("Software") is licensed, not sold, to you by Pearson Education, Inc. Publishing as Pearson Longman ("We" or the "Company") for academic purposes and in consideration of your purchase or adoption of the accompanying Company textbooks and/or other materials, and your agreement to these terms. This license allows instructors teaching the course using the Company textbook that accompanies this Software (the "Focus on Grammar") to use, and display the data on a single computer (i.e., with a single CPU) at a single location for academic use only, so long as you comply with the terms of this Agreement.

   We reserve any rights not granted to you. You own only the disk(s) but we and our licensors own the Software itself.

2. **RESTRICTIONS ON USE AND TRANSFER:** You may not transfer, distribute or make available the Software or the Documentation, except to instructors and students in your school in connection with the Course. You may not reverse engineer, disassemble, decompile, modify, adapt, translate or create derivative works based on the Software or the Documentation. You may be held legally responsible for any copying or copyright infringement that is caused by your failure to abide by the terms of these restrictions.

3. **TERMINATION:** This license is effective until terminated. This license will terminate automatically without notice from the Company if you fail to comply with any provisions or limitations of this license. Upon termination, you shall destroy the Documentation and all copies of the Software. All provisions of this Agreement as to limitation and disclaimer of warranties, limitation of liability, remedies or damages, and our ownership rights shall survive termination.

4. **DISCLAIMER OF WARRANTY: THE COMPANY AND ITS LICENSORS MAKE NO WARRANTIES ABOUT THE SOFTWARE, WHICH IS PROVIDED "AS-IS." IF THE DISK IS DEFECTIVE IN MATERIALS OR WORKMANSHIP, YOUR ONLY REMEDY IS TO RETURN IT TO THE COMPANY WITHIN 30 DAYS FOR REPLACEMENT UNLESS THE COMPANY DETERMINES IN GOOD FAITH THAT THE DISK HAS BEEN MISUSED OR IMPROPERLY INSTALLED, REPAIRED, ALTERED OR DAMAGED. THE COMPANY DISCLAIMS ALL WARRANTIES, EXPRESS OR IMPLIED, INCLUDING WITHOUT LIMITATION, THE IMPLIED WARRANTIES OF MERCHANTABILITY AND FITNESS FOR A PARTICULAR PURPOSE. THE COMPANY DOES NOT WARRANT, GUARANTEE OR MAKE ANY REPRESENTATION REGARDING THE ACCURACY, RELIABILITY, CURRENTNESS, USE, OR RESULTS OF USE, OF THE SOFTWARE.**

5. **LIMITATION OF REMEDIES AND DAMAGES: IN NO EVENT, SHALL THE COMPANY OR ITS EMPLOYEES, AGENTS, LICENSORS OR CONTRACTORS BE LIABLE FOR ANY INCIDENTAL, INDIRECT, SPECIAL OR CONSEQUENTIAL DAMAGES ARISING OUT OF OR IN CONNECTION WITH THIS LICENSE OR THE SOFTWARE, INCLUDING, WITHOUT LIMITATION, LOSS OF USE, LOSS OF DATA, LOSS OF INCOME OR PROFIT, OR OTHER LOSSES SUSTAINED AS A RESULT OF INJURY TO ANY PERSON, OR LOSS OF OR DAMAGE TO PROPERTY, OR CLAIMS OF THIRD PARTIES, EVEN IF THE COMPANY OR AN AUTHORIZED REPRESENTATIVE OF THE COMPANY HAS BEEN ADVISED OF THE POSSIBILITY OF SUCH DAMAGES. SOME JURISDICTIONS DO NOT ALLOW THE LIMITATION OF DAMAGES IN CERTAIN CIRCUMSTANCES, SO THE ABOVE LIMITATIONS MAY NOT ALWAYS APPLY.**

6. **GENERAL:** THIS AGREEMENT SHALL BE CONSTRUED IN ACCORDANCE WITH THE LAWS OF THE UNITED STATES OF AMERICA AND THE STATE OF NEW YORK, APPLICABLE TO CONTRACTS MADE IN NEW YORK, EXCLUDING THE STATE'S LAWS AND POLICIES ON CONFLICTS OF LAW, AND SHALL BENEFIT THE COMPANY, ITS AFFILIATES AND ASSIGNEES. This Agreement is the complete and exclusive statement of the agreement between you and the Company and supersedes all proposals, prior agreements, oral or written, and any other communications between you and the Company or any of its representatives relating to the subject matter. If you are a U.S. Government user, this Software is licensed with "restricted rights" as set forth in subparagraphs (a)-(d) of the Commercial Computer-Restricted Rights clause at FAR 52.227-19 or in subparagraphs (c)(1)(ii) of the Rights in Technical Data and Computer Software clause at DFARS 252.227-7013, and similar clauses, as applicable.